THOU SHALT NOT KILL
Poles on Jedwabne

THOU SHALT NOT KILL

Poles on Jedwabne

Texts revised and edited by William Brand on the basis of translations by:
LLC Tłumaczenia, Lawrence Fahrenholz (1, 2, 4, 13, 14, 19, 24, 26, 31, 32, 34, 35)
William Brand (3, 9, 10, 11, 12, 17, 20, 30)
Ryszard J. Reisner (5, 6, 7, 16, 25, 27)
Academia Polonica (15, 18, 23, 28, 33)
Krzysztof Kotkowski (8, 29)
Translation of the text by Jan Nowak-Jeziorański: Courtesy of SIEC POLSKA,
Michael Szporer, mietek@erols.com

Cover design: AgrafA
Typesetting: "Nowy Dziennik"
Printing and Binding: Petit

Printed in Poland
ISBN 83-88032-38-0

TABLE OF CONTENTS

PARTITION OF POLAND
1939

The map above depicts the state of affairs in the fall of 1939 resulting from the Soviet-German pact and the subsequent invasion of Poland by the armies of both those states. When the German army began attacking the USSR on June 22, 1941, the first areas that came under its control were the parts of the Polish state that had been occupied by the USSR.

ISRAEL GUTMAN

INTRODUCTION

The publication of Jan Błoński's groundbreaking essay "Poor Poles Look at the Ghetto," in *Tygodnik Powszechny* in 1987, brought to an end the long period of silence on the subject of the attitudes of the Poles toward the Jews during World War Two. At the same time, a hollow, tedious credo about the Holocaust crumbled. This credo had been endlessly repeated by the communist regime, was not based on the analysis of research, and failed to shock public awareness in the way that public awareness in the West had been shocked by the disclosure of the truth about those times.

Błoński wrote about the shared guilt falling upon the countries and peoples of Europe, stressing that this guilt should be expressed with particular force in Poland, a country in which so many Jews had lived for so many centuries. He touched upon painful truths without hesitation, but he also expressed relief that the worst evil had passed Poland by: "When one reads what people wrote about the Jews before the war, how much hatred there was in Polish society, one often wonders how it is that words were never followed by deeds. Well, they were not (or were seldom) followed by deeds. God stayed our hands. Yes, God, because if we did not take part in this crime, it is because we were still somewhat Christian, and realized at the very last moment what a satanic venture this was...."

That is what Błoński thought, and that is also what many friends of Poland thought until recently. In the light of the Jedwabne massacre, one can no longer claim that genocide was alien to the Poles during the Holocaust.

We know full well that the horror of the Nazi occupation in Poland did not root out anti-Semitism, and that anti-Semitism also did not

9

disappear during the Holocaust, or even later. The plague of *szmal-cownicy**, evil-minded bounty hunters who sought out Jews hiding among the Poles, is a case at hand. The underground publications churned out by nationalists of all stripes did not shy away from anti-Jewish accents and anti-Semitic prejudices. Here and there, armed groups "liquidated Jewish bandits" or, in truth, murdered scattered remnants of Jewish groups seeking shelter in the woods.

Nor can one gloss over the depravity which Kazimierz Wyka attributed to certain social segments in his collection of essays entitled *Życie na niby* [A Pretense of Life]: "...the economic-moral standpoint of the average Pole toward the tragedy of the Jews boils down to this: The Germans committed an atrocity by murdering the Jews. We would never do such a thing. For this atrocity the Germans will be punished, they have stained their consciences, but we—we have nothing but advantages today, and in future, too, we will have nothing but advantages, not having burdened our consciences or stained our hands with blood." But such opinions were rare. Generally, within the framework of a consensus adopted by people of good will in and outside Poland, it was said that the only glaring sins against our neighbors were sporadic excesses committed by crazed hooligans or incurable fanatics who were morally lost in an inhuman reality. It was thought that the majority, or the overwhelming majority, of Poles, suffering under and paralyzed by brutal terror, were wrapped up in their own fears and worries.

Jedwabne clearly goes far beyond the pattern of universal indifference or marginal deviation. This is the murder of a major part of the inhabitants of an impoverished town by their compatriots and neighbors, with whom the victims had lived for generations. These people knew each other's names and faces, they knew their neighbors' parents and children, had worked together in order to survive the difficult times and, just as in other towns, had visited each other at family celebrations and festivities. This massacre—committed only because the victims were Jews—is an unheard of, incomprehensible atrocity. The tools and the methods by which mass murder was

---

* Terms marked with an asterisk: see Explanatory Notes (ed.).

committed against defenseless people, completely at the mercy of their tormentors, illustrate an incredible breakdown of humanity.

Prof. Tomasz Szarota, the author of one of the publications in this collection, says in the interview with Jacek Żakowski: "These unquestionable facts are so shattering that they force even me, a historian who has read much and written a good deal about various instances of disgraceful behavior by Poles under German occupation, to come to completely new conclusions.... Through his publications, Gross has forced us to change our views on the subject of the attitudes of the Poles during the Second World War, and that is an unquestionable service." Another author, Zdzisław Krasnodębski, asks why Jan T. Gross's book *Neighbors* "affects the Polish reader to the core when, for example, Christopher Browning's *Ordinary Men. Reserve Police Battalion 101 and the Final Solution in Poland*, which is also set in Poland... can be read with much more distance. The answer is simple. *Neighbors* invokes the national identity of the reader."

Such an approach is justified, but it offers only a partial explanation of the matter. I have never agreed with Browning's claim that the perpetrators of this crime were "ordinary men." The uniformed Germans who murdered women, old people and children in "special operations" were not "ordinary men," but a product of Nazi ideology and the Third Reich regime. Yet the murder in Jedwabne and—as it turns out—in several other nearby towns, was committed by Poles, who were united by their view of the Germans as the implacable foe. The Poles were not uniformed ruffians. So how was this atrocity possible, and where did all the pent-up fury and bloodlust come from?

The authors of a few articles, including Professor Szarota, state unequivocally that the Poles were the murderers ("there is no denying the fact"). They suggest further investigation into the details, and add that it is necessary to carefully establish the influence and contribution of the Germans to this atrocity, which might diminish, if only partly, the responsibility of the Polish inhabitants of Jedwabne.

11

The appointment of a commission of experts to establish a complete fundamental picture of the events is an understandable and desirable step. But it is also necessary to check Gross's remark that the order to exterminate the Jews was given by the Germans on July 10, 1941. Gross provides no specifics as to who gave the order or who was charged with carrying it out, or even as to his source. The reports of witnesses and documents from the beginning of the occupation of territories taken over in the summer of 1941 indicate that, during "Operation Barbarossa,"* the Jews were deprived of all rights and local communities were encouraged to commit pogroms and robberies with impunity. However, mass killings were carried out by special uniformed German units (*Einsatzgruppen*), assisted by volunteers from among the local riffraff. But Poles did not engage in such collaboration.

A question comes up as to whether the atrocity was fuelled by a desire to rob and pillage. Our knowledge of the pogroms committed in Russia in the final decades of the 19th century suggests that a desire to plunder led to the theft and destruction of property, the torment of people and the rape of women—but rather not to mass murder.

The next absorbing and vexatious question is: What brought about the mass murder of Jews in Jedwabne? No less surprising is the fact that many residents of Jedwabne took an active part in the orgy of destruction and murder in a visible way and that, apart from one documented case where seven Jews were saved, we know of no efforts to rescue and protect even children. Neither do we now of any local conflict or event with inflammatory consequences that could cause such fury and bad blood in Jedwabne.

And finally: How is it that the murder of some 1,600 people in the heart of a town, like the "court case" now being played out, has caught us by surprise 60 years after the event, like an unexpected archeological discovery?

Knowledge of the mass murder committed in Jedwabne is an enormous, astonishing shock to Poles, and a shock that clashes with the national myth about the war years. The continuing series of articles in the press, the public debates and discussions, have concentrated not solely on Jedwabne, but also on a wide range of issues such as anti-Semitism in Poland, Polish-Jewish relations at the time of the profound changes that occurred during and after the turbulent war years, and the question and dimensions of the responsibility for Jedwabne.

Generally speaking, the wide-ranging debate has been conducted in a mood of contemplation, without any whitewashing of the truth, and with frequent expressions of contrition and grief. The Polish people's readiness to recognize the fact that Polish history is not a glorious chain of heroism and justice, but contains episodes of harm done to weak and innocent people, does not signify spiritual collapse, but is a test of fortitude on the path to a better future.

The Polish nation has traveled a long road of bondage and martyrdom. The well-worn self-portrait of Poland has always shown the country as a victim fighting for its due right to existence. Now is the time—and not only because of the shadow of Jedwabne—to accept the fact that the inter-war history of independent Poland, followed by successive chapters of its history, are tarnished with harm wrought upon its own citizens who looked to their country for aid and understanding.

In Polish-Jewish relations, the Jews are repeatedly accused of disloyalty and of welcoming the Red Army with demonstrative joy upon its entry into eastern Poland in September 1939. They are also accused of occupying key posts in the Soviet administrative-police apparatus.

These accusations are not unfounded. The arrival of the Soviets came as a great respite and relief to local Jewish residents and refugees, because the only alternative was a Nazi onslaught and the prospect of a threat that embraced the Jews. In the land of the Soviets, the Jews, like everyone else, could expect the evil and cruelty of that regime, but under the Germans the Jews could expect nothing aside from a Jewish fate. It is true that a certain percentage of young Jews were favorably inclined toward communism, but collaborators were to be found everywhere, among "us" and among "others." It is

13

true that the Jews occupied posts in Soviet offices (and it is worth remembering that in the prewar independent Poland, posts like these, especially toward the end of Polish independence, were barred to Jews), but young Jews—Zionists and members of the Bund*—also formed clandestine groups in the Soviet zone, and many disappointed refugees were even prepared to return to their town and families in the German zone. The Soviet regime was a misfortune for the masses of religious Jews and for those engaged in "traditionally Jewish" trades. Just like the Poles, the Jews were arrested and deported to the depths of eastern Soviet Russia and Kazakhstan. One of the paradoxes of this war was the fact that a considerable portion of what was left of Polish Jewry survived in exile and in Soviet camps.

So it was with no small surprise and disappointment that I read an exhaustive article by Prof. Tomasz Strzembosz, the doyen of historians of the Polish underground, entitled: "Covered-Up Collaboration." He claims that: "the Jewish population, especially youths and the town-dwelling poor, staged a mass welcome for the invading [Soviet] army and took part in introducing the new order, some with weapons in hand." The Jewish poor with weapons... Strzembosz's rumors and generalized accusations, which he lays on thick, are the products of fantasy and are not worth discussing. Although he does not say so clearly, these words suggest a certain tit for tat approach to Jedwabne—you hurt us, so now we'll hurt you!

It is difficult to hold a conversation when we keep returning to "the Jews, all Jews," to a stereotype of hostility, and when we keep imitating the Bourbons in "never forgetting anything and never learning anything." Those who are pained by the memories of the misfortune, and there are many of them in Poland, pay a high price for the publication, here or there, of someone's defamatory comparisons. And, as usual—well-worn stereotypes, difficult to dispense with, give rise to diametrically opposed stereotypes.

I believe that the sources of the disasters, the savagery, and the annihilation of the Jews were the Nazi style of racism, brutal German aggression, and the inhuman occupation regime. This is best expressed by Paul Celan in his poem *Fugue of Death*: *"Der Tod ist ein Meister aus Deutschland"* [Death is a master from Germany].

Are the Poles a nation of incorrigible anti-Semites? I have never thought so or believed so. I think that such a sweeping statement itself bears something of the plague of anti-Semitism. It is true that anti-Semitism has embedded itself deeply among Poles over the past few generations, that it existed during the war and occupation, and that it made itself sharply felt after the war. It was expressed in the Kielce pogrom* and the wave of killings in the 1940s, and in the expulsion of Jews in 1968*–1969, the result of squabbling between Communist party factions.

At the same time, a relatively large number of Poles occupy an honorable place among the Righteous among Nations for helping hunted Jews at the risk, and sometimes with the loss, of their lives and the lives of their families. They did so selflessly, for people whom they did not know, and lived in constant fear and in ceaseless effort. Their fate—even the fate of those not discovered by the Germans—was colored with tragedy. There is no doubt that the task of rescuing Jews was more difficult and dangerous in Poland than anywhere else.

Nor do I think that the institutions representing the Polish people during the occupation—the government-in-exile in London and the underground Home Army* in Poland—are responsible for atrocities against the Jews, even if they did little to alleviate Jewish misery.

So is no one responsible for the massacre in Jedwabne? A lot has been said about individual responsibility or limited local responsibility, and various aspects of responsibility and guilt have been examined in detail. It has also been said that responsibility for the sins of a small, remote town do not weigh on the nation and its future generations.

I think such a manner of gauging responsibility is mistaken. There is such a thing as the personal responsibility of the perpetrators, but that is only one side of the coin. There is no denying that the evil force of what happened in Jedwabne was nourished by a widespread dislike of Jews. This hostility, which reached its peak in Poland in the 1930s, required the Jews—who had lived in Poland for centuries—to be seen as a threat to the state, and a threat that ought to be eliminated. This anti-Semitism was not just imported from outside, but grew on Polish soil, on Polish home ground.

The regime of lawlessness and disregard for human life imposed by the Germans provoked the tragedy of Jedwabne, a tragedy which is but a small part of the enormous tragedy of the Holocaust—yet it is a misfortune for the Jews and a blow to the Poles.

The settling of historical scores is primarily a lesson in the community of life and existence. Anti-Semitism is an illness that is not easy to eradicate. After the experience of our century, on the threshold of mankind's self-destruction, we must be on full guard against all forms of totalitarianism, racism and anti-Semitism. Leszek Kołakowski* wrote in a brief treatise on anti-Semitism in 1956: "A necessary condition for bloody Jewish pogroms, slaughters and atrocities has always been a social atmosphere of emotional tolerance of anti-Semitism, even in its mildest, watered-down form. Wherever atrocities occurred, the system of discrimination and suspicion, even if apparently harmless, always gathered reserves of destructive social energy beforehand which nourished and bred criminals."

The world we live in now—and it will never be perfect—is engaged in a struggle for the freedom of the individual, nations and social strata. In this struggle, it is also our task to try to shape and educate human beings whose consciousness is an independent store of memory and knowledge, and an independent signpost to the future.

Israel Gutman

Danuta Wroniszewska and
Aleksander Wroniszewski

To Survive

"Kontakty" July 10, 1988

"Misfortune came to the man
like a wild animal
and fixed him with its eye.
Misfortune waits.
Will the man flinch?"
Cyprian Kamil Norwid

Misfortune did not come unexpectedly; it had been lingering for years, emitting ominous echoes in the form of tumults, strikes, and political trials, and then it drew strength from the wave of fascism abroad and nationalism at home.

In provincial towns such as the Jedwabne of the 1930s, with a population of almost 3,000, not many people knew anything about world affairs. Apart from the communists, to whose ranks mainly Jews were recruited, and a small number of Peasant Party supporters, the only people who had any contact with the "outside world" were the lady of the manor, the parish priest, the doctor, the mayor.... For everyone else in the town and its environs, the entire world consisted of the town itself, and the scene of the most important events was the town square.

"In the middle of the town square stood a building shaped like an airplane" is how some residents recall Jedwabne's prewar appearance. The square was paved with cobblestones, there was some grass, and around it stood Jewish-owned buildings nestling close to each other. There were numerous shops, workshops and tobacco stalls. On workdays, there was more bargaining in the shops than selling. But the seasonal fairs and market days in Jedwabne attracted farmers and merchants from outside town. On market days, there was already traffic on the roads at dawn.

On holidays, these same people, dressed in their best, separated into two groups—some went to the synagogue, and others to church. In 1935, a new brick church on the town square, was consecrated in place of the wooden one which had burned down during World War I. Inside the new church, Father S., a supporter of the "nationalists," expressed new ideas imported directly from Nazi Germany. On market days, pickets would appear in front of Jewish shops, with the slogan "Do Not Buy From Jews!" However, such slogans had no major effects because there was virtually no shops or workshops at all in the hands of Poles. There were only two small Polish "colonial" shops [selling spices, tea, tropical fruit, etc.—ed.] that somehow managed to survive. The majority of the Polish traders had gone bankrupt in the face of Jewish competition. Even among the Jews, not everyone could afford noodles with cheese and cinnamon. Others had to make do with a dish of buckwheat, onion and turnips, and received financial support from the Jewish *kahał* [religious community—ed.], who effectively protected them against ruin. In addition, what was in Poland an ethnic minority was in Jedwabne a majority, and in order for a Pole to be elected mayor of a Polish town, it was necessary to gerrymander three hamlets into the boundaries of the town.

Despite frequent differences of interests and mutual ill feeling, there were never any violent events or displays of hostility in Jedwabne. Only the advent of war caused a flare-up of human emotion and the elimination of two-thirds of the inhabitants. The "Jewish question" was "solved" one month before civil administration was introduced to Jedwabne. This is commemorated today by an inscription on a memorial stone opposite an old Jewish cemetery overgrown with hazel: "SITE OF THE SUFFERING OF THE JEWISH POPULATION. THE GESTAPO AND THE NAZI GENDARMERIE BURNED 1600 PEOPLE ALIVE JULY 10, 1941."

Written reports and memoirs by witnesses on the subject of the Jedwabne holocaust also remain. The memoirs are controversial—some of them are flavored with a feeling of co-responsibility, others express the enormous harm suffered, and others still are full of accusations against the Poles, such as this report by Szmul Wasersztajn written on 5 April 1945.

"On July 10, 1941, eight Gestapo came to town. They held talks with representatives of the town authorities. Asked by the Gestapo men what they intended to do with the Jews, all the municipal officials replied as one man that the Jews must be eliminated. The Germans suggested that one Jewish family representing each of the crafts should be kept alive, but the local carpenter, Bronisław S., said: 'We have our own craftsmen. We have to get rid of all the Jews.' Mayor K. and all the others agreed. It was decided that all the Jews would be gathered in one place and burnt. For this purpose, S. provided the use of his barn, situated not far from the town.

After this meeting, the massacre began. Local hooligans, armed with axes, special clubs studded with nails and other tools and instruments of torture, forced all the Jews out into the streets. They chose 75 of the youngest and healthiest males to be the first victims of their diabolical instincts, and ordered them to remove the big statue of Lenin which the Russians had put up in the town center. This statue was extremely heavy. Nevertheless the Jews, with terrible blows raining down upon them, had to comply. In addition, while carrying the statue, they were forced to sing until the statue had been brought to its appointed place. There, they were ordered to dig a hole and throw the statue into it. After this had been done, these same Jews were beaten to death and thrown into the same trench.... Older Jews had their beards singed, and infants were killed while clinging to their mothers' breasts. The Jews were beaten, murdered, forced to sing and dance, etc. Finally, the main operation—the horror of the burning—began. The whole town was surrounded by guards so that no one could get out. Then the Jews were lined up in four rows, with the rabbi, aged over 90, and the Kosher butcher at the front. They were given a red banner and marched off, singing, to the barn...."

The daughter of Bronisław Ś. claims she no longer remembers all the details of the events that took place 47 years ago, but she is sure her father did not stain his hands with Jewish blood as others say he did. *"He was a town councilor before the war, and that is probably why he took part in the mayor's official turnout. But the story that he offered his barn in which to burn the Jews is utter nonsense. It's as if the Germans were asking for permission. The barn was very convenient because it stood near the Jewish cemetery and at a safe distance from other buildings. I bore no grudges against the Jews, and I don't think my father had anything against them, either. For many years we lived next door to a Jewish family of hat-makers without the slightest quarrel. I grew up with Jews, played with them. When on July 10th the Germans began to round the Jews up in the town square, allegedly in order to weed the grass growing there, my mother and I, together with two female Jewish neighbors, watched the whole thing from an upstairs window. One of them translated for us what the Germans were saying to the assembled Jews. The Germans were telling them that they were going to be moved out of Jedwabne because they were not allowed to live there. They must have already heard about the ghettoes, because they formed themselves obediently in four rows, and behaved as if they believed the whole thing. Not until the Jews were directed towards the graves did some of them begin to think that they were being sent to their deaths. Two days earlier, Jews had been burnt in Radziłów, and news of this must have reached the Jews in Jedwabne. They began to moan and wail, and in the town itself such tension arose that no one felt like doing any work, and all they could do was talk about what was going to happen to the Jews. Later, when we saw the black smoke, we knew. None of us betrayed these neighbor women. They survived the pogrom. Later they ended up in the ghetto in Łomża."*

In fact, the actual people responsible for this deed, as the daughter of Bronisław Ś. claims with conviction, were the Germans. But only the Poles were punished for it, and innocent Poles at that. She herself saw how a strapping young Gestapo man went up to one of the Jewish houses. Ż. only peeked out from behind the door, but was immediately noticed by the German. "Come here, you. Go and find the Jews!" So it was actually a Pole who sought them out. Well, who would have had the courage to oppose an armed German? And yet that man died in prison after the war for what he had done.

> *"Until at last death became a common possession,*
> *Edible and easily digestible like bread.*
> *We partook morsels of it,*
> *A slice blossoming with flavor but without a name,*
> *Our daily bread"*
>
> Rafał Wojaczek

Eugeniusz Ś. has no doubts about who was behind this tragedy. *"It was Hitler's policy to exterminate the Jews, and he achieved his aims one way or another—by means of ghettoes or concentration camps. However, the 'Endlösung'* occurred sooner in Radziłów, Wąsosz and Jedwabne. The Nazis took advantage of reluctant assent and resentment among the Poles, and found a few hooligans for good measure. Although we have peace, law and order today, how much violence theft and even murder there still is. And one must remember that forty-odd years ago was a period when the law and people's characters were regularly broken, a period of killing. For some people, it was enough to be told by the Gestapo 'You are allowed to kill,' whilst others had to be told 'You have to burn the Jews.' And the price of obedience was your own life and that of your family."*

Says Jan S: *"K. played a not insignificant role in the pogrom. He had just been appointed mayor by the Germans, more or less at random. On July 10, as I was sweeping the road outside my property, he said to me: 'You know what? Today they're either going to burn the Jews or shoot them.' He didn't look particularly worried. A little later he repeated this news to other people. I heard shouts of joy, as if they were pleased that they were going to have fun. I went to Drozdów on business, and when I returned, all I saw was billowing black smoke...."*

After the liberation, Mayor K. disappeared somewhere and was never seen again. His older children fled to Warsaw, while his wife and youngest child stayed in Jedwabne. In the mayor's absence, vengeance was wrought on her. While she lay in the street, murdered, the little one still sucked at her breast. No one looked for the perpetrators of this atrocity. Is it because this atrocity was considered more just, more noble?

The findings of historians leave no doubt about the role played by the Germans in the murder of the Jews of Jedwabne. In his *Polityka okupacyjna III Rzeszy w Okręgu Białostockim 1941–44* [The Occupation Policy of the Third Reich in the Białystok Area 1941–44], Jan Karlikowski writes that special operation groups (*Einsatzgruppen* A, B, C and D), set up by the RSHA (Reich Main Security Office), were engaged in exterminating the Jewish and Polish population. These groups were divided into *Einsatzkommandos*, and these in turn consisted of *Sonderkommandos* and smaller units attached to armies and tactical formations. The Białystok region belonged to the area of operations of *Einsatzgruppe* B, commanded by Arthur Nebe.

In the opinion of Waldemar Monkiewicz, chairman of the Białystok branch of the Commission for the Investigation of Nazi Crimes*, the pogrom in Jedwabne was carried out by a special police unit, the so-called "Birkner *Kommando.*" It consisted of some 200 ruffians, people deprived of all scruples. They drifted from one locality to another, carrying out a new pogrom every other day. They were capable of exploiting the tiniest element of ethnic animosity. In Rajgród, for instance, they found a woman who said that the Jews had murdered her son. That was enough to fan a flame of vengeance in people's hearts.

However, Waldemar Monkiewicz objects when he hears people say that the Jews of Jedwabne were murdered by the Poles. *"That can only come from the lips of people who have no idea about the reality of those times. There was a period in 1941 when the Russians were already retreating and the Germans had not yet arrived. The local ruffians took advantage of this interregnum and committed robberies and settled all kinds of scores. To prevent complete anarchy, a police force began to be formed. When the Germans arrived, some of these people in the police resigned, whilst others resolved to collaborate with the Germans. During the pogrom they escorted the doomed Jews, though they probably had no idea what was going to happen to them. I don't deny that there were also a few who gave the Jews a rough time, but they were on the margins of society, the kind that exists in any community. In any case, these people, too, had their justifications. When the Russians came to Jedwabne in 1939, they were ordinary invaders to the Poles, but most of the Jews immediately took the side of the Soviet authorities. They had no scruples about swapping their Polish eagles for Russian stars, and willingly attended meetings. Anti-Semitic moods also rose for certain just before the arrival of the Germans, when people who had been denounced by Jews returned after serving time in the prison at Łomża."*

Many residents of Jedwabne also believe that the Jews themselves brought the "lash of God" down on their own backs. *"They were Polish citizens, but they never felt Polish,"* says Jan Czesław S. *"I remember how pleased they were when the Poles passed eastwards through this area in 1920*. They said 'Our men are heading for Wilno!' Later, when the Russians were advancing on Warsaw, they said: 'Our men are coming!' But after the 'miracle on the Vistula'* came crowding around, joyfully saying, 'It's God's will, our men are coming back.' Ethnic discord flared up between the wars. The Jews acquired strength and significance. Under the Russians, the Jews developed a fighting spirit. Some of them sensed that blind obedience would turn against them one day. Kuropatwina once told me: 'My Pesa and Chaja are happy, but I know the old prophecy: our death is nigh.' I remember how the Russians loaded the Poles onto carriages to be taken to Siberia. On top of each carriage was a Jew armed with a rifle. Mothers, wives and children knelt before the carriages, begging for mercy and help. The last time this happened was 20 June 1941. So when the Germans came.... There was only a handful of these zealous, revengeful Poles, but that* *was enough to bring shame down on all Poles. Because the Germans had not just machine pistols, but also cameras...."*

Jan C. of Wizna, himself of Jewish extraction, thinks it correct to say that the behavior of Poles was dictated by a desire for revenge. *"In Wizna, after the Soviets had left, Poles held kangaroo courts on fellow Poles who had worked in the selsovets.* * *The Jews were dealt with solely by the Germans: shooting, plunder, deportation to ghettoes like everywhere else."*

One way or another, the participants in the Jedwabne pogrom were called to account after the war. A trial was held and severe verdicts handed down. Waldemar Monkiewicz has more to say on this topic than anyone else, for he was a prosecutor in that trial. Today he admits he acted against his own conscience. "Those people," he stressed, "had to be convicted, regardless of the extent of their guilt. After all, that was the time of Jakub Berman* and people like him."

Bronisław Ś., whom Szmul Wasersztajn considers to be the Polish ringleader of the pogrom, did not even live to see a trial.

"Our homegrown evil spirit was Miss Z.," the daughter of Bronisław Ś. recalls. *"She married a Soviet lieutenant. She came from a poverty-stricken home, so this marriage meant advancement. It also helped her win the trust of the Soviet authorities later. She 'turned the Russians loose' against various people. Because she was our neighbor, she knew what sort of valuables we had. Under some pretext she arranged a search of our house. They didn't notice the jug full of home-brewed vodka in the corner, but they fished out the gold from underneath the mattress. When the Russians returned with the Poles in 1945, Z. immediately made her presence known. She told the commanding officer lies about my father. In the night, some people dismantled the barn which had just been rebuilt on a formerly Jewish-owned field, and they beat my father up so hard that he died from his injuries. They had sentenced him without a trial, without witnesses or an explanation. It was necessary to find guilty persons, and the Nazis were no longer around."*

This search for the guilty was never easy. The people of Jedwabne most readily point to anonymous "farm hands and stable boys" as the guilty. To this, the peasants say: "It's the local people who took them into their houses. They stripped them of all their possessions—beds, pots and pans, everything. What peasant had anything to gain from abandoning his land and house?"

And yet some of them did just that. 70 year-old Maria K., points to one side of the town square and says: "*Here, where about 30 Jewish families used to live, there are these four villas built of brick. There are not many people left here who were born and bred in Jedwabne. Most people, like my husband and I, moved into deserted houses after the war. I never saw the burning, only my husband secretly helped some escapees get away. Two days later, I visited my mother in town. What a lot of people had arrived on carts, looking for loot! The Germans did not interfere in any way, not even when gold was found on a dead body. When they fought over the gold, the Germans simply laughed and said: 'You're going to end up the same way.' I'm not afraid to say this because I never got any advantage out of the burning. A quilt and two pillows are all I got, plus a cupboard which my mother took for me. And think of all the trouble I went to transporting all these goods! We lived at my mother-in-law's, and she was a bit of a member of a tertiary religious order. She prayed for the Jews, lamented their misfortune, and heaped curses on those who had enriched themselves at the expense of the Jews.*"

> "*There was a need for life, there was a need for death*"
> Rafał Wojaczek

In Janczewko, a village of the righteous, 5 kilometers from Jedwabne as the crow flies, everyone still remembers old Karwowski, who was famous for having successfully hidden seven Jews in storeroom throughout the German occupation. Apart from Franciszek and Józefa Karwowski and their daughter Antonina Wyrzykowska, no one in the village knew anything about this, though a few must have wondered suspiciously why their neighbors' appetites (or those of their animals) had grown so much. In any case, the Gestapo men who turned up in the village one day searched the premises of only these two families. The remaining peasants stood in front of their properties with raised hands, with the full knowledge that if the Karwowskis and Wyrzykowskis were hiding anyone and the Germans found them, the entire village would go up in smoke. Luckily, the Germans found no one, and not even families suspected of hiding Jews suffered any harm. Nevertheless, to this very day some people in Janczewko find it difficult to make a clear assessment: "They saved the Jews, but they rather recklessly endangered the entire village." No one knows if any of the neighbors belonged to the band of people who whipped the hide off Karwowski and his daughter for their wartime services. When they describe Franciszek Karwowski, their voices contain a hint of ironic forbearance. "He wasn't a hero, rather he was a good, God-fearing man. He would practically break down crying even for an animal that was about to be slaughtered. When he lay half-dead after being beaten by partisans, he said: 'May God forgive them and keep them healthy.'"

Out of the Jedwabne Jews hidden in Janczewko, only one decided to return to Jedwabne. He converted to Catholicism and received the Christian forename Józef. He returned to his home and to his Polish neighbor, Feliks Ż., who had been a grave-digger before the war. Józef G. did not reproach Ż. for having taken part in the Jewish pogrom and for having dragged Józef G. out of his house and onto the square. After all, Józef G. had survived. First, he managed to hide in the town hall, and later he crawled his way to Janczewko through the woods. This was not easy in view of the fact that there were man-hunts and rumors that the Jews might burn down Jedwabne in revenge.

G. did not ask how his wife and children had died. Nor did he tell his neighbor about the long years spent in hiding in a hole beneath a cowshed, about the luxury of breathing fresh air on special nights, or about the slow learning to live with lice, which bit into his body and left wounds. Details of his story were known only to his wife, a Pole, who had worked in his house as a servant before the war.

"My husband was very pious," G.'s widow says today, *"and that is probably why he meekly bore all kinds of persecution. In the night, shootings and a hammering on doors were to be heard all the time. We never opened the door. After a while, Felek Ż. moved away to the "Recovered Territories"* in western Poland, because his family had become larger and he had neither a farm, nor a trade that was in demand. Once he had resettled, he developed a new life. He also built a house for his children in Ełk. While paying a visit to his former neighborhood, he learned about my husband's death. He came to me, complaining that I had not told him of the funeral. Then I could stand it no more. 'Józef would have turned in his coffin if I had told you.' Well, Felek himself is now lying in the cemetery, and my time is almost up, and soon no one is going to reminisce about old wrongs and misfortunes any more."*

Both sides are forgetting the past. The cousin of Feliks Ż. married a girl of Jewish descent...

After 1956, Antoni Ch., with his wife Helena, of Jewish origin, also settled in Jedwabne, and no one gave them any trouble. *"My wife owes her life solely to Providence and human kindness,"* he says. *"God watched over her even when she was lying in the corn and the Germans were combing the cornfield. Her nightmare began on July 7, 1941, when the local ruffians led her father, the village blacksmith, off to Radziłów and burnt him together with others there. The Gestapo came to Kubra to collect her mother and three children. But the village did not betray them, even though everyone knew that they could die for hiding a Jew or for so much as giving him a glass of water. The peasants staged a fictitious man-hunt so as not to fall foul of the Germans, but they did not want to have any part in the atrocity. Earlier, the peasants had slept in the fields or gone into hiding in order to avoid being picked to lend a hand in the burning of the Jews in Radziłów. My wife, her mother and her brothers hid among various people, including those in Chrzanów, Kubra, Doliwy and Trzaski. The people who hid them did not do so for money, which no one had in any case. But they put their own lives and those of their families at risk. One by one, my wife's brothers unfortu-*

nately fell into the hands of the Gestapo and, after being tortured, were shot. My wife and her mother were luckier...."

Despite the passage of time, Helena Ch. holds in grateful memory the people who hid her. *"How can I say anything bad about the Polish people when they saved my life and that of my cousin?"* she asks.

After reading Szmul Wasersztajn's report, she comments without hesitation: *"My grandfather and my mother's two sisters, with their husbands and children, died in the fire at the Jedwabne barn. How this came about I know only from what people have told me. But I don't believe the people of Jedwabne could have been as cruel as that. Szmul's words must have been dictated by grief and despair, so he wasn't objective. A rabbi from Costa Rica visited Jedwabne recently, one of the seven Jews whom Karwowski saved. First he prayed at the Jewish cemetery, and later he came to us. He had good memories of one of those who, according to Wasersztajn's account, had murdered the Jews; 'That was a very good man,' the rabbi said, and I believe him."*

Wars have always been hard on Jedwabne. What was once a flourishing industrial town during the partitions* turned into a settlement of merchants and artisans after World War I. World War II cost the town even its shops and workshops. For 40 years it was incapable of rising again, or of regaining more than a fraction of its former importance. It shared the fate of other small Jewish towns, similar to those which Antoni Słonimski describes in his *Elegy to the Jewish Towns*:

"These towns are no more.
They have passed like a shadow,
And this shadow shall descend between our words
Ere these words come fraternally together and
Rejoin two peoples raised on the same suffering"

Danuta Wroniszewska and Aleksander Wroniszewski

ANDRZEJ KACZYŃSKI

BURNING ALIVE

"RZECZPOSPOLITA" MAY 5, 2000

In Jedwabne, the German extermination of the Jews was carried out by Polish hands.

On July 10, 1941 in Jedwabne, in the Łomża region, the Germans ordered that the entire Jewish community of the small town be exterminated. Local Poles carried out the death sentence. Recently revealed eyewitness accounts by Jews who survived the Holocaust confirm this. Nor do Polish residents of Jedwabne who witnessed the tragedy deny it. From these same sources, it is also known that the Germans used Polish hands to commit similar massacres of Jews in Wąsosz, Wizna and Radziłów. Many of these documented testimonies were previously known to Polish scholars. These scholars did not, however, contribute to exposing the shocking truth about Polish involvement in the Nazi extermination of the Jews. This knowledge has reached us from abroad.

One tragedy, two histories

A boulder with a memorial tablet is the only trace of more than two hundred years of Jewish presence in Jedwabne, near Łomża. But the inscription on it accusing the Nazis alone of carrying out the destruction of the Jewish residents of the town does not tell the entire truth. Nor did historians living in Poland reveal that truth. Only recently, Professor Jan Tomasz Gross of New York published Szmul Wasersztajn's account describing the general participation of local Poles in the murder of the Jedwabne Jews. This document, written in 1945 and preserved in the archives of the Jewish Historical Institute* in Warsaw, had been known to, or at least referred to by Polish historians who nevertheless concealed its true significance. A collection of later Jewish testimonies, which also accuses a certain number of Poles from Jedwabne and the nearby villages of involvement in the crime (it accuses them by name, and there are at least thirty names), has recently been placed on the Internet in the United States.

A discussion on the subject of the murder of the Jedwabne Jews has developed over the Internet, based on this documentation as well as on a lecture by Professor Jan Tomasz Gross at an American university. One posting, from a month or so ago, reads in part: "The Germans entered Jedwabne. The Poles asked them to leave town for eight hours. Eight hours later, there were 1,100 fewer Jews." The author got her distorted information second hand, or she heard about it, but not accurately. Another author confuses the dates and informs the world that [in Jedwabne—trans.] the Poles murdered Jews who had survived the Nazi Holocaust. The June 3, 1946 pogrom in "Kielce,* in comparison was small beer" he states. Both authors display considerable curiosity about, and a degree of familiarity with Polish affairs. These are the results of covering up the truth. The reaction of Internet readers who know little or nothing about Poland is something that it is better not even to think about.

I checked to see what Polish Shoah researchers had written on the subject. It turns out that there are two different, and even contradictory versions of the destruction of the Jedwabne Jews. Polish sources attribute responsibility for the massacre exclusively, or almost exclusively, to the Germans, the Nazi *gendarmerie* and police. The Polish role in them is downplayed, silenced, or denied outright.

Are they going to take away formerly Jewish property?

Many Jedwabne citizens refused to talk, and yet without great difficulty I obtained general confirmation of the Jewish accounts of the perpetrators of the extermination. Not only older people who lived in town throughout the war knew and stated that Poles committed the murderous acts, but so did young people who knew the truth only through family stories. "None of the murderers is still alive," they assured me. Yet almost all of them demanded anonymity. When our photographer approached some youngsters gathered in the town square and asked them to point out any mementoes of the Jedwabne Jews, or the monument to them, they first asked with a hint of sarcasm whether he had come to take back the property that formerly belonged to the Jews.

Only one Jewish apartment house remains in Jedwabne. The author of one of the accounts placed on the Internet visited the town some 20 years ago and lamented that he saw hardly any Jewish buildings left.

During World War I about 75% of the town was destroyed. A few years before World War II, the church and synagogue were rebuilt. The Germans burned down the splendid new synagogue, the pride of the Jedwabne Jews, in September 1939.

On September 28, 1939, the two invaders, the Third Reich and the Soviet Union, agreed on their division of Poland. For 20 months, Jedwabne was under Soviet occupation. The Germans again entered the town on June 23, 1941, the second day of their attack on the USSR. Eighteen days later, almost all the Jedwabne Jews were burned alive.

The Jewish version

The few Jews who survived the burning or who heard about it from eyewitnesses, accuse the Poles, their neighbors and fellow townspeople in Jedwabne, as well as others from the nearby villages, of the crime. According to their accounts, Poles were the sole perpetrators of this crime. Germans may have issued the orders or incited the pogrom, but it is not certain whether they were in town at the time, and they may have even tried to moderate or limit the extermination. The first source is two depositions that Szmul Wasersztajn, an eyewitness to the tragic events in Jedwabne on July 10, 1941, presented to the Jewish Historical Committee in Białystok in 1945. These statements are preserved in the archives of the Jewish Historical Institute* in Warsaw. The JHI archives also contain depositions on the events in Jedwabne and the vicinity by, among others, Menachem Finkelsztejn, Abraham Śmiałowicz, and A. Belawicki. All of them accuse the Poles. These documents have been known to scholars for a dozen or more years—at least they are cited by all Polish scholars in their lists of sources. Jan Tomasz Gross was the first to publish one of Szmul Wasersztajn's two depositions (the longer one) in its entirety (in a *festschrift* for Professor Tomasz Strzembosz, *Europa nieprowincjonalna* [Non-Provincial Europe], Warsaw, 2000). While indicating that while he found several discrepancies between Wasersztajn's two depositions, Gross did not engage in any basic criticism of them as sources (obviously regarding them as credible). He also outlined plans for further research on Polish attitudes to the extermination of the Jews in the period following the [1941] German attack on the Soviet Union.

Among the testimonies on the Internet (http://www.jewish-gen.org/Yizkor/jedwabne/) are those of three eyewitnesses: Herszel Piekarz-Baker, Rywka Fogel and Icchak (Janek) Neumark.

Wasersztajn claims that on the third day of the German occupation of Jedwabne, June 25, 1941, "local Polish bandits" started robbing Jewish property, brutally beating and even killing Jews. "With his own eyes" he saw three people murdered. "Jakub Kac was stoned with bricks; Eliasz Krawiecki was stabbed repeatedly with knives, then his eyes were gouged out and his tongue was cut off. He suffered inhumanly for twelve hours before drawing his last breath." Rywka Fogel names four other victims of the massacre.

Wasersztajn continues: "That same day I observed a horrible scene. Chaja Kubrzańska, twenty-eight years old, and Basia Binsztejn, twenty-six years old, both holding newborn babies, when they saw what was going on, they ran to a pond, in order to drown themselves with the children rather than fall into the hands of bandits. They put their children in the water and drowned them with their own hands: then Baśka Binsztejn jumped in and immediately went to the bottom, while Chaja Kubrzańska suffered for a couple of hours" [Gross's translation]. Rywka Fogel offered different details. The two women exchanged babies. They slashed their own veins before throwing themselves into the pond. According to Wasersztajn, the hooligans treated the tragedy as a spectacle. Fogel claimed some Poles rescued the women the first time they attempted suicide. Their husbands, communist activists, escaped with the Russians.

The pogrom lasted one day. Wasersztajn stated that it was stopped by the priest, explaining "that the German authorities would take care of things by themselves" [Gross's translation].

On July 7th and 8th, Jewish refugees from pogroms in Wizna and Radziłów tried took shelter in Jedwabne. About 1,000 Jews lived in Jedwabne and it is not known how many fled with the Russians. Some place the number of fugitives as high as 700. Some hid outside of town, expecting a catastrophe since the Nazis were organizing a pogrom in a different locality each day.

Early in the morning of July 10th, the people in hiding watched as many peasants from the outlying hamlets arrived in town by cart —like on a market day. Germans also arrived. Eight Gestapo functionaries held a meeting with representatives of the town's Polish authorities. According to Wasersztajn, the Germans wanted to kill most of the Jews while sparing skilled craftsmen who would be useful to them, while the Poles demanded that none of the Jews be left alive, because there were enough skilled Christian craftsmen to do any work. Other Jewish accounts give a similar account of the meeting. Some Polish witnesses also overheard the local side taking just such a stance in the negotiations with the Gestapo.

The Jews were ordered to gather in the town square. "Local hooligans armed themselves with axes, special clubs studded with nails, and other instruments of torture and destruction and chased all the Jews into the street" [Gross's translation], testified Wasersztajn. They forced the Jews to weed and clean the square. A statue of Lenin was toppled from its pedestal and young Jews were ordered to carry it around the square while singing Soviet songs and chanting: "This war is our work." According to some accounts, the Poles selected dozens of strong young men and ordered them to carry Lenin's statue to the Jewish cemetery outside of town. There, they forced them to dig a large pit and bury the statue in it. After that, they murdered all these men and threw their bodies into the same pit. The rest of the Jews were kept in the town square all day under the scorching sun, without a drop of water. They were insulted and beaten. Polish hoodlums tormented the gray-haired rabbi, Awigdor Białostocki, and did not spare the women and the children. In the evening they marched all the Jews, in rows of four, towards the Jewish cemetery. According to some accounts, the rabbi was ordered to march in the front rank carrying a red banner. Everyone was forced into a barn. The barn was doused with a flammable liquid and set alight. Icchak Neumark, a former citizen of Jedwabne, testified that a Pole whom he recognized stood guarding the barn door, axe in hand. "He was ready to kill anyone who tried to get out. My family and I were standing near the door because, fortunately, we were among the last to be pushed into the barn. Suddenly, the barn door fell apart in the flames. The one guarding the door raised his axe to strike me, but fortunately I managed to knock it away. My sister, her five year-old daughter, and I managed to escape to the cemetery. I saw how my father collapsed in flames on the earthen floor [of the barn]."

Those who were not burned alive in the barn were beaten to death wherever the Polish perpetrators found them. Rywka Fogel heard the terrible screams of Józef Lewin, a boy whom the bandits clubbed to death. "The goys grabbed little Judka Nadolna, cut off her head, and played with it like a soccer ball," testified Fogel. Icchak Neumark said that one woman, nine months pregnant, had her abdomen ripped open by her father-in-law's farm hand. "I saw with my own eyes how Aron lay dead in the street with a cross carved into his chest. Three-year-old Chana hid in a chicken coop. The goys found her and threw her into the fire like a piece of wood," said Neumark.

"Not even one German participated in the killing that day. On the contrary, two officers came to the barn of destruction to save at least the craftsmen, tailors, cobblers, blacksmiths, and carpenters, whose labor the Germans required. But the goys told them: 'Not one Jew can remain alive. There are enough skilled craftsmen among the Christians,'" Neumark reported. "Even though the Germans gave the order, it was Polish hooligans who took it up and carried it out, using the most horrible methods," said Szmul Wasersztajn. "The Poles decided to kill all the Jews and they did so. The Germans looked with disdain upon the overt bestiality of the Poles," testified Herszel Piekarz-Baker, the author of one of the accounts published on the Internet.

The Polish version

In 1966 article in the *Bulletin* of the Jewish Historical Institute,* Szymon Datner charged the special operational groups [*Einsatzgruppen**—trans.] of the German police with the crimes committed on a mass scale against the Jewish population of Białystok region after the attack on the USSR by the Third Reich. "Those units were supported by 'native' police formations consisting of traitors, fascists, degenerates and criminals. Often playing on the lowest instincts of these people, the [German—Kaczyński's note] units organized outbursts" of popular fury, "supplying arms and giving instructions without themselves taking part in the slaughter themselves. As a rule, they photographed the scenes that were played out as evidence that the Jews were hated not only by the Germans." Datner goes on to write about the Łomża region: "the Germans dragged the dregs of the local community, as well as the so-called 'Blue Police'* into these crimes. This was a phenomenon that was relatively rare in occupied Poland, as well as in the rest of the Białystok area, where the local population—Polish and Belorussian alike-refused to be hoodwinked by German provocation.... In a few cases, the local scum and criminal elements allowed themselves to be used as henchmen pawns by the Germans. However, the majority" of the work "was done by

German hands." Szymon Datner did not write anything unequivocal about who perpetrated the crime in Jedwabne.

The most detailed Polish account of the events in Jedwabne was presented in 1989 by Waldemar Monkiewicz, a public prosecutor and member of the Białystok Regional Commission for the Investigation of Nazi Crimes in Poland,* in *Studia Podlaskie* [Podlasie Studies] published by the University of Białystok. "In early July 1941, 200 men from the 309th and 316th [German—Kaczyński] police battalions were detached to form a special unit, called *Kommando Bialystok*, under the command of Wolfgang Birkner, who was seconded from the Warsaw Gestapo. On July 10, this unit arrived in Jedwabne by truck. Both the *gendarmerie* and the auxiliary police were engaged in the operation carried out against the Jews. The auxiliary police were involved only in leading the victims to the square and escorting them out of town. There, the Nazis committed unspeakable cruelty, driving some 900 people into a barn that they next closed, and the walls of which they splashed with gasoline and set alight, causing the martyr's deaths of the men, women, and children inside. Two days later, these same perpetrators murdered almost all the Jews in Radziłów [according to most sources, the massacre in Radziłów occurred on July 7, and thus earlier than the one in Jedwabne]. There, they burned approximately 650 people in a barn. In both Jedwabne and Radziłów, the Nazis attempted to drag some auxiliary policemen of Polish nationality [i.e., ethnic background—trans.] into the pogrom. Those among them against whom any sort of involvement was proven-and this was most frequently in acts of subsidiary importance-bore severe punishment."

Three years earlier, during a ceremonial oration at ceremonies marking the 250th anniversary of Jedwabne's municipal charter, prosecutor Monkiewicz stated that 150 German police came to Jedwabne by motor vehicle on the day of destruction in Jedwabne, estimated the number of dead Jewish victims at "about 900, and in any case not fewer than 600," and admitted that he had managed to establish the names of only a few families who perished then. He added that he "would omit for understandable reasons" mentioning the names of the Polish auxiliary police who had anything to do with the crime.

Twenty-two Poles were tried in Łomża in 1949 for cooperating with the Germans in the murder of the Jews of Jedwabne. A death sentence was pronounced against a *Volksdeutsch** from Cieszyn. The others were sentenced to eight to fifteen years' imprisonment. None of them admitted his guilt. Unfortunately, the records of the trial are at present unavailable since the archives of the Main Commission for the Investigation of Crimes against the Polish Nation,* where they are preserved, are being moved to new premises.

Prosecutor Waldemar Monkiewicz also states that Nazi state functionaries have been tried in Germany for the Jedwabne crime.

To clarify, not to justify

Discussing "anti-Jewish outbreaks and pogroms in occupied Europe" in an article in the book *Holocaust z perspektywy półwiecza* [The Holocaust from the Perspective of Half a Century], published by the Jewish Historical Institute*, Professor Tomasz Szarota writes that "each time it was probably a provocation prepared by the Sipo* and SD*, and in the east by the *Einsatzgruppen*.* The primary purpose was one of propaganda. The world was thus shown that the Germans were not the only ones who felt the need to eliminate the Jews, and that the strength of hatred of the Jews was even stronger in other countries than in Germany. As a by-product, there was a demonstration of the alleged approval of the occupied countries for the way in which Nazi ideology brandished anti-Semitic slogans. By intervening at a certain moment as a factor for law and order, the German achieved yet another aim—they suddenly appeared as the defenders of the Jews against an assault by the Poles...." This scenario fits the events in Jedwabne perfectly.

Andrzej Żbikowski of the Jewish Historical Institute stated in 1992 (in the JHI Bulletin) that, in the western regions of the Soviet Union, the former Polish eastern marches,* "after June 22, 1941, the Jewish population became the protagonists of two simultaneous tragedies. One of these, incomprehensible to the majority of the

37

Jews, was the German desire to physically exterminate the Jewish people. The second was the explosion of long-suppressed hatred, founded on an economic and emotional-ideological basis, among the native local population." He added: "the aggression by the local community was not exclusively a result of German manipulation."

During the period of the Soviet occupation (less than two years) the relationship between Poles and Jews in the eastern marches* worsened significantly.

"The Jews have supported us and only they were always visible. It has become fashionable for the director of every institution to boast that he no longer has even a single Pole working for him," said the head of the Łomża NKVD* at a meeting with activists in 1941. He said that, from the point of view of the Soviet state, this was a highly unfavorable situation.

Someone heard a farmer from the vicinity of Łomża complaining during the war: "Now we have a Jewish empire. They are chosen everywhere, and the Pole is like a horse: he only hauls, and they strike him with a whip. Bad times have come for the Poles." Historians, and not only Polish ones, cite these and similar statements in order to show the reasons for the exacerbation of Jewish-Polish relations between 1939 and 1941.

In a collection of accounts by Poles who joined the army of General Władysław Anders* (published as *W czterdziestym nas matko na Sybir zesłali* [In 1940, Mother, They Sent Us to Siberia] by Irena and Jan Tomasz Gross), there is a report by a member of a clandestine Polish military group from the neighborhood of Jedwabne blaming his imprisonment and deportation on a denunciation by a Jew who collaborated with the NKVD.

In Jedwabne in 1940, the NKVD smashed two underground resistance groups: "The Partisans," numbering about 35 members, and Armed Combat Union,* whose 80 soldiers came from the Białystok region and the Jedwabne area. After their organization was penetrated by NKVD agents, about 100 members of the Polish underground gave themselves up in December 1940. Documents unearthed in Soviet archives and published recently in *Studia Łomżyńskie* [Łomża Studies] indicate that the NKVD recruited eighteen of these former non-Jewish partisans as agents, a fact that was not known at a time when public opinion placed most of the blame for denunciations on the Jews. In June 1941, the NKVD began arrests in Jedwabne of the partisans who had turned themselves in, along with their relatives and those who helped them, including one priest. Some were deported eastward just before the German-Soviet war broke out. Others avoided that fate only because of the panicky flight of the Soviet authorities.

"After what happened here during the Soviet occupation, you shouldn't be surprised at the Polish rage that was directed against the Jews," one Jedwabne resident told me.

There are two war memorials in this small town. One commemorates the 180 people murdered between 1939 and 1956 by the Soviet, German and Polish communist authorities. The other commemorates the 1,600 Jews who were burned alive on July 10, 1941.

The Wyrzykowski family of Janczewko saved the lives of 7 Jews from Jedwabne by hiding them on their farm. Antonina Wyrzykowski received a Yad Vashem medal as one of the Righteous among the Nations. However, she moved out of her native village. She feared that she could pay with her own life for saving Jews. "They beat her black and blue," recalls her son.

Memory

The memorial to commemorate the murdered Jews of Jedwabne was erected in 1962 or 1963 by the Łomża branch of ZBoWiD,* remembers Eugeniusz Adamczyk, who looked after the memorial. The inscription bears signs of attempts to vandalize it. Adamczyk was the first commander of the Citizen's Militia* post in Jedwabne. He lucked out twice when he happened to be away from his post during an attack by the underground-and also had the bad luck to lose his job for that reason. "The UB* suspected me, although it was a pure coincidence," he explains. He also remembers arresting three men for the massacre of the Jews, and delivering the suspects to Łomża. "The other accused were arrested by 'security,'" he adds. Adamczyk hails from the Cracow region, but his wife, Henryka, remembers the massacre even though she was only twelve at the time. "My parents ordered me to hide but I can still hear the screaming of the Jews being led to their death, and I can smell the stench of the burning."

No one has ever verified the figures on the memorial plaque. All that is known is that more or less that many Jedwabne Jews were never seen again. The remains of those who were burned were never exhumed after the war. None of the residents of Jedwabne can point out to me the place where they were buried.

The institute in Jerusalem for research and commemoration of the Holocaust is named Yad Vashem. These two Hebrew words mean "a name and a place"—the minimum that the living owe to the victims of the Holocaust or, to put it differently, of those who were burned alive. The Jedwabne Jews, who died just such a cruel death by being burned alive, have not been granted even that minimum of memory.

Yet something has started to change: In Wąsosz, a Jewish-Polish committee erected a monument in memory of the town's Holocaust victims. In Jedwabne, the Bishop of Łomża recently held an expiation service at the place where the Jews were killed. When Pope John Paul II spoke in Rome and Jerusalem about the guilt of Christians towards the Jewish people, they began considering in the Łomża diocese about how parishes in which Poles were involved in any way in the persecution and extermination of the Jews ought to examine their consciences and perform an act of repentance.

Andrzej Kaczyński

GABRIELA SZCZĘSNA

THE BLOOD OF JEDWABNE

"KONTAKTY" MAY 7, 2000

Poles from Jedwabne burned alive 1,600 Jews from the town and its environs, in a barn near the cemetery. The Germans didn't have to do anything, apart from taking pictures and thus documenting the barbarity of the Poles. Official propaganda as promulgated by communist Poland subsequently presented the line that the Gestapo and Nazi *gendarmerie* burned the Jews.

1.

A letter from Montevideo in broken Polish: "*Dear Mayor, I Ester Migdal, born in Jedwabne, Łomża district, Białystok voivodship, journeyed to Uruguay in 1937—me, my sisters, brothers and mother. My grandmother, Chana Yenta Wasersztejn, stayed behind. I know that Poles killed all of the Jews, I know who killed my Grandmother, her daughters—her entire family. He took her home, and now lives in this house. Forgive me, as I don't remember much Polish now, I haven't spoken the language for 62 years. I know no Jews remain in Jedwabne because the Poles killed them all and took everything, and now there are no Jews. What a bunch of bandits and thieves you are. You will get your just deserts before God. Not a single Jew is left. You bandits, the marks of what you have done are visible on your hands. You have worked the destruction of a whole town—you bandits, you bandits. What does your priest have to say about this? Your people live better now? Kill the whole town. How do you commit such evil? Now that you have homes that didn't cost you anything, you can dance. Your God will repay you for this. Bandits, bandits. What evil did my grandmother ever do? You didn't leave even a single Jew. Can you sleep at night? Write me and tell me how it is now in Jedwabne. I can throw out these bandits, these bandits from my house. Sir, write me telling me how you killed all of the Jews in the town. Can you sleep at night? Killed the whole town? Is life better now? Bandits, bandits! God will punish you. Write me, I want to know who lives there still."*

Someone still lives there.

"How did you feel, to have lived for so many years among people who murdered your loved ones?"

"May God forgive them."

"Have you never felt hatred?"

"May God forgive them."

"Are you afraid of anyone?"

"May God forgive them."

2.

"Since that July 10, 1941 the names of the murderers have remained an open secret," says Jerzy Ramotowski, a secondary-school teacher from Jedwabne. *"According to documents of the Jewish Historical Institute* in Warsaw and Yad Vashem, Jerusalem, the instigators of the crime were the Germans. Shortly after entering Jedwabne, the Germans began to search for a place to hold the executions, and for executioners to carry out 'the sentence.' Then a session of the local town council was held in their presence. The Germans proposed sparing one Jew from each profession. But in the end things turned out the way they turned out. This brings shame onto the people of Jedwabne, but you can't pick and choose with history. The Jews were joint creators of the history of the town from the eighteenth century on, and they and the Poles formed a common social organism."*

All these bonds were suddenly severed.

In broad daylight, the Poles of Jedwabne hauled Jews from their homes. They beat them with sticks, spades, clubs spiked with nails, forks and fists. First of all they were herded onto the town square. Then, from a six-meter high plinth, they removed a bust of Lenin which was left in the wake of the "Ruskies," and were ordered to carry it, while repeating the words "This war was caused by us, this war was caused by us...." They were herded down Sadowa and Cmentarna streets, then along a country road, where a barn with open doors awaited them. The barn was made available by a resident, a member of the town council. The Germans walked alongside, and did nothing. They took photographs, which served as evidence of the Poles' crime.

"A few Jews were able to escape from the column of death," says Krystyna Raszczyk. *"I know this from my grandfather. Five of them hid in his orchard. Among them were Hańcia and Szmujeł; he could see who was murdering his son. Szmujeł also told Grandfather that before herding them into the barn, the Poles ordered the Jews to remove their shoes, good clothes and jewelry...."*

The barn doors were closed; a moment later it burst into flames.

This torturous death rose into one great cry, heard in the neighboring villages. The stench of charred bodies hung over the town for several days.

"I was just returning that way from my parents' place," recalls Jadwiga Michałowska. *"I cried as I walked along, over this tragedy and the war. My husband was in Auschwitz. Today there's a gravestone for Jews in the field; this is also Auschwitz for me."*

Hańcia and Szmujeł hid in Krystyna Raszczyk's grandpa's orchard only a week. They did not want to endanger the life of their benefactor or that of his family any longer. All of a sudden they announced to him that they were going to Łomża, to the Ghetto; whatever will happen will happen, and off they went....

It's known that the Jedwabne murderers were no more than a dozen or so people. All of them so-called respectable types. They were joined by Poles from neighboring villages. It started with Wizna.

They got worked up about "beating a Jew," and were joined by others from the outskirts of Radziłów and the outskirts of Stawiski....

"There was no ideology behind it. For me it was an ordinary thuggish murder, from envy and for profit. A saying came out of it: 'He who in Jedwabne wears a signet ring is...,'" says an old man. *"The Jews, however, bore their share of the blame. From the start of the war they sided with the Ruskies and informed them as to who the wealthiest Poles were, and together with the Ruskies they drew up lists of Poles to be deported. It was difficult to forget about this all of a sudden. I won't give my name. From the newspaper it will get on the Internet and then Jews from around the world will make me out as a defender of Polish thugs and an anti-Semite from Jedwabne. My family had nothing to do with the slaughter, but as far as the Jews are concerned every Pole who was of age then played some part in their extermination. Today the Holocaust is also a business for them."*

3.

The town square, Przytulska Street, Przestrzelska Street. The Polish homeland of Fajgełe, Sara and Rebeka; Moryc, Icek, and Aron. The synagogue, the Hades House of Culture. Honek Gerber's grain purchase center, Zimny's mill, Hania Stryjakowska's haberdashery shop, Hania Kanowicz's dry goods store. It was from her that Antonina Narewska, after passing her seamstress exam, received a present for her profession in life: a fine pair of scissors.

"My family always had acquaintances and good friends among the Jews," she recalls. "My best friend at school was Dwercia Łojewska. Just before the war she left for Palestine. I missed her. And, then when 'this' happened I thanked God that he had spared her life."

When only bricks remained of the Jedwabne synagogue after the war, the authorities sold them to home builders. There was no shortage of takers.

"I refused: it's not right from a house of God," says Antonia Narewska. "Those bricks would always remind me of the people...."

Not long after that, those with lesser scruples occupied Jewish homesteads and drew up notarized deeds of ownership.

4.

In the fifties, the criminals of Jedwabne came before a court. A few served sentences. The remainder immediately left town with their entire families.

"But the memory of them was constantly kept alive for us by Marianna Gosiewska, a pre-war teacher," recalls Krzysztof Godlewski, the mayor of Jedwabne. "For her, life always had clear laws: black is black and white is white."

5.

A fenced-in stone sits in an open field. An inscription is engraved on it: "SITE OF THE SUFFERING OF THE JEWISH POPULATION. THE GESTAPO AND THE NAZI GENDARMERIE BURNED 1600 PEOPLE ALIVE JULY 10, 1941."

"The truth is sacred. It's obvious that the inscription must be changed," says the mayor. "However, I'm not in favor of simply naming the perpetrators of the crime. The assassins from Jedwabne were a handful, so the statement 'Poles' would be hurtful to all the residents. Each nation is made up of people; it isn't exclusively good or evil. I think the inscription 'Victims of the Second World War' would be the most fitting. As a warning to all of what hatred is."

"And what will you write back to Ester Migdal?"

"That wounds should be left to heal and not be opened anew."

Gabriela Szczęsna

ANDRZEJ KACZYŃSKI

THE PURIFICATION OF MEMORY

"RZECZPOSPOLITA" MAY 19, 2000

Three important things need to be done in the recently revealed matter of the mass murder of the Jedwabne Jews who
were burnt alive on July 10, 1941 by a group of local Poles
acting on Nazi orders (we wrote about this in *Rzeczpospolita*, May 5,
2000).

First, determine the place where the remains of the victims of the
tragedy were buried and arrange a cemetery for them according to
the laws of the Jewish religion. Second, reveal the true course of the
crime, its causes and circumstances, its perpetrators and victims, as
well as the witnesses and their mindset, in order to rectify the
half-truths and lies propagated so far on the subject. Third, commemorate not only the tragic end of the town's entire community of
Jewish fellow-citizens, but also their presence through the centuries
in a way that would help to unite rather than to divide.

The will to collaborate on these issues was agreed upon at a meeting in Jedwabne on May 8 by representatives of the local government, the Polish Union of Jewish Religious Communities, and the
prime minister's office.

A new monument, a memorial grove and an educational program

For close to forty years, the commemorative plaque at the place where Jews were burned alive in Jedwabne, near Łomża, has proclaimed a falsehood by ascribing responsibility for their death only to the Gestapo and Nazi *gendarmerie,* while everyone in the village are aware that the Germans gave the orders or provided the inspiration for the crime, but the majority of its perpetrators were local Poles. Those at the meeting agreed that the plaque bearing lies must be replaced by one that reflects the true course of the tragedy, and that it would be best if this were done before its sixtieth anniversary next year.

Piotr Zandberg, on behalf of the Warsaw Jewish Community, declared a willingness to fund a plaque commemorating the Poles who saved Jewish lives in Jedwabne and the nearby villages during the Nazi occupation. He also proposed that young trees, modeled on those at Yad Vashem in Jerusalem, be planted in Jedwabne jointly by Jews in honor of Poles who saved Jewish lives and by Poles to mark the memory of their Jewish fellow-citizens. He outlined a proposal by the Union of Jewish Religious Communities to organize an educational program to familiarize young people with the lives of the Jews in Jedwabne and elsewhere in Poland (their religion, culture and customs), in collaboration with the local government, educational authorities, parental committees, and maybe also with the town's Catholic parish. The most important thing of all, however, says Piotr Zandberg, is to create a cemetery for the victims of this murder.

Aerial photographs and archeological survey

This may not be easy. The existing monument probably stands on the site of the barn that was the site of the suffering and death of many hundreds of Jews. How many exactly is not known. The figure of 1,600 victims is only an estimate. A certain number died before July 10, 1941, and some the same day but not by being burned alive. Others survived the pogrom in Jedwabne and died in the Łomża

47

ghetto or extermination camps, or were murdered after their hide-outs were revealed. Nor is it possible to indicate precisely where the July 10 murder victims were buried. On the basis of clues from local residents, it can be deduced that the remains were buried near the site of incineration, not at the nearby Jewish cemetery but next to it, in pits or ditches. Irregularities in the ground level indicate numerous excavations, but it will require special research to reveal which holes were dug for burial and which ones were dug for sand extraction. The outline of the burned barn is visible on old aerial photographs, but archaeological investigation may prove necessary to identify the burial sites.

Witnesses

After the story was published in *Rzeczpospolita* on May 5, the response from former Jedwabne residents permitted new facts to be established. The monumental bust of Lenin that the perpetrators forced the Jews to carry stood not in the main town square in the center of Jedwabne (there was also another town square, smaller one known as the "old square," in the old Jewish neighborhood; nearby, I was shown several formerly Jewish-owned houses that are still standing, rather than the single one about which I was earlier in-formed), but in a small square not far away. This has made it possible to retrace the probable death route from the main town square to this small square (now a sort of small plaza) and then by way of Sadowa and Cmentarna streets to the place of suffering and death.

The reconstruction of the tragedy, based on the testimony of living witnesses, is made difficult not only because of the passage of time. As many of those who are still alive and residing in Jedwabne tell me, the massacre should not be thought of as taking place in the midst of a large crowd. Whoever could do so, especially women and children, sheltered from the danger, which threatened everyone, from criminals who had assumed the role of executioners, drunken outlaws caught up in a frenzy of murder. Despite this, there were people brave enough to stand up to the murderers. To the list of names previously known, it is possible to add further ones. Kozłowski the butcher saved a girl (Chajka, or perhaps Chaimka) and kept her for several months until her aunt came for her; both were later in the Łomża Ghetto and probably died in Treblinka or Auschwitz. I also was shown the turning off Sadowa Street where two little girls escaped from the death march and hid in a shed or outside toilet—in any case, they managed to survive the pogrom. In the end, however, they too found themselves in the Łomża Ghetto.

When he put forward the education project, Piotr Zandberg quoted the line by George Santayana: "Those who do not know the past are condemned to repeat it." In Jedwabne, everyone knew the truth, but they previously refused to speak it aloud. During a mass for the Motherland on Saturday, May 13, the parish priest asked the faithful to pray as well for those victims of the war who lost their lives because of the uninhibited, criminal desire of others to enrich themselves.

Andrzej Kaczyński

MARIA KACZYŃSKA

IN MEMORY AND ADMONITION

"GAZETA WSPÓŁCZESNA" JULY 11, 2000

Yesterday, July 10, was the fifty-ninth anniversary of the extermination of the Jedwabne Jews. Many visited the site of the mass murder and burial of about 1,600 people, although no one officially announced the commemoration. This case represents one of the blackest pages in the contemporary history not only of the region but also of Poland.

The local Jewish community of Jedwabne, consisting of some 1,600 people, was ruthlessly exterminated on July 10, 1941. A commemorative boulder was placed at the site of the killing and mass burial of the victims in the 1960s. It states that the Gestapo carried out the murder.

Burned in the barn

For several months, publications have been appearing that state unequivocally that the German occupation forces were only observers, and that the then mayor of Jedwabne at the time and his aides initiated the pogrom, with perpetrators coming from the ranks of those living in the town or nearby.

Recently, an account by one of the Jewish survivors was published along with documents from the 1949 Łomża trial of the Jedwabne murderers. From these sources, it transpires that in July 1941, men, women and even children were dragged from their homes and killed with clubs, axes and knives. Most of them, over a thousand, were herded into a barn outside of town and burned alive there.

Yesterday, about 20 people from Jedwabne and nearby villages came to the site of the massacre and the grave. Some brought memorial candles.

Here lie my friends

"We've been coming here for three years now and we light small candles," says an elderly woman from Jedwabne who was eight years old on July 10, 1941. "The girls I played with as a child and their parents are buried here. They all died in the barn."

The woman states that she knows how the tragedy occurred, for she was standing about twenty meters from the blazing barn. Earlier on, she saw how people were dragged out of their homes in town. She also saw the murderers, but will not say who they were. She refuses to give her own name or to agree to meet a reporter for an interview.

"Let the truth be found by those whose duty it is. I'm scared," she says, breaking off and wiping her eyes.

"There are no words for this," says 74-year-old Leon Dziedzic from Przestrzele. Several days after the crime, he was picked by the Germans to gather up the remains of the murdered Jews.

"We used rakes to push the piles of corpses into a great ditch dug along the north wall of the barn. I recognized people I knew," he says.

Jedwabne mayor Krzysztof Godlewski and the town and district council chairman Stanisław Michałowski came to the monument yesterday before noon. They brought a mourning wreath with a ribbon decorated with the words: "For the murdered Jedwabne residents of Jewish nationality—in memory and admonition—society." They placed it at the foot of the boulder.

"If it is confirmed that the truth is different from what is inscribed on the plaque, then it should be changed," said Godlewski, surprised by the presence of the group of local residents, journalists and a crew from Polish national television.

The truth above all

In the Mayor's opinion, recent publications on the murder have a sensational tone and should not be given full credence.

"An investigation should be conducted and the truth should be established, one which all will adhere to," said Godlewski. "We cannot allow the new monument to divide people. This monument should unify and not divide. It should be a warning for the future."

"We've been stuck with the reputation of a criminal town," added council chairman Michałowski. "This is unfair. As in every community, various sorts of people lived here. It's necessary to differentiate the criminals from the normal people—this was just as much a tragedy for the latter as for those murdered."

Will there be an investigation?

As Krystyna Michalczyk-Kondratowicz, regional prosecutor in Łomża informed us yesterday, the case has provoked interest from the Main Commission for the Investigation of Crimes against the Polish Nation,* now being transformed into the Institute of National Remembrance.*

"The former head of the commission, professor Kulesza, has asked us to question one of the witnesses. Two weeks ago, one of my prosecutors questioned that person," Kondratowicz said. "I don't know what stage the present case is at, however. Most likely, the investigation hasn't started because of the reorganization of the Institute."

Yesterday we were unable to contact the Institute of National Remembrance.

Maria Kaczyńska

MARIA KACZYŃSKA

BURN THE JEWS IN THE BARN

"GAZETA WSPÓŁCZESNA" JULY 14, 2000

July 10 was the fifty-ninth anniversary of the extermination of the Jedwabne Jewish community. This year's anniversary differed from all the previous ones, which went unnoticed by Jedwabne residents and the general public. For the first time, the Mayor and the chairman of the City Council placed a wreath from society at the commemorative boulder.

The events that took place on the 10th of July 1941 in Jedwabne near Łomża belong on the darkest pages of the recent history of that region—and of the country.

There was an anti-Jewish pogrom on an unprecedented scale. Approximately 1,600 people, almost all the town's Jewish residents, were murdered.

For many years it was officially stated that the Gestapo and Nazi *gendarmerie* did the killing. That is what it says on the commemorative stone that appeared on the site of the atrocity in the 1960s.

Publications appearing over the last several months indicate unequivocally that the instigators and perpetrators of the crime were residents of the town and the outlying hamlets. The only role played by the Germans was that of "observers."

53

MARIA KACZYŃSKA

On the Radziłów model

Jan Tomasz Gross has produced the most fully documented new perspective so far in *Neighbors*, published by Fundacja *"Pogranicze"* in Sejny. Reading this book is a mighty shock. The author introduces, among others, the account of Szmul Wasersztajn, one of the survivors of the pogrom. Wasersztajn's account was the basis for a 1949 criminal investigation aimed at identifying and bringing to trial those responsible for the murder. The second source for the reconstruction of the circumstances and course of events is the records of this trial, held in May 1949 before the Regional Court in Łomża. At that time, eleven of the offenders named by Wasersztajn were sentenced to jail terms of eight to fifteen years, one was sentenced to death penalty, and ten were found not guilty.

According to these sources, an explosion of anti-Semitism occurred in Jedwabne and places like, for example, Radziłów and Wąsosz, after the retreat of the Soviets and the invasion by the Nazis in June 1941, and "Polish hooligans" murdered Jews with a feeling of total impunity. In their savagery, these massacres resembled the Cossack pogroms of the Jews in seventeenth-century Ukraine during the Chmielnicki uprising, described on the pages of Sienkiewicz's *With Fire and Sword.** On July 7, the extermination of 600 Jews occurred in Radziłów. The German *gendarmerie* took an approving attitude as the Jews were burnt alive in a barn. On July 10, the Jedwabne Jews were dealt with. According to Wasersztajn, many out-of-towners appeared armed with knives, clubs, axes and the like on that day. Together with "local hooligans" they herded the Jews into the town square. During this frenzied roundup, there were murders in various parts of town. Patrols on horseback armed with plow handles circled the town, catching those who tried to escape.

According to Wasersztajn and the witnesses appearing at the Łomża trial, the collaborationist authorities in Jedwabne, headed by mayor Marian Karolak, made an agreement with the Germans to settle the question of the Jews once and for all. Karolak allegedly received permission from the Germans for the extermination of the Jews, and arranged for them to be herded into the town square.

54

Gross suggests that, until the very end, the ringleaders of the slaughter had no clear concept of how to kill 1,600 people efficiently. The Germans refused to issue firearms, and killing by means of clubs, knives, and axes took a long time. Because the Germans had given them only eight hours, the ringleaders decided, as evening approached, to implement the Radziłów model and burn the Jews in a barn.

This mass murder occurred on the outskirts of town, opposite the Jewish cemetery. The victims were packed into a barn, gasoline was poured on, and the building set on fire.

Drag the corpses any which way, just get it over with

Leon Dziedzic from Przestrzele is 74. As a young boy, two days after the crime, he was picked by the *gendarmerie* to rake up the remains of the murdered Jews.

"It was here." He points out the exact spot where Śleszyński's barn stood. "A long ditch was dug, two meters wide, the length of the north wall, in line with the foundation."

When Dziedzic started working here, there was already one layer of human remains covered with earth. Piles of corpses remained in the smoldering ashes of the barn. "They gave us pitchforks with bent teeth, the ones used for manure. I dragged however I could. If I hit a leg, I dragged by the leg, a head—by the head, just to get it over with," the old man recounts.

He is one of the few witnesses who speak about the mass murder without much reluctance. "Sure, there are those who won't like it, but I don't care," he laughs. A moment later, he starts sobbing.

"It's from what I've been through," he explains. "This has been tormenting me all my life. You can't have a conscience, you can't be a human being...."

Dziedzic was not an eyewitness to the murder. In Przestrzele, about 3 kilometers from Jedwabne, there were only the shouts, the muffled sound of people being murdered, as night fell on July 10, 1941. A column of smoke then rose in the sky.

Before everything quieted down, eighteen-year-old Szmul, the son of the seamstress Wasersztajn, appeared at the Dziedzic farm, having managed to slip through the mounted patrols and escape from the small town. For several days, Szmul hid in Przestrzele. He told Leon Dziedzic what had happened. Later, Dziedzic had the chance to more stories, different stories. "I could go on about it for ages," he says, waving his hand.

"I was eight and I saw how they were dragging them out of their homes. When they set the barn on fire, I was standing right there," says an elderly woman, pointing to a spot in a field of sparse rye some twenty meters from the commemorative boulder that marks the site of the slaughter.

On July 10, she came to the plaque to light a commemorative candle. She's been doing this for three years. "The girls I played with as a child and their parents are buried here. Someone must remember them," she adds.

The woman doesn't want to give her name, and doesn't want to make an appointment to meet with a reporter. "I remember the faces and names of the murderers but I'm afraid to talk," she declares bluntly.

This is unjust

Publications on the subject of the crime have caused a stir in Jedwabne. The town authorities at the moment are not accepting the image of a "town of criminals" on the basis of what has been written.

"This is an overblown and unfair image," says the chairman of the town council, Stanisław Michałowski.

Michałowski is a native of Jedwabne, and the uncovering of the truth is important to him. As he sees it, Gross condemns all the Polish inhabitants in his book and lumps them together by accusing them of the collective murder of the Jews. "It's not possible to agree with this," protests Michałowski. "This matter is far from clear, and requires thorough investigation."

In the opinion of Jedwabne mayor Krzysztof Godlewski, an investigation should be conducted and an official finding issued. "A truth should be established that is convincing to all, to us in Jedwabne, to all Poles, and to all Jews. Only then, if reports of voluntary Polish involvement in the murder are confirmed, will it be possible to change the inscription on the boulder."

The Mayor says that he will not allow for a change of the inscription before the facts are ascertained: "That monument should contribute to reconciliation and not to dividing people anew. It should pay homage to the victims and be a warning for the future that this crime and the sacrifice made by the victims, had significance at least in this context."

In Godlewski's opinion, there are certain symptoms of an effort being made by someone to exploit this dark page in the history of Jedwabne for ulterior motives. "After all, Jews have been coming to the scene of the crime for many years," he says. "They haven't just started coming now. I have never heard of anyone having any objections to the inscription on the boulder."

In the West, the first reservations about this inscription appeared many years after the crime. Nor did anyone propose a review of the case in Poland after censorship ended in 1990. In the last ten years, most of those who were alive during the occupation have died. Amongst the living, only a few witnesses and potential suspects remain. "In my opinion it's no accident that only now is the truth being sought," Godlewski reiterates.

After the recent publications, the Main Commission for the Investigation of Crimes against the Polish Nation,* at present being transformed into the Institute of National Remembrance,* has become interested in this case. "From what I know, the gathering of materials in this matter has begun," says Krystyna Michalczyk-Kondratowicz, regional prosecutor in Łomża. "Among others, at the request of the Commission chairman, one of our prosecutors has questioned a relevant witness."

In the light of the reorganization and creation of the Institute of National Remembrance,* the momentum in the case has slowed. Everything indicates, however, that an investigation will be conducted.

Maria Kaczyńska

ADAM WILLMA

MY SON'S BEARD

"GAZETA POMORSKA" AUGUST 4, 2000

On a single day, the Polish residents of Jedwabne in the Łomża Province murdered fifteen hundred Jews.

Horse-drawn wagons kept arriving in Jedwabne all night. Drivers cracked their whips and excited people had been gathering in the streets since dawn. The old Honks spent the night at the Bukowskis.' In the morning, however, they packed their gear and went to the town square. Józef Bukowski tried to convince them to wait it out—to no avail. The Honks were reticent and composed. "Our time has come," old Honk remarked upon departing.

Krzysztof Godlewski, the Mayor of Jedwabne, has distanced himself from the events of 59 years ago. He comes from Olsztyn Province. He has been taking frequent walks around the town lately: "I try to visualize what it was like. For long years no one would as much as mention the events of 1941, and then suddenly all hell broke loose. I keep seeing snapshots of Jedwabne in the 1960s. No sidewalks, cobblestone streets, gutters and those little rundown houses. Straight out of a Bruno Schulz* novel."

"The memories start pressing back. I can see these faces more vividly now. I can hear the voices more distinctly. It is time to settle accounts in my old age," the voice of Halina Popiołek (the daughter of Józef Bukowski) begins to waver. "On the night that the Honks came over, father brought home terrifying news. He said they were going to burn the Jews."

Stanisław Ramotowski lived right outside of Radziłów, a town a few kilometers away from Jedwabne. What lay in wait for the Jedwabne Jews took place in Radziłów two days earlier. Stanisław learned about the preparations for the pogrom from his friend in the neighboring village. He rushed to the Finkelsztajns, the owners of a grain mill in Radziłów. He hid the whole family in the henhouse attic: the old Mrs. Finkelsztajn, her son, two daughters and two grandchildren. He then went to Radziłów to take a look. "I saw 60 families rounded up in the town square. They were pulling up weeds in the scorching sun. Meanwhile, their Polish neighbors were plundering their homes. A German soldier was taking pictures from a balcony. It was about to begin."

Szmul Wasersztajn asked his mother to take some "rags" to Jedwabne. Leon harnessed the horses to the wagon and set off for his schoolmate's village. He packed his clothes and a sewing machine. "When we arrived, a band of young men surrounded the wagon, metal-spiked clubs in their hands. They shoved our load off the wagon and started sorting through it. I lost sight of Szmul."

The next morning, Halinka Bukowska was running around the streets of Jedwabne along with a bunch of other kids. She was eight but nevertheless remembered a lot: "First they walked from door to door, telling people to come to the square and cut off Jews' beards. My father didn't go. The Jews stood in the square all day. The sun was beating down mercilessly. They made them pull up the grass growing there. They battered them with clubs. Mr. Bielecki rode his horse past our house chasing a young Jewish woman by the name of Kiwajko—I can't remember her first name. Dripping sweat, she cried for help but no one would come to the rescue. Everyone knew that she had taken care of Bielecki's children while he was in prison."

The barn belonged to Bronisław Śleszyński. Large, located on the outskirts of town, it was perfect. Marian Karolak, the Mayor, went to get the keys to the padlock. Śleszyński and his daughter, Jaśka, removed the thresher and the wagon.

Janina Biedrzycka (née Śleszyńska, the daughter of Bronisław) sits down to relax by the well. I find a place next to her on the freshly mowed grass. The farmer turns her face toward the orange setting sun: "Have you got some sort if identity card to show me? Your name doesn't sound Polish. At any rate, I don't care. Everyone listens to the Jews. No one is interested in the truth."

"What truth?"

"The truth is that when the Russians came in, the Jews welcomed them with bread and salt. They informed on us, made threats. Within a week, the Ruskies arrested twelve Poles. I remember. I can recite all the names."

"And what about the barn?"

"You think my father had anything to say about it? They came and asked for the keys. There was no way to say no. But it was not the Poles' idea. The Poles would never have come up with anything of that sort. After all, the Jews could have been locked up in a ghetto."

Halina Popiołek does not claim to have seen everything. "I wasn't there when they were cutting off heads or stabbing the Jews with sharpened stakes. I found out about that from my neighbors. Neither did I see them make those young Jewish women drown themselves in a pond. My mother's sister did. Her face was covered in tears when she came to tell us about it. I did see them make young Jewish boys lug Lenin's monument around and shout 'This war is our fault!' I saw them whipping the boys with rubber truncheons. I saw them torturing Jews in the synagogue and how Lewiniuk, all beaten up, was buried alive, before he stopped breathing."

A black cat leaped into Popiołek's lap. Halina Popiołek gasped: "They drove them all into a barn. They doused it with kerosene on four sides. It was all over in less than two minutes but that screaming.... I can still hear it in my ears."

The cry of fifteen hundred burned people turned into a dull wail when it reached the house of Leon Dziedzic, three kilometers away. Then the wind brought the black smoke and the smell of burned bodies.

The next morning, German *gendarmes* told young men to come for work with their shovels. The workers included Leon Dziedzic. "It was covered with a thin layer of sand. We had to clean it up to prevent an epidemic. When we started digging, we released the carcass gas. Each of us vomited about two dozen times, but when the gas was gone only the smell of baked meat remained." Dziedzic adjusts his cap. The warm wind tousles the leaves of the pear tree that gives us shade. Puppies, few weeks old, play with our trouser cuffs. "After an hour or so, the Germans themselves decided the work was hopeless—the bodies were entangled like roots. Someone came up with the idea of tearing them apart piece by piece and throwing them in the pits. They brought us pitchforks and we started jabbing randomly at the heads and legs."

Leon Dziedzic falls silent. An unripe pear falls out of the tree. An aggravated dog growls at her puppies. Leon Dziedzic sprawls out comfortably in his garden chair: "At night, toward the end, only isolated human shreds were left. We scooped them all up. At one point, my pitchfork hit upon a shoeshine box. The box opened and gold coins fell out. People ran over and started picking them up. Then the Germans shooed us away with their rifle butts and searched everyone. 'The gold is ours, the rest is yours,' they said, pointing to the dead bodies."

Dziedzic remembers another detail: "I heard there was a problem later—the Germans had told the Poles to save at least one craftsman for every craft. But the Poles didn't, and then they searched frantically for craftsmen among Christians."

Ramotowski succeeded in hiding the Finkelsztajns until 1943. Then someone informed on them. Everyone was taken off to a ghetto and then, reportedly, on to Treblinka. Stanisław followed the Jews. Even then, he was in love with Rachela Finkelsztajn. She was well educated and refined. She had worked for the Buick and Chrysler dealer in Kielce. Stanisław was lucky—one of the *gendarmes* was Feliks Godlewski, who cooperated with Home Army.* He helped Stanisław sneak Rachela out.

"This is when the Holocaust started for me too. They searched for me with more vengeance than they did for the Jews," reminisces Stanisław Ramotowski. "Finally, I made a dug-out in a field for us to live in. Before the liberation, a German soldier accidentally stumbled upon the camouflaged dug-out. He was a frontline soldier, however, and had little interest in the extermination of the Jews. The Germans did not respond even when a neighbor informed them that a Jewish woman, Finkelsztajn, lived there. Instead, the Germans gave Rachela a job in a field kitchen."

After the war, Stanisław let the girl choose. "He said 'You're free to do as you please,'" recalls the former Rachela Finkelsztajn, now Marianna Ramotowska. "I was sure of what I wanted."

They have lived happily for 54 years. "Perhaps we have been so happy together because we went through all the worst things at the start."

In the late 1940s, Stanisław was summoned to the prosecutor's office regarding the pogrom. "Who burned the Jews?" asked the prosecutor. "Poles." The prosecutor shook his head in disdain. Ramotowski fumed: "If you know, why do you ask?" The prosecutor said, "You need to calm down, Mr. Ramotowski, you don't need this. Let's just say it was the Germans."

A few days after the burning of the Jews, Leon Dziedzic walked into his barn to get hay for his horse. A pile of hay moved and Szmul's face emerged. Wasersztajn had seen everything that had happened in Jedwabne from his hiding place. "He was preparing a hideout in Janczewko. He stayed there for three years. After the war, the forests still teemed with guerrillas. My brother was in the Home Army* and found out that guerillas wanted to 'take care of' Szmul. As a witness to the Jedwabne killing, Szmul had to die. He fled to Białystok in the nick of time. He sent us a soft, tanned hide as a token of his appreciation."

In 1949, Szmul Wasersztajn testified before the Jewish Historical Committee in Białystok. His account became the main source of information on the Jedwabne events.

With Mayor Godlewski, we ascend a hill where, in the 1960s, a stone with a commemorative plaque was placed in the memory of Jews burnt alive by the "fascists." Across the road, the only reminder of the Jewish cemetery are the wildly spreading hazel trees. As late as the 1980s, stones from the cemetery were taken away by Poles who returned here to build houses with money earned in the United States. Dozens of houses have tombstones embedded in their foundations.

"Why don't we have the Star of David? What good is a monument that won't last a year? It would attract anti-Semites from all over Poland," Godlewski says. "It shouldn't irritate people. The same goes for the inscriptions. The monument stands outside of town. It is too easy to deface it with graffiti."

One day, the Ramotowskis were visited by a neighbor. He told them about his trip to the Holy Land. "'I saw a tree planted in your honor,' he said. 'It grows on the Mount of Remembrance in Jerusalem.'"

Hanna (black bushy eyebrows, lively blue eyes, hair covered with a flowery handkerchief) feeds chickens in a yard by her house on Jedwabne town square. The magazine *Niedziela** is spread out on the table; her husband is sick in bed in the adjoining room.

Hanna was the only survivor in her family. Her name then was Sara; she was 15 when neighbors from a village outside of Jedwabne gave her a place to hide. She spent three years and three months hiding with her mother. They came out in January 1944. Her mother enjoyed her freedom until March, then died of exhaustion.

"Don't use my name. Why would you even want to? The name is gone, as are the people. God wanted them all to die in that barn. I hold no grudges. Poles gave me life." Hanna wipes her hands on her a blue apron and holds them together in an imploring gesture. "It was so quiet for years. Why go back to all that? Don't use my name, not for my sake but for my children's sake. When my son was studying in Białystok, he grew a beard. I had to plead with him to shave it off so that people didn't get the wrong idea. Then he wanted to name my grandson 'David,' but I explained that it might make people angry. I don't want to make anybody upset. I want to die in peace. As quietly and peacefully as possible."

P.S. A few weeks ago, Professor Jan T. Gross published *Neighbors*. The first printing sold out in record time. A second, from *Pogranicze* publishers, will be in bookstores in mid-August.

We would like to thank Henryk Bagiński and other residents of Jedwabne for their help in compiling the report.

Adam Willma

TOMASZ SZAROTA
INTERVIEWED BY JACEK ŻAKOWSKI

THE DEVIL IS IN THE DETAILS

"GAZETA WYBORCZA" NOVEMBER 18–19, 2000

Jacek Żakowski: *All the readers of Jan Tomasz Gross's* Neighbors *that I have spoken to are walking around in pain. The book is too cruel and too emotional, and the weight of its accusations too great for anyone to be able to read it and go on living as before. Although doing so will not be easy, we must therefore absorb Jedwabne into our image of ourselves. First, however, we must understand it. In order to understand, we need to know exactly what happened there. The more spotty our knowledge, the harder it will be to understand, and the easier to be emotional—and there is too much emotion in Polish-Jewish relations in any case. After reading this book I feel distinctly unsatisfied and uncertain about what happened in Jedwabne. Gross deliberately provokes these feelings—in the first place, through his emotional, journalistic style, and in the second, through his uncritical attitude to arbitrarily chosen sources. He proclaims this attitude himself. In rejecting the principles of the historian's and even the reporter's craft, he writes that "we must take literally all fragments of information at our disposal, fully aware that what actually happened to the Jewish community during the Holocaust can only be more tragic than the existing representation of events based on surviving evidence." As a journalist, I know that the truth can differ in many important particulars from what is suggested by* *"fragments of information." As a historian, can you help me build up a true image of what happened in Jedwabne?*

Tomasz Szarota: I, too, am in less than total agreement with Jan Tomasz Gross's assessments of accounts by miraculously rescued Holocaust victims. Gross is surely right when he states that rescued victims could not lie in 1945. They could, however, be mistaken as to details, and surely they made mistakes on more than one occasion. Every lawyer, psychologist, and historian understands perfectly well that witnesses—who are often convinced that they are telling the truth—are unable for many various reasons to recount the truth. The more emotional the event that they are telling about, the greater the risk of error. That is why I think that, in spite of the existence of a considerable number of accounts, no one will be able to completely reconstruct that image today, for no one has seriously researched the Jedwabne affair.

— *Why not?*

— I think that there were simply too few of us who knew about it. I myself only learned about the crime in Jedwabne from Szmul Wasersztajn's account, which Gross quoted in the article that he contributed to *Europa nieprowincjonalna* [Non-provincial Europe], the *festschrift* for Professor Tomasz Strzembosz (published in 2000; Gross's article was titled "Lato 1941 w Jedwabnem. Przyczynek do badania udziału społeczności lokalnych w eksterminacji narodu żydowskiego w latach II wojny światowej" ["The Summer of 1941 in Jedwabne: A Contribution to Research into the Role of Local Society in the Extermination of the Jewish People during the Second World War]). Reading that article was just as much of a shock to me as reading *Neighbors* was for you. Only afterwards did I begin to work on the Jedwabne affair, so I have been at it for only a few months. Yet I have been working hard, and have perhaps managed to acquaint myself with everything that has been published on the subject of Jedwabne.

— *And so things have been published?*

— Szymon Datner published a lengthy article in *Biuletyn Żydowskiego Instytutu Historycznego* [The Bulletin of the Jewish Historical Institute*] in 1966. There have been publications by Waldemar Monkiewicz, the public prosecutor who in 1949 represented the prosecution in the trial of those involved in the pogrom, and who later worked for many years in the Białystok branch of the Main Commission for the Investigation of Nazi Crimes*. There was also a very important article by Danuta and Aleksander Wroniszewski in *Kontakty* of Łomża.

— *So in all your years of working on recent history, you never came across even a mention of the pogrom in Jedwabne?*

— In general, I knew little about what happened in the Łomża region in 1941. After all—as I am now beginning to realize—Jedwabne was no exception. In his 1966 article, Datner described the large-scale extermination campaign that the Germans carried out against the Jews in the Białystok region between June and August 1941. We know that the scenario in Radziłów was similar to that in Jedwabne. Three days earlier, 1,500 Jews were also burned alive in a barn there. There too, the perpetrators were local Poles. In the dozen or more other cases that Datner described, as far as is known, the Germans themselves committed the murder. They shot 1,800 people in nearby Stawiska, 2,000 in Kolno, 2,100 in Tykocin, 3,500 in Łomża, and 1,900 in Szczuczyn. On June 27, the German 309th police battalion locked several hundred Jews in the synagogue in Białystok and burned them alive.

— *For the time being, however, let us attempt to reconstruct what happened in Jedwabne.*

— The basic facts seem indisputable. In July 1941, a large group of Poles living in Jedwabne took part in the brutal murder of almost all the local Jews, who in fact made up the clear majority of the inhabitants of the town. At first, they murdered them individually, using clubs and stones, torturing them, cutting off their heads, profaning their corpses. Later, on July 10, the almost 1,500 Jedwabne Jews who remained alive were forced into a barn and burned alive there. Gross describes this massacre on the basis of the extant accounts. He uses documents from the collection of the Jewish Historical Institute*—primarily the account by Szmul Wasersztajn —and memoirs by other people, including those known from *Yedwabne: History and Memorial Book*, which was published in the

United States in 1980, and the testimony of the defendants from the 1949 trial.

These unquestionable facts are so shattering that they force even me, a historian who has read much and written a good deal about various instances of disgraceful behavior by Poles under German occupation, to come to completely new conclusions. We already knew about the *szmalcownicy** and about the fact that relatively few Poles dared to shelter Jews in their homes. We knew that there had been anti-Semitic outbursts after the arrival of the Germans in Warsaw in 1939, and that Jews were assaulted, robbed, and beaten by young Polish hoodlums. Yet we did not realize that Poles were also perpetrators of the Holocaust. In Jedwabne, they were—and these were not some isolated deviants, who are found in every society, but a crowd with the town authorities at its head. Through his publications, Gross has forced us to change our views on the subject of the attitudes of the Poles during the Second World War, and that is an unquestionable service. Like you, however, I have the impression that he wrote *Neighbors* too hurriedly and examined the Jedwabne affair too superficially for us to be able to understand what really happened there.

— *What does this mean?*

— He did not, for instance, explain the matter of the presence of Germans in Jedwabne and their role in organizing and carrying out the pogrom. Gross assumes that there were practically no Germans in Jedwabne, aside from a small group of 11 *gendarmes* in the local police post and perhaps a few Gestapo functionaries. In a 1983 article, however, the prosecutor Monkiewicz states that the so-called *Kommando Bialystok*, led by Wolfgang Birkner from the Warsaw Gestapo, was involved in the Jedwabne pogrom. This unit was made up of functionaries from two German police Battalions, the 309th and the 316th. According to Monkiewicz, 232 Germans under the command of Birkner went to Jedwabne in trucks on July 10, 1941.

— *In* Neighbors, *Gross rejected similar information provided by a cook who worked in the German* gendarmerie *post.*

— I do not know if he was right to do so. I am not yet able, as a historian, to confirm the information provided by Monkiewicz. But

Gross did not deal at all with Monkiewicz's texts, and I doubt that the prosecutor made up those 232 Germans, the trucks, and the figure of Birkner out of whole cloth. One way or another, there is something wrong when the name of Birkner does not even appear in Gross's book. After all—and this is something I have confirmed—such an officer did indeed work in the Warsaw Gestapo, he held the SS rank of *Hauptsturmführer*, and he probably died in Poznań in 1945. Following this lead, someone might try to find documents on the German presence in Jedwabne and German involvement in the pogrom. Gross did not do so.

— *Should he have done so?*

— Every solid historian would surely do so before publishing a book. As a sociologist and writer, Gross might have felt that doing so was not necessary to explain the matter.

— *Yet is it necessary when we already know that Poles murdered Jews in Jedwabne?*

— There is no denying the fact that Poles committed murder. To understand this event properly, however, it is necessary to become familiar with the circumstances of the crime in detail. What Gross has written in *Neighbors* is enough to rattle our consciences. But it is necessary to know the details to understand the whole situation. Every historian knows that a multiplicity of details can often be the devil's workshop. After all, it is not a matter of indifference for understanding the whole Jedwabne affair whether the massacre was carried out spontaneously by the town's residents taking advantage of permission from the local *gendarmes*, or whether the German, who sent a police battalion to Jedwabne, incited a group of the dregs of society to "purge" the town of Jews.

— *This would also explain why the Jewish majority did not try to defend themselves against a pogrom carried out by part of the Polish minority, and why one of the Polish witnesses quoted by Gross told a Jew who was being murdered, "I cannot help you."*

— Yes. Obviously, not all the Poles took part in the massacre. However, as far as we know, no one interfered with the criminals.

— *Over the previous days, when what was still a small group of the dregs of society was tormenting and killing individual Jews in their*

69

homes and on the streets, no one interfered either—not Poles, and not even Jews. There are no accounts of any opposition aside from the priest mentioned by Wasersztajn who told them to "stop the pogrom, and that the German authorities would take care of things by themselves."

— Perhaps the town was terrorized. Or perhaps a part of the population felt that these murderers were settling accounts from the time of the Soviet occupation.... In his book, Gross quotes Tomasz Strzembosz's article "Uroczysko Kobielno" [The Kobielno Forest Range]. This is the story of an act of betrayal in the anti-Soviet resistance movement, which led to the breaking up of a partisans camp and the arrest by the NKVD* of a large group of Poles, including some from Jedwabne. One of the victims of this betrayal was Jadwiga Laudańska, who was murdered by the Soviets. Gross does not tell how she was connected with the Laudański brothers, who are often mentioned in *Neighbors* as the most active and brutal participants in the pogrom and the preceding individual murders. It is quite probable that the death of Jadwiga Laudańska at the Kobielno forest range influenced the behavior of the Laudańskis in July 1941, because it was then felt in Jedwabne that one of the local Jews had informed to the NKVD about where the partisans were. This went on top of the stereotype of the "Jewish communist"* and the universal conviction at the time that the NKVD were Jewish. Finally, as Gross does not mention either, a group of former underground anti-Soviet soldiers returned to Jedwabne before the pogrom. They had been freed from the NKVD prison in Łomża by the German invasion. Returning after long months of interrogation and Soviet imprisonment, they must, of course, have been baying for bloody revenge. Not only the perpetrators, but also the witnesses, both Jewish and Polish, might have assumed that a settling of accounts was taking place. Today, thanks to research by Tomasz Strzembosz, we know that the informant was probably Polish, but what people knew at the time is more important to understanding the situation.

— *Firmly grounded in an anti-Semitic stereotype.*

— Of course, traditional anti-Semitism was the basis for what happened. But not only. In the article by the Wroniszewskis, one of the witnesses describes the cooperation of a group of Jews with the

NKVD at the time of the Soviet deportations. Of course, Gross is correct when he writes that Jews were also victims of the deportations and of the Soviet system, for the Soviet authorities also confiscated their property and prevented them from taking part in religious services. However, the outbreak of hatred of the Jews that occurred after the arrival of the Germans also had its sources in generalized observations of the behavior of some Jews under Soviet occupation. And again, Gross is right when he writes that all generalizations are unjust. Yet they functioned and were "covered" by personal experiences.

It is impossible for us to conceive today of the scale of hatred of the Jews there. Not only among Poles, but also among Lithuanians. In my recently published book *U progu zagłady* [On the Threshold of Destruction], I describe, among other incidents, the pogrom in Kaunas. And Kaunas was not a small town perhaps gone mad with pain, like Jedwabne for example, but rather a large, modern city, and the capital of independent Lithuania. Yet things just as terrifying, which would have been unthinkable before the war, happened there. Soviet totalitarianism not only brought about new wrongs to be settled, but in its cruelty it also deprived people of a feeling of moral sensitivity. The deportations and NKVD* crimes taught the local people that there is no longer anything that is absolutely impermissible. Not everyone succumbed, but many did.

— *To the extent that someone like the carpenter Śleszyński could urge the Gestapo to permit the burning of all the Jews, without sparing the master craftsmen whom the Germans supposedly wanted to leave alive?*

— Unfortunately, knowing the economic aspects of prewar anti-Semitism and the sort of criminal emotions that sprang up under Soviet occupation, it is quite easy for me to imagine such a situation. An occasion simply sprang up suddenly to liquidate the Jewish competition once and for all, and a person completely devoid of inhibitions could feel that full advantage should be taken of the situation. Various accounts of Jedwabne indicate that an Aryan shop could not survive there before the war. All retail commerce was in the hands of Jewish merchants. The economic competition, including that among craftsmen, could arouse powerful emotions. Unfortunately, even such a statement fits in with the reality and criminal madness of the times. That's one thing. The second thing is the question of whether those words, among the most shocking in the book, were actually said.

— *Gross summons them up on the basis of the account by Szmul Wasersztajn, who could not have heard them. For Wasersztajn, they were hearsay.*

— If Gross had tracked down the German documents on Jedwabne, he might have found confirmation of Śleszyński's request. But he might have found information there that contradicted it. For instance, he might have found an earlier German order to kill all the local Jews—or perhaps even to burn them in the barn. Again, that would not cancel out the monstrous eloquence of the facts. It would, however, modify it in an important way.

— *Perhaps those documents would also make it easier for us to arrive at a view on the question of how many people took part in the crime out of their own free will, and how many were terrorized by a group of criminals (whom Wasersztajn calls "hooligans"), and who were thus following orders in forcing their victims into the town square, and later into the barn. Gross quotes the testimony of Jerzy Laudański, one of those involved in the crime, who says that, on July 10, after discussions with the Germans, "Marian Karolak told us Poles to call Polish citizens to the town hall. After calling in the Polish population, he ordered them to round up the Jews to the square, presumably to work, and this was done."*

— In order to understand Jedwabne, it would be necessary to know what proportion of the figure, given by Gross, of 92 persons involved in the crime did so out of criminal motivations, and how many were there and helped out of cowardice, out of fear of the dregs of society and Gestapo functionaries who controlled the town, backed up by the *gendarmes* present in Jedwabne and a battalion of German police.

— *On orders, or under protection and with permission?*

— Today, we cannot say. However, perhaps we are pointed in a certain direction by the information that the German authorities rebuilt the barn belonging to Bronisław Śleszyński, in which the Jews were burned.

— *So who is guilty in your opinion: the Germans, the dregs of local society, members of the anti-Soviet underground out for revenge, or the anti-Semitic society of Jedwabne? I have the impression that Gross accepts too easily the view that the crime was the work of the whole town when he writes that "the 1,600 Jedwabne Jews... were murdered by... society"* [thus reads the Polish edition—trans.].[1]

— Such a conclusion may be justified by emotions, pain, and anger. This is understandable, but it is not justified by the documented facts. The accounts published by the Wroniszewskis would rather indicate that a relatively small group supported by the Germans terrorized the rest of the inhabitants and committed the massacre that later covered all of Jedwabne with shame. Today, that shame weighs on the whole Polish community of Jedwabne. But just think how much courage would have been needed under those circumstances to stand up to them.

— *It is, of course, very difficult to imagine. However, a good deal of food for thought about the intensity of the terror and fear can be found in the fact that in the first days, before the Gestapo arrived, it was not only Poles who were passively watching the crimes being committed against the Jews. Other Jews were watching, too.*

— I shall not attempt to explain this. It is possible, of course, to summon up negative stereotypes. According to one stereotype, Poles are anti-Semites by nature and even those who did not murder Jews observed the crimes approvingly. According to a second stereotype, Jews are victims by nature, and do not attempt to defend themselves even when they are in the majority. However, stereotypes never explain history, although they often falsify it. One way or another, it is hard to understand—and Gross does not attempt to explain in his book—how 1,500 healthy, able-bodied people could be led to their death by fewer than a hundred criminals armed only with clubs, without attempting to defend themselves or even to flee.

---

[1] The corresponding words on page 170 of American edition of *Neighbors* are: "the 1,600 Jedwabne Jews... were killed [by]... their neighbors." [translator's note].

This does not in any way diminish the guilt of their murderers, yet there is some sort of tragic mystery here—even if 232 German police were waiting somewhere nearby. A situation described in Gross's book may shed a bit of light on this mystery. This is the story of Michał Kuropatwa, a Jewish drayman, who sheltered a Polish officer in his home during the Soviet times. At the door of the barn, someone pulled him out of the crowd in order to save his life. Kuropatwa refused. He chose death with the other Jews. Gross compares Kuropatwa's decision with the attitude of Janusz Korczak* but, unfortunately, he does not quote the words that, according to eyewitness accounts, Kuropatwa then uttered: "Where the Rabbi goes, I will follow." It would also be worth understanding these words if we want to comprehend the phenomenon of Jedwabne.

— *Didn't Gross know about those words?*

— He knew about them, but did not quote them. However, there are facts about which Gross might not know, such as the fact that the wife of mayor Karolak, who was the main organizer of the pogrom, was murdered after the war. This, of course, has nothing to do with the circumstances of the pogrom, but it might shed some light on the repercussions that the events of July 10, 1941, had on the people of Jedwabne after the war.

— *Was that revenge?*

— I am convinced that it was, especially because she was not the last victim. Bronisław Śleszyński, in whose barn the massacre was carried out, was also beaten to death after the war. Gross does not mention this, either. I do not know whether he had an obligation to write about this in his book. However, these devilish details are very important to anyone who wants to understand Jedwabne. They are lacking in *Neighbors*.

— *Why aren't they there?*

— Because the author did not know about them. At a certain moment, he felt that he had enough material to write the book. In his position, I would have had a different opinion. I would have thought that I needed to keep on searching.

— *Do you think that documents that will help us to understand Jedwabne will still be found?*

— It's likely. I would not even rule out finding the film of the event, which the Germans shot according to many accounts. In the same way, German film shot in the Warsaw ghetto in 1942 was found in the *Stasi* archives. Accounts could be found in the records of one of the war crimes trials held in Germany. We might find the personnel records of one of the Gestapo functionaries who was present at Jedwabne. There might be German documents on the pogrom in various archival collections. No one has yet carried out a serious search for them. That is why Gross's book leaves so many question marks. From a historian's point of view, the subject has not been exhausted.

In a sense, however, Gross's thinking was correct. He must have felt, accurately, that the time had come when it was possible, and also when there was a need to examine seriously the dark side of Polish-Jewish relations during the Second World War. Polish historians have not taken this up over the last half-century. Not even the accounts gathered in the Jewish Historical Institute* have been adequately introduced into scholarly circulation, not to mention the popular Polish mind. Now we can no longer avoid a serious approach to this material. For that, despite all my reservations, I am grateful to Jan Tomasz Gross.

JACEK ŻAKOWSKI

EVERY NEIGHBOR HAS A NAME

"GAZETA WYBORCZA" NOVEMBER 18–19, 2000

Jan Tomasz Gross writes [in the Polish edition of his book—trans.] that *"the 1,600 Jedwabne Jews were killed neither by the Nazis, nor by the NKVD,* nor by the UB,* but by society."*[1] **On this basis, he explains the enduring resentment that the Jews have towards the Poles. The Jews who continue to feel such "enduring resentment" towards the Poles are unconsciously upholding the logic of that crime. Every one of us is responsible for himself. None of us has the right to rebuke anyone else for his countrymen or forebears.**

This book is an atomic bomb with a time-delay fuse. Jan Tomasz Gross planned and wrote it that way. He does not conceal the fact that his intention is to place the emotional charge of *Neighbors* in the Polish conscience and detonate it. This would be the end of Polish self-satisfaction, the end of false pride in being the righteous ones of wartime Europe, the end of the myth about being the only ones who had nothing to do with Hitler's crimes.

---

[1] In the American edition, the corresponding passage reads: *"... the 1,600 Jedwabne Jews were killed neither by the NKVD, nor by the Nazis, nor by the Stalinist secret police. Instead, as we now know beyond reasonable doubt, and as the Jedwabne citizens knew all along, it was their neighbors who killed them."* Jan T. Gross, *Neighbors* (Princeton and Oxford: Princeton University Press, 2001), p. 170. (translator's note).

To a large degree, Gross has succeeded at this. To such a large degree that it is hard to recover your equilibrium after reading *Neighbors*. If anyone wanted to broadcast a work of comparable emotional power and comparable cruelty on Polish television, they would have to put a "for mature audiences" warning in the corner of the screen. And yet I am afraid that even those Jews and Poles who do not have nerves of steel and who will never read *Neighbors* are now going to be living not only in the light of newly discovered truths, but also in the dark shadow of this book.

The good Lord scatters the words that people write, and it is obviously too early to say who will understand what in *Neighbors*, and what conclusions they will come to as a result. We cannot say how much truth will be added to the public awareness and how much hostility, how much light and how much threatening gloom. We do not yet know the balance. We do not know how many consciences will be awakened or how many dangerous emotions stirred up, how many historical ghosts Gross will finally impale on his aspen spike or how many he will awaken to life.

Yet I would be lying if I said that this book does not fill me with fear.

Torturous questions

This fear has three sources. First, there are the facts: the monstrous crime committed in Jedwabne—terrifying, repulsive, and shameful, regardless of the details over which the historians will long argue, for it may prove impossible to definitively verify certain details after 60 years.

Terryfying, repulsive and shameful regardless of exactly how many victims there were and how many people were involved in the crime, of how many bloodthirsty onlookers there were and of how many Poles—terrified by the madness of their neighbors—shut themselves up in their houses so that there were so few people courageous enough to offer aid to those who were being persecuted, regardless also of how many Nazis were sent to Jedwabne and what proportion of the quilt is borne by Polish, and what part by German criminals. It is simply hard for me to believe that people could do such a thing so recently and so near—less than 60 years ago and less than 200 kilometers from the place where I live. Ordinary, simply people. Europeans, perphaps our neighbors.

And it is terrifying to think that whatever it was that impelled them to that crime may still lie somewhere deep within them (within us? within me?). Now that we know about it, we are beginning to look differently into the eyes of our neighbors, and also into our own eyes. Would the man across the way know how to bludgeon a little girl with a plow handle? Would he and his brother-in-law play with her lovely sawed-off head afterwards, as if it were a soccer ball? Would he smash her father's skull with a stone? Would the lady on the first floor rush to loot the apartment on the eighth floor while the man from the fourth floor was burning its tenants in a barn? Where would any of us be at the time? ...Who would be sitting terrified, locked in their apartment, while their neighbors were being murdered?... Who would be running around town, like Laudański, in a raging lust for murder? Who would be watching in curiosity? And since, as the poet assures us, "We know as much about ourselves as we have been put to the test," where would I be? What would happen to my neighbors and to me if we lived through the war and two years of Soviet occupation in Jedwabne? Would we yield to the moral break-down that supposedly prevailed there at the time?

It is hard to ward off such questions when reading *Neighbors*.

In the shadow of Auschwitz

It is true that Gross may perhaps not tell us much that is new about human nature. After Bosnia and Rwanda, it is hard for us to be shocked by human cruelty. Nor, alas, does Gross say much that is new about Polish culture, because it is already well known that neighbors of various ethnic groups, including the Poles, did monstrous things to each other in eastern Małopolska during the war. I even have the impression that he adds little to the litany of guilt towards the Elder Brothers, because it was possible long before this to read about what armed Polish groups sometimes did during the war to Jews hiding in the forests.

After the Holocaust, however, mass murder carried out with Polish involvement against their Jewish neighbors, whom they had known by name for generations, has an additional eloquence, no matter how much controversy there may be around it, and especially when it was committed in some sort of connivance with the Gestapo. Although every life has the same value, there is among the generations that lived in the proximate shadow of the chimneys of Majdanek and Auschwitz it is a natural reaction to feel a heightened sensitivity to the particularly terrible fate of the Jews. (In 1941, Karolak and Laudański could not have had the slightest inkling about either Majdanek or Auschwitz. Would the experience of the Holocaust have restrained them from their crime?)

In this sense, I too am grateful to Jan Tomasz Gross for the fact that his book attempts to maintain, or rather to awaken this awareness. Yet the way in which he does so also fills me with fear. I do not know if this kind of discourse is permissible, especially in the shadow of Auschwitz and the shadow of Jedwabne. I am not saying that it is not permissible. But is it, indeed? Is it prudent to talk in this way? Proper? Just? Is it responsible?

Can "society" kill?

Responsibility is the key issue in this book—even more so than truth, towards which Gross has an attitude (judging by his approach to the sources) that is "postmodern" and "subjectivist." He is more concerned with guilt. Who is guilty of this crime? Who did the killing?

Gross answers: "Society did the killing."[2] His exact words [in the Polish edition—trans.] are: *"the 1,600 Jedawbne Jews were killed neither by the Nazis, nor by the NKVD,* * *nor by the UB,* * *but by society."*

---

[2] In the American version, *"it was their neighbors...."* See the previous note (translator's note).

He means the polish society [or, in the American version, "their neighbors—trans.] in the town of Jedwabne.

This thesis, based on the factual material that Professor Tomasz Szarota analyzes, was posed by a reputable sociologist, a Yale graduate, a professor at a serious university in New York City. He posed it in a book that will soon be published in the United States, and afterwards, surely, in Germany and a few other countries.

This thesis is not something that Gross tosses off in passing, just for the sake of posing a thesis. This thesis is needed to exemplify another thesis that stating that, in occupied Poland, *"the so-called local population involved in the killings of Jews did so of its own free will"* (p. 133). And this thesis, in turn, leads to what would seem to be the crucial journalistic argument of *Neighbors*:

"Might there not lie concealed here an important part of the answer to a question that haunts Polish public opinion: Why do the Jews have such an ingrained resentment towards the Poles, seemingly even more deeply rooted than their resentment towards the Germans themselves who, after all, were the inventors, initiators, and principal perpetrators of the Holocaust? [there is no equivalent to this sentence in the American edition—trans.] *And if, in collective Jewish memory, their Polish neighbors in numerous localities murdered them of their own free will—not on orders or as part of an organized, uniformed formation (and therefore, at least on the level of appearances, acting under compulsion)—then are the Poles not somehow, in the perceptions of the victims, particularly responsible for those acts? After all, a man in uniform who kills us is at least to a degree a state functionary; a civilian in that role is nothing more than a murderer."*[3]

---

[3] The entire corresponding paragraph in the American edition (p. 133) reads: *"And if in collective Jewish memory this phenomenon is ingrained—that local Polish people killed the Jews because they wanted to, not because they had to—then Jews will hold them particularly responsible for what they have done. A murderer in uniform remains a state functionary acting under orders, and he might even be presumed to have mental reservations about what he has been ordered to do. Not so a civilian, killing another human being of his own free will—such an evildoer is unequivocally but a murderer"* (p. 133—translator's note).

When I come to that paragraph, I feel that I must somehow resist—because, in appealing to the language of ethnic quantifiers, Gross runs the risk of causing or contributing to further misfortunes.

This is the language of misfortune

Previously, the thesis that "Jews blame the Poles more than the Germans for the Holocaust" was something that I came across mainly in anti-Semitic hate literature. That was enough to negate it. Now I see it asserted, with a supporting rationale, by an accomplished fifty-year-old American professor of Polish-Jewish background, a participant in the March events,* a prisoner in 1968, an emigrant in 1969, who is surely no anti-Semite.

What is a Pole to do? The first temptation that some of us will face is to follow the path trodden by that hate literature. "The Jews have always felt contempt for what is Polish and hated the Poles, which is why they joined the UB* and murdered Polish patriots there, and now they are making us repulsive in the eyes of the world...." "The Jews were always fascinated by German culture and German power, and are still fascinated, and that is why they can forgive the Germans everything...." "American Jews could never believe that the cultured Germans were capable of such monstrousness. It was more comfortable for them that way, since they did not lift a finger at the time of the Holocaust...." "The Jews need good relations with the powerful Germans. The Holocaust is an impediment to them in this, and so they must find a different guilty party. We are the easiest prey. That is why international Jewry puts the blame on the Poles."

I cannot rely on such argumentation. Nor can I take such argumentation into consideration (by evoking, for instance, Reich-Ranicki,* who chose Germany, or Edelman,* who chose Poland) or even carry out a polemic against it, because I reject the language in which such views can be expressed. This is not a legitimate language for any sort of discussion. It is the language of misfortune, of many terrible misfortunes. It is the language of Marian Karolak and the Laudański brothers. It is the language of ethnic war, of genocide. If "the Jew was treacherous (and in the original, there would be no capitalization), then the Jew should be punished." Then it is not important to the user of such language which particular Jew they batter with stones. In certain circumstances, surely, "better if it's all of them" ("not excepting the skilled craftsmen").

Gross clearly pushes us in the direction of such language when he decides to resort to it himself. For the Jewish users of such language (whose relatives or countrymen were murdered by Laudański), with *"ingrained resentment towards the Poles"* [Żakowski follows the Polish edition here and in the foregoing—trans.] it must not be particularly important whether or not the Poles (here, too, there would often be no capitalization) who feel the existence of that *"ingrained resentment"* were in fact involved in the catastrophe of the Holocaust. For in such language, totalitarian language ("the individual is a zero, the individual is nonsense"), there is no place for individual wrongs or for justice.

It sounds obvious.

I had the impression that we in Poland had learned to a considerable degree how to avoid that language—not only in writing and in speech, but also in emotions and in thinking about the world. And not only in Poland. I think that, in Europe, we were reminded of the danger of such quantifiers when we saw what happened in Bosnia. Perhaps not all of us. Perhaps not completely. Yet, in general, we reject that language. And we tremble when we observe its strange renaissance in nearby Austria, in Germany, in France, or in Polish stadiums. Still, we are wary. We know what the threat is.

Perhaps Nietzsche's admonition that "it is wrong to love or to hate nations," and therefore also to judge them, came too late, after all. Love and hatred (as well as "ingrained resentment" and "gratitude") can properly only be felt towards a specific person. After the catastrophes of the twentieth century, more and more of us seem at last to understand that, in the world of emotions, large-scale quantification is, in the first place, false, and that, in the second place, it leads sooner or later to crimes.

The cost of incaution

I will agree that this language is natural. For thousands of years, we recognized our enemies and our friends by their dress and language, just as animals recognize their enemies by their smell and their coloration. In nature, it is safer that way. In Europe over the last half century, however, we have undertaken a great many efforts to suppress this nature, to expunge hostility (mistrust, dislike, fear) and all generalizations about others from the catalogue of reflexes, to suppress ethnic emotions with reason, to use culture to de-claw dangerous nature. I think that we have had considerable success in that suppression, especially since the suppression of ethnic emotions fits in well with the evolution of culture, which emphasizes the value of the person (the individual, the citizen, the consumer, the human being) in various fields (from economy through theology).

These successes, however, are fresh and surely impermanent. It is doubtful in the end whether ethnic emotions can ever be removed totally, for culture has never yet conquered nature completely. Even if we succeeded in doing this in some sort of future, we have spent too little time learning to speak (to think, to feel) the language of "persons" to make it impossible for the language of "tribes" to ever burst forth in us again. That language, indeed, can still be heard. It has quieted down in Poland of late, but in many other countries it resounds more clearly than it did a few years ago. Sometimes, it sounds threatening. I am all the more astonished at Jan Gross—who himself once heard that language in Poland—for now being ready to call it forth again and to run the risk of nourishing ghosts that are on their way to extinction.

This is neither an accident nor an oversight. It is, as I understand it, a risk taken consciously as part of an intellectual design in which the acknowledgement that *"when reflecting about this epoch, we must not assign collective responsibility"* nevertheless permits Jan Tomasz Gross to formulate the question of whether, in thinking *"about the national pride and sense of identity rooted in the historical experience of many generations, we are not equally responsible for the shameful deeds of our forebears and countrymen?"* [from the Polish edition—trans.].[4]

It sounds apparently logical. But something that is logical, that might be correct to a large degree in terms of values, something that is in agreement with nature and even psychologically authentic in some way, may nevertheless be too dangerous for us to accept it insouciantly. Our world is too threatening, human nature too incalculable, the evil of this world too real and (as we go on convincing ourselves) too lightly covered by a thin layer of culture ("those cultured Germans") for intellectuals to pose this sort of question incautiously and with impunity. This does not mean that I would like to see anyone punished for the views they express. Yet I know that history sometimes presents people with macabre bills to be paid for incautious thinking and for the overly bold speculations of outstanding minds—even if they are solidly rooted, from the standpoint of values in, for example, the ideal of equality.

Words and ideas can murder indeed. That is why I would like to call in no uncertain terms for self-restraint, in the name of our common safety.

The boundaries of responsibility

In itself, the placing of collective pride and collective responsibility on the same level strikes me as being artificial, a product of the ivory tower (although collective responsibility has been invoked by intellectuals of the caliber of Hannah Arendt or Jerzy Jedlicki). It is no accident that merits and responsibility are measured by different principles in the world we live in. Meting out justice to a common criminal requires a burdensome court trial subject to the rigors of refined procedures. Yet no one in their right mind would demand

---

[4] In the American edition, the corresponding passage (p. 135) reads: "*if people are indeed bonded together by authentic spiritual affinity—I have in mind a kind of national pride rooted in common historical experiences of many generations—are they not somehow responsible also for horrible deeds perpetrated by members of such an 'imagined community'?*" (translator's note).

comparable procedures before a prize is awarded. Similarly, it would be difficult today to accept the imposition of collective punishment (for those involved in a riot, for instance), while a collective prize (for the police who restore order, for instance) tends not to evoke objections.

Now, in order to bring this thread to a close, I shall refer to a thought from Father Tischner's* book *Jak żyć* (How to Live). "A person's responsibility," Tischner writes, "does not extend beyond the limits of the possibility of effective action" (Tischner's master, Roman Ingarden,* wrote something similar in his famous essay on responsibility). Period. The rest is unreasoning and dangerous. Behind the Tischnerian barrier, we are safe. There is no place for tribal hatred, because tribal responsibility does not exist. The one who did evil or who did not prevent evil although he could have done so is the one who will be called to account. Any further claims are groundless.

There is no responsibility for grandfathers and great-grandfathers (and furthermore there is no law to make anyone bear such responsibility), because those not yet born had no way of restraining them. Nor is there any responsibility for contemporary countrymen or non-countrymen if we can have no influence on their actions. Jan Tomasz Gross is responsible for himself, and I am responsible for myself. Neither of us has the right to complain to the other about his countrymen or forebears.

I am ready to surrender even my pride in Tischner or Copernicus, and in Plato as well, for the sake of such a consensus, for it raises the hope of avoiding misfortunes and offers a greater chance of biological survival.

And yet when I read in Gross's book about the crime in Jedwabne and about the lie on the monument that has been standing there for half a century, I feel it far more sharply than when I read in Kapuściński* or Jagielski* about crimes in Africa. This is not only because I am irritated by the language of large-scale quantifiers, which attempts to implicate me in culpability for a crime committed half a century ago only because I am a Pole. Nor is it because it has to do with another monstrous episode in the exceptional Jewish fate.

It is because, in spite of everything, the affair has something to do with an important fragment of my personal responsibility.

Here is the third source of my unease as a reader of *Neighbors*. In a certain sense, I agree with Jan Tomasz Gross that *"such a mass murder affects all in a community across time."* What is more, it plays a part in creating a map of collective responsibility in which I admit that I, too, have a place—but not in the sense that I am, or feel myself to be, responsible for a crime that Laudański or Karolak—with the help of some number of other residents of the town of Jedwabne—committed more than half a century ago, before I was born, no matter how monstrous the things that were done there. I have a place there rather in the sense that all of us share the responsibility for whether or not such things ever happen again. According to the Tischnerian thought that I subscribe to, it is impossible to accept the concept of collective, *a priori* responsibility for the past on the basis of being a member of any given nation. Yet, according to this same thought, there is no questioning the principle of collective responsibility—including national, but not *a priori* responsibility—for the future.

There was nothing that I could do to save the Bromsztajns, Hurewiczes, or Piekarzes. But to some degree it is up to me whether others will share their fate someday. No one can shirk such responsibility. It is only here, in accordance with the directives of Tischner* and Ingarden*—whether we like it or not—that the principle of shared responsibility connects us with the communities to which we belong—local, ethnic, denominational, cultural, and political—for these communities mark our "limits of possible effective action."

It is not ties of blood or language, or place of residence, or even cultural heritage, which I experience and draw on in perhaps a different way than the Laudański brothers, but rather the Tischnerian "limits of possible effective action" (Ingarden would add that additionally, this is always a matter of action that is "one's own" and "conscious") that decide about participation in responsibility. These borders are obviously different for each of us, so that each of us has a different dimension (Ingarden would say "degree") of responsibility.

Ingarden was an eyewitness to wholesale Nazi crimes. He devotes a great part of the subtle considerations in *Książeczka o człowieku* [The Little Book about Man] to the gradation of responsibility. By the nature of things, each person is more responsible for what happens and will happen close at hand than for what is farther away. All of us are more responsible for the attitudes of others with whom we share a language and a culture, for this is where we usually have more "possibilities of effective action." Those who have more possibilities are more responsible than those who have fewer. Those who know more and understand better bear more responsibility than those who are unable to learn or to arrive at a correct assessment.

This increases my unease. I have the impression that, as a community, we have not fully come to terms with our responsibility and have not yet faced up to the challenge posed to us by the experience of Jedwabne. This impression is accompanied by the onerous feeling that the people whom fate has endowed with privileged positions in terms of access to knowledge and the opportunity for communicating with others (intellectuals, politicians, the clergy, teachers and journalists—and thus I, too) have failed in a particular way—and go on failing. We remain unable to rise to this challenge.

Why we have failed

Now I must ask an unpleasant question. Why is it that the traces found, for instance, in Szymon Datner's 30-year-old article were never followed up and checked, never entered into public circulation, and never became the subject of debate in Poland?

Out of unconcern? It would be colossal unconcern. Out of forgetfulness? Or perhaps by oversight? I myself missed the trail. I was lacking in knowledge and, perhaps, intuition. Yet there were people who read Datner's article. Someone also read the articles in *Kontakty*. Someone listened to and read the report by the prosecutor, Monkiewicz. Why, then, did the falsehood inscribed on the monument at Jedwabne, where it is written that the "Gestapo and Nazi *gendarmerie*" alone committed the crime, endure until 2000? Why is there not even a mention of places like Jedwabne in the history textbooks?

Could those who knew have regarded it as insufficiently significant? Were they falsely ashamed? This cannot be excluded, for the natural feeling of collective responsibility still lives in us. Could they have feared the questions that this knowledge raises? Or perhaps Gross is right: it is easier to convince oneself that one is a victim than to acknowledge responsibility for a crime that has been committed. When one is in fact a victim (of war, occupation, or a political system imposed from the outside) and is fighting to survive and maintain one's own identity, then perhaps it is difficult also to see oneself as a victim. Or perhaps we were simply not allowed to write about such things? Still, the censor cannot be blamed for everything. If the censor had made trouble, then Datner and his readers of the time could have published the results of further investigations in *Kultura* (Paris).* Could it have therefore been the case that they were afraid of touching the subject out of a fear of stirring up those vexed Polish-Jewish emotions? Could a partial reason that the truth about Jedwabne did not come out for so many years have been the fact that the emotions and prejudices that motivated Karolak and Laudański had still not disappeared from Polish culture? Such an answer is disquieting. Yet is it not true in part? If there is a grain of truth in such a suspicion, it would mean that some of us could someday once again become dangerous to our neighbors only because they are Jews, or Roma, or Vietnamese.

It is therefore worth wondering long and hard whether we might not fail today by some chance, just as our forebears and the contemporaries of Mayor Karolak failed. Do we have the will and courage to stand up to symptoms of hatred that could signal a readiness to commit such crimes? Are we sure that, if they saw the shadow of a pogrom approaching, our bishops would now have the courage to leave their palaces, stand in the pulpit of the Jedwabne church, and restrain the maddened crowd before they murdered their neighbors? Would enough of the righteous be found in today's Jedwabne (or Warsaw or Radom) to restrain the murderers? Is there no town left in Poland today where a Karolak could become mayor? Do we have the systematic courage and insight to demand proofs when we hear hasty generalizations and accusations based on assumptions? In the year 2000, are we capable of finding an appropriate response to a politician who reacts to skinheads chanting "*Jude raus!*" on the streets by calling them "young people blowing off steam"? Do we have the will to stop the racists before they feel that "their moment has come"? This is the domain of our responsibility. We must do something about it.

The truth without emotion

I share with many other people a fear of opening up Polish-Jewish wounds. Justifiable emotions, as well as unjustified and completely irrational ones, are still too fresh for an unimpassioned, rational, public debate to be possible. This much we know about ourselves. There is no use pretending that this is a history like every other one—for it is not. The element of the irrational is incomparably greater here than anywhere else.

However, this does not mean that history can be built with impunity on silence and lies. I know of no better antidote to irrational emotion than solid knowledge, just as I know no better way of avoiding misfortune than cultivating the memory of past misfortunes. This means that it is our duty to reveal and tell about the truth. The history of *Neighbors* teaches us that we must constantly engraft and attempt to understand the truth. Yet this must be the truth told forthrightly, without fear and without favor, but also without emotion, undue haste, unnecessary simplifications, stereotypes, injurious generalizations, and large-scale quantifiers.

Therefore I am very much opposed to the idea of inscribing on the monument in Jedwabne, under the influence of Jan Tomasz Gross's book, a declaration that the 1,600 Jews of Jedwabne were murdered by "society."[5] That would be a lie that not only reinforced dangerous emotions and threatening stereotypes, but that also obscured the responsibility of those who committed murder and wronged those who took no part in the crime. A more powerful

---

[5] The term used in the Polish edition; in the American edition, it is "neighbors" (translator's note).

argument might be the fact that the memory of the victims demands from us today that we inscribe on the monument the names of the murderers, since their hate-filled faces, and not some formless "society," were the last thing that the victims saw.

I would very much like to see Jan Tomasz Gross draw the attention of the Jewish readers of the American edition of his shocking book to the fact that, despite all the guilt and omissions of our grandfathers and fathers, and also of ourselves, those Jews who have an "ingrained resentment" towards Poles preserve the logic of that crime, which is still dangerous today. They do so unconsciously, and perhaps unwillingly. In the name of the memory of the victims and responsibility for the future, we cannot permit ourselves to lie about the past. Even more so, we cannot repeat its mistakes.

Jacek Żakowski

JAN TOMASZ GROSS

"COMPREHENSIBLE" MURDER?

"GAZETA WYBORCZA" NOVEMBER 25–26, 2000

As the author of the book about the tragic murder of the Jews who were annihilated by their neighbors in the little town of Jedwabne on July 10, 1941, which was the point of reference for Jacek Żakowski's interview with Professor Tomasz Szarota and for Żakowski's essay "Every Neighbor Has a Name," I feel obliged to provide a few words of explanation. On the one hand, I should show restraint, since I have already had my say on the Jedwabne massacre in my book *Neighbors*. On the other hand, *Gazeta Wyborcza* has almost a million readers, while only 2,000 copies of the book were published. The majority of the public can therefore learn about its contents only from what is written in *Gazeta Wyborcza*.

I will begin with a reminder about what happened in Jedwabne. In order to make it clear that my reviewers agree with the diagnosis that follows, I will use their own words.

Szarota says: "The basic facts seem indisputable.... We already knew about *szmalcownicy**.... Yet we did not realize that Poles were also perpetrators of the Holocaust. In Jedwabne, they were—and these were not some isolated deviants, who are found in every society, but a crowd with the town authorities at its head.... At first, they murdered them individually, using clubs and stones, torturing them, cutting off their heads, profaning their corpses. Later, on July 10, the almost 1,500 Jedwabne Jews who remained alive were forced

91

into a barn and burned alive there.... These unquestionable facts are so shattering that they force even me, a historian who has read much and written a good deal about various instances of disgraceful behavior by Poles under German occupation, to come to completely new conclusions."

Żakowski writes: "It is simply hard for me to believe that people could do such things so recently and so near—less than 60 years ago and less than 200 kilometers from the place where I live. Ordinary, simple people. Europeans, perhaps our neighbors."

What a shame it is that, while they accept the obviousness of the Jedwabne crime, Żakowski and Szarota quickly distance themselves from the heart of the matter either by misreading parts of the book or by appealing to unreliable sources. After all, in view of Szarota's qualifications as a historian and Żakowski's reputation as a journalist, the readers of *Gazeta Wyborcza* could take their reading of *Neighbors* as an accurate commentary on what was actually written in the book.

*

The most misleading thing is Szarota's reference in his discussion with Żakowski to the findings of the prosecutor Waldemar Monkiewicz. He states that the guilt for the murder of the Jews in Jedwabne rests on a 232-strong unit of the German *gendarmerie*, commanded by someone called Birkner, who came to the town in trucks for that purpose.

These theses have appeared twice so far in the press discussion on Jedwabne, in Andrzej Kaczyński's first article (*Rzeczpospolita*, May 5, 2000) where they are immediately undercut by statements by the residents of Jedwabne, and in *Nasz Dziennik** (May 13–14, 2000), where Jerzy Robert Nowak uses them in an assault on Kaczyński's article and my scholarly reputation. In the light of several excellent articles and, I suppose, the arguments developed in my book, no one else mentioned Monkiewicz again until Professor Szarota brought him up. I cannot understand why Szarota is "not yet able, as a historian, to confirm the information provided by Monkiewicz." All the more so, since Szarota met Monkiewicz personally. On May 19, 2000, Professor Jerzy Holzer, director of the Institute of Political Studies at the Polish Academy of Science, organized a meeting of a group of historians, staff members from the Main Commission for the Investigation of Crimes Against the Polish Nation,* and interested persons from the Office of the Prime Minister and the Ministry of Foreign Affairs to discuss the circumstances surrounding the murder of the Jews on July 10, 1941. Prosecutor Monkiewicz made opening remarks reviewing the matter from the point of view of a Commission staff member who was researching war crimes in the Białystok region. Professor Szarota and I were both at that meeting.

Szarota erroneously identifies Monkiewicz as the prosecutor at the 1949 Łomża trial. On that occasion, as is written on the first page of the court records, charges were brought against Ramotowski and his accomplices by "prosecutor C. Jagusiński." We therefore do not know exactly which case Monkiewicz handled. In a time line on the Jedwabne crime in *Gazeta Wyborcza* (Nov. 18–19, 2000), Jan Tomasz Lipski states that Monkiewicz was in charge of an investigation in the Białystok region in the 1960s.

The records of the interrogations that Monkiewicz carried out must surely still be extant in the archives of the Main Commission. Those records could tell us whom Monkiewicz questioned, when he questioned them, what he questioned them about, and what answers he got. This is significant because when residents of Jedwabne, Radziłów, and the vicinity were interrogated years later about crimes committed during the occupation, they were induced by the head investigators to give false testimony. Here is what a reporter from *Rzeczpospolita* wrote (July 10, 2000) about an account of such an interrogation, as provided by an informant from Radziłów: "After the war, people from Radziłów were summoned to be interrogated in Białystok. My informant was not able to tell me who questioned them or when. He was one of those summoned. He testified that the massacre was committed by Poles. The interrogator violently denied this. 'Why did you call me here if you know better?' my informant asked. Then the interrogator allowed my informant to recount his own version. Afterwards, [the interrogator] advised him to keep it to himself. The trial took place in Ełk. 'I did not testify truthfully in court,' [the informant] admitted."

I do not know if Monkiewicz was one of the officials carrying out the investigation, but he too states that it was the Germans who committed the crime. I hope that, as part of the effort to reach the truth about the genocide in Jedwabne, the Institute of National Remembrance* will identify the persons responsible for this equivocation and call them to responsibility before the law.

In the Ministry of Foreign Affairs palace on Foksal street [in Warsaw—trans.] where we met on May 19, Monkiewicz began his explanation by stating that Poles did not murder Jews in the Białystok region in 1941. Of course, he did know about a case in which a group of Poles was made to assist in forcing Jews to the place where they died. Monkiewicz said that the Poles did this by linking their hands together to form a human chain that prevented the Jews from escaping. After this declaration it would already have been possible to thank him for any further explanations, since we know full well that the Polish crowd beat Jews mercilessly that day in Jedwabne, and that the reason that we are pondering the whole affair today is not that people linked their hands together there!

Nevertheless, prosecutor Monkiewicz continued his statement and revealed to us further reasons why the murderers of the Jews in Jedwabne could not have been Poles. He stated that gasoline was not freely offered for sale during the war, and so Polish civilians could not on their own have poured gasoline onto the barn for the purposes of burning it down. In this context in Monkiewicz's analysis, trucks appeared in Jedwabne. Gendarmes from these trucks simply poured gasoline on the barn and set it on fire.

Given the vastness of the lack of knowledge on the subject of this crime—a lack of knowledge that we are now trying to make up for—there is one detail that has been noted. The kerosene poured on the barn was distributed from storage by Antoni Niebrzydowski to Eugeniusz Kalinowski and his brother Jerzy: "They brought the eight liters of kerosene that I had issued to them, eight liters, and doused the barn filled with Jews, and lit it up; and what happened next, I do not know."

However, Szarota should already have been aware that Monkiewicz had nothing to say about what happened in Jedwabne, and was only presenting his own deductions. From the facts that Jedwabne lies in the Białystok region, and that Jews were murdered in the Białystok region, and that the Germans were also in the Białystok region and murdered Jews, he concludes that Germans murdered the Jews in Jedwabne. It is a likely scenario, but flawed reasoning, and the conclusion is false. Szarota should also have asked himself: Is it possible that three dozen eyewitnesses (including people involved in the crime) who mentioned in their testimony the arrival of several Gestapo men from Łomża in a "taxi" would have said not a word about some ten army trucks carrying 232 functionaries from "the two German police battalions, no. 309 and no. 316" that would have had to arrive in the little town that day?

Tomasz Szarota concludes that "there is something wrong when the name of Birkner [introduced into the "Jedwabne issue" by Monkiewicz—J.T.G.] is not even mentioned in Gross's book.... Following this lead, someone might try to find documents on the German presence in Jedwabne and German involvement in the pogrom. Gross did not do so.... Every solid historian would surely do so before publishing a book." However, I remain skeptical as to the results of any possible following of the trail of Birkner, in the conviction that matching historical forthrightness with Monkiewicz is an oxymoron. It is unfortunate that Szarota used his authority as a historian to corroborate a delusive version of the Jedwabne tragedy.

*

Szarota says that I wrote the book "too hurriedly." He is surely correct. I did not come upon Monkiewicz's texts before writing *Neighbors*—not that I regret this. Nor did I come upon Szymon Datner's article [on the extermination of the Jews in the Białystok region, published in the *Bulletin of the Jewish Historical Institute** in 1966—ed.]. Even though it contains only confirmation of the theses of my book, I regret very much not having noted it in my references. It would have been possible to research the Jedwabne affair more thoroughly, and to write the book more painstakingly. But I do not know whether my reviewer's suggestions would have been helpful in such an effort because he, in turn, read *Neighbors* too hurriedly. Otherwise, when speaking of facts "about which Gross might not know," would he have mentioned "[the fact] that the wife of mayor Karolak, who was the main organizer of the pogrom, was murdered after the war"? After all, I write about this on page 60 of *Neighbors*.

Szarota is a slipshod reader not only in regard to this detail. It is impossible to say why he repeats several times in his discussion with Żakowski that I give "the figure... of 92 persons involved in the crime" in the book. In fact, I wrote something quite differently on pages 62 and 63 of *Neighbors* [the page numbers refer to the Polish edition—trans.]:

"Sources at our disposal cite, by my count, ninety-two names (and, often home addresses to boot) of people who participated in the murder of Jedwabne Jews. Perhaps not all of them should be labeled murderers—after all, nine of the accused in the Łomża trials were found not guilty. Various people who guarded the Jews in the square may perhaps have just been there, uninvolved in acts of brutality. On the other hand we also know that people mentioned by name are only a fraction of those who were there at the time. 'Near the assembled Jews,' states Władysław Miciura, another defendant in Ramotowski's trial, 'there was a mass of people not only from Jedwabne, but also from the environs.' 'A lot of people were there, whose names I do not remember now,' we are told by Laudański père, who with his two sons was among the busiest on this day, 'I'll tell them as soon as I recall.'

"The crowd of perpetrators swelled somehow as Jews were being herded toward the barn where they were incinerated. As Bolesław Ramotowski put it, 'when we were chasing them to the barn, I couldn't see, because it was very crowded.'

"The accused, who all resided in Jedwabne during the war, could not identify many participants, because a large number of these were peasants who flocked into town from neighboring hamlets. 'There were many peasants from hamlets whom I didn't know,' explains Miciura. 'These were for the most part young men who enjoyed this catching of the Jews, and they tortured them.' In other words, a lot of people took an active

part in the massacre. It was a mass murder in a double sense—on account of both the number of victims and the number of perpetrators."

So much for what I wrote in the text of *Neighbors*. On the basis of this, Szarota formulates an entirely unhistorical problem: "It is possible, of course, to summon up negative stereotypes.... According to one stereotype, Poles are anti-Semites by nature, and even those who did not murder Jews observed the crime approvingly. According to a second stereotype, Jews are victims by nature and do not try to defend themselves even when they are in the majority. One way or another, it is hard to understand—and Gross does not attempt to explain in his book—how 1,500 healthy, able-bodied people could be led to their death by less than a hundred criminals armed only with clubs, without attempting to defend themselves or even to flee."

I am not going to ruminate over whether or not these 1,500 people (including the elderly, women, and children) were "healthy [and] able-bodied" after being subjected to a whole day full of murder and torture in the hot July sun, without water, crowded since morning into the town square, surrounded and tormented by a crowd armed with stakes, axes, plow handles, rubber truncheons, and God knows what else. It is clear that Szarota read my book "too hurriedly," if he can permit himself such assertions. All the more so since he gives voice to his methodological consciousness when he explains to Żakowski that "To understand this event properly, however, it is necessary to become familiar with the circumstances of the crime in detail. What Gross has written in *Neighbors* is enough to rattle our consciences. But it is necessary to know the details to understand the whole situation. Every historian knows that a multiplicity of details can often be the devil's workshop."

Yet where did this spokesman for history come up with the details that he shares with the readers of *Gazeta Wyborcza*? Those "fewer than a hundred" perpetrators, armed, for good measure, "only with clubs"? Certainly not from a reading of *Neighbors*. Otherwise, he would have to explain how, let us say, Kobrzyniecki "knifed to death eighteen jews [lower case in the original—trans.]" that day, not to mention many other gory details that fill the accounts, which I quote, by the Polish witnesses and the perpetrators of the crime.

I will not make things even more uncomfortable for my reviewer by quoting fragments from the articles on Jedwabne in *Rzeczpospolita* (May 19 and July 10, 2000) or *Gazeta Pomorska* (August 5) which poke holes in Szarota's astounding thesis about "1,500 healthy, able-bodied people led to their death by fewer than a hundred criminals armed only with clubs." However, I recommend these articles to readers of *Gazeta Wyborcza* who are interested in the pogrom committed against the Jedwabne Jews. And let us remember: the Jews who were led to their death were no more "healthy" and "able-bodied" than their murderers were armed "only with clubs."

*

Szarota's next oversight appears in his unawareness that Jews escaped from that hell all day long, and that they defended themselves. There are many places in *Neighbors* where one can read about this. Two of the people with whom I spoke escaped from Jedwabne twice that day. In the first pages of the book, in the relation by Wasersztajn that I cite at the beginning, we learn that "some tried to defend themselves, but they were defenseless." That is one of the most moving sentences written there about the fate of the Jews of Jedwabne.

Of course, Szarota did not deliberately distort my book. So what? It would be hard indeed for a historian who poses some questions that are based on false premises (Why did the Jews not "defend themselves or even flee" that day?), and others that are profoundly unhistorical, to excuse himself through absent-mindedness. After all, in 1941 and in territory just conquered by the German army, how was the Jewish community supposed to defend itself from a criminal attack by the local civilians? The Jews could flee or hide to avoid aggression, and they did so. But what else could they do? In what further way could they stand up to an attack by criminals, even if those criminals were armed "only with clubs"? By engaging them in a free-for-all? And then what? Would they be left standing victorious on the battleground?

In this cavalier aggravation of the problems surrounding the Jedwabne massacre, I discern echoes of the boyhood reading of a historian from Warsaw—titles like *Chłopcy z Placu Broni* [The Boys from Arms Square*]. Otherwise, I would have to suppose that he is referring by implication to the negative stereotype according to which "Jews are victims by nature and do not try to defend themselves, even when they are in the majority." In a more common variant, this anti-Semitic cliche proclaims that the Jews "went like sheep to the slaughter" during the war. Yet Szarota knows full well —I am quoting him—"that stereotypes never explain history, although they often falsify it."

I am hardly splitting hairs. The response to Jedwabne is an issue of immeasurable significance for the self-image of Polish society in the twenty-first century. Żakowski and Szarota are prominent intellectuals and each of them, in his own way, has a real influence on that self-image. How could it come to pass, for instance, that—having read *Neighbors* and the distinguished articles about Jedwabne published in Polish newspapers since May—an accomplished journalist who is aware of the power of words could express his thoughts by asking (I am quoting from one of Jacek Żakowski's questions): "why the Jewish majority did not try to defend themselves against a pogrom carried out by part of the Polish minority?"

Let us imagine that a family of five, consisting of a grandmother, an able-bodied mother and father, and two small children, is attacked by three teenage hooligans who begin striking them with baseball bats. One might obviously describe this situation as a confrontation in which the "family majority" fails to attempt to defend itself against the "teenage minority," but we feel that such a formulation would not be the most accurate way of grasping the essence of the event.

*

And one more objection. In his first question to Szarota, Żakowski says: "After reading this book I feel distinctly unsatisfied and uncertain about what happened in Jedwabne. Gross deliberately provokes these feelings—in the first place, through his emotional, journalistic style, and in the second, through his uncritical attitude to arbitrarily chosen sources. He proclaims this attitude himself. In rejecting the principles of the historian's and even the reporter's craft, he writes that 'we must take literally all fragments of information at our disposal, fully aware that what actually happened to the Jewish community during the Holocaust can only be more tragic than the existing representation of events based on surviving evidence.' As a journalist, I know that the truth can differ in many important particulars from what is suggested by 'fragments of information.'"

I have inexpressible appreciation for Jacek Żakowski's journalistic abilities. But the conclusion he quotes from the chapter in *Neighbors* titled "New Approach to Sources" is preceded by a line of explanation that I follow in order to enable readers to decide for themselves whether or not I in fact suggest an "uncritical attitude" to sources by rejecting the principles of the historian's craft. And perhaps it would be worthwhile for Żakowski to explain what he means when he says that the sources I rely on are "arbitrarily chosen"—because he lightly tosses off that remark without providing any justification for it.

I wrote in *Neighbors* that *"The mass murder of Jedwabne Jews in the summer of 1941 opens up historiography of Polish-Jewish relations during the Second World War.... To begin with, I suggest that we should modify our approach to sources for this period. When considering survivors' testimonies, we would be well advised to change the starting premise in appraisal of their evidentiary contribution from a priori critical to in principle affirmative. By accepting what we read in a particular account as fact until we find persuasive arguments to the contrary, we would avoid more mistakes than we are likely to commit by adopting the opposite approach....*

"I make the point, to some extent, on the basis of my own experience. It took me four years, as I stated at the beginning of this volume, to understand what Wasersztajn was communicating in his deposition. But the same conclusion... suggests itself as we consider the general absence in Polish historiography of any studies about the involvement of the ethnically Polish population in the destruction of Polish Jewry. It

is a subject of fundamental importance that has been extremely well documented. In the Jewish Historical Institute* in Warsaw alone one can find over seven thousand depositions collected from the survivors of the Holocaust immediately after the war.... But, in the last analysis, it is not our professional inadequacy (as a community of historians of this period) that calls most compellingly for revision in the approach to sources. This methodological imperative follows from the very immanent character of all evidence about the destruction of Polish Jewry that we are ever likely to come across. All that we know about the Holocaust—by virtue of the very fact that it has been told—is not a representative sample of the Jewish fate suffered under Nazi rule. It is all skewed evidence, biased in one direction: these are all stories with a happy ending. They have all been produced by a few who were lucky enough to survive. Even statements from witnesses who have not survived—statements that have been interrupted by the sudden death of their authors, who therefore left only fragments of what they wanted to say—belong to this category. For what has reached us was written only while the authors were still alive. About the 'heart of darkness' that was also the very essence of their experience, about their last betrayal, about the Calvary of 90 percent of the prewar Polish Jewry—we will never know."

Then comes the part that Żakowski quotes. As to whether or not what I said here is arbitrary and uncritical, I will leave it to the readers to decide for themselves.

*

And finally a brief clarification in connection with an article by the same Jacek Żakowski, "Every Neighbor Has a Name." Żakowski is outraged after reading *Neighbors*, and gives vent to his feelings: "This book is an atomic bomb with a time-delay fuse.... It is hard to recover your equilibrium after reading *Neighbors*." Żakowski notes that "all the readers of Jan Tomasz Gross's *Neighbors* that I have spoken to are walking around in pain." In the face of the Jedwabne crime as evoked by *Neighbors*, Żakowski feels strangely defenseless —I am even thinking of the unusual form of his text, which is probably more than a mere stylistic device. Never before have I read a long article by a seasoned journalist that is made up mostly of questions.

Nevertheless, I have the impression that the starting point for this series of undoubtedly important questions is an erroneous reading by Żakowski of the last paragraph of *Neighbors*. He writes: "Responsibility is the key issue in this book—even more so than truth, towards which Gross has an attitude (judging by his approach to the sources) that is 'postmodern' and 'subjectivist.' He is more concerned with guilt. Who is guilty of this crime? Who did the killing? Gross answers: 'Society did the killing.' His exact words are: *'the 1,600 Jedwabne Jews were killed neither by the Nazis, nor by NKVD,* * *nor by the UB,* * *but by society.'* He means the Polish society in the town of Jedwabne" [see the notes to the translation of this passage in Żakowski's article—trans.].

In fact, it sounds somewhat different. I shall quote the entire last paragraph of the book, a particularly important passage, of which Żakowski quotes the final sentence. I lead up to that paragraph by writing that Poland is no exception in Europe: *"And like several other nations, in order to reclaim its own past, Poland will have to tell its past to itself anew."* After this assertion that the truth about our history in the period of the Second World War still remains to be written, comes the paragraph that reads thus:

"An appropriate memento is, of course, to be found in Jedwabne, where there are two monuments with inscriptions carved into the stone that will have to be chipped away in order to liberate the historical truth in them. One says simply that the Germans killed the Jews: 'THE PLACE OF THE SUFFERING OF THE JEWISH POPULATION. THE GESTAPO AND THE NAZI GENDARMERIE BURNED 1600 PEOPLE ALIVE JULY 10, 1941.' The other one, erected in a Poland that was already free, either implies that there were no Jews at all in Jedwabne—or else it bears witness, in spite of itself, to the crime that was committed: 'TO THE MEMORY OF APPROXIMATELY 180 PERSONS INCLUDING TWO PRIESTS MURDERED IN THE TERRITORY OF JEDWABNE DISTRICT IN THE YEARS 1939––1956 BY THE NKVD, THE NAZIS, AND THE UB [signed:] SOCI-

ETY' For, in fact, the 1,600 Jedwabne Jews who are omitted here (even though they were 'murdered in the community of Jedwabne in the years 1939–1956') were not murdered by any Nazis or NKVD or UB, but rather by society" [translation of the Polish edition—trans.].[1]

In other words, my point is that it is necessary to write the truth, because the truth will always out.

Yet I make haste to explain that my attitude to truth is not "postmodern," as Żakowski supposes, but only Aristotelian. In other words, I regard it as impossible for the statements "A" and "not A" to be simultaneously true. On reflection, I nevertheless feel that the final word in the book [in its Polish edition—trans.], "society," should be put in quotation marks, to make it immediately plain that it unconsciously reveals the truth hidden in the lies inscribed on the Jedwabne monuments.

Permit me to conclude by posing two questions to my readers.

Let us say that a German police battalion was, indeed, in Jedwabne that day, and that Poles, acting under pressure (from the dregs of the local community? the local government? public opinion? the German *gendarmerie*?) and embittered by the certainty that Jews had collaborated with the NKVD* under Soviet occupation (even though all we know for certain in the case of Jedwabne is that two of the defendants in the Łomża trial, Laudański and Bardoń, had previously cooperated with the NKVD), murdered their Jewish neighbors—women, children, old people, and everyone they came across that day. Are there any parameters of pressure or embitterment that

---

[1] The beginning and end of the passage in the American edition differ from the Polish edition as translated above. In the American edition, the paragraph begins thus: "An appropriate memento is to be found—where else?—in Jedwabne. Inscriptions were engraved there on two stone monuments commemorating the time of war. One of them simply propagates a lie by stating that 1,600 Jedwabne Jews were killed by the Nazis" (p. 169). The conclusion, in the American edition, reads: "For, indeed, the 1,600 Jedwabne Jews were killed neither by the NKVD, nor by the Nazis, nor by the Stalinist secret police. Instead, as we now know beyond reasonable doubt, and as Jedwabne citizens knew all along, it was their neighbors who killed them" (p. 170—translator's note).

would make the Jedwabne murder carried out by the Poles against the Jews "comprehensible"? Can we imagine a sequence of events leading up to the murder in Jedwabne that would permit us to say in conclusion something like, "Aha, I understand," or, "That was a monstrous crime, and yet…," or "It's terrible, it's unforgivable, but nevertheless…"?

And the second question: What inscription should be placed on the monument commemorating the tragic death of the Jedwabne Jews?

Jan Tomasz Gross

TOMASZ SZAROTA

DO WE NOW KNOW EVERYTHING FOR CERTAIN?

"GAZETA WYBORCZA" DECEMBER 2–3, 2000

A discussion of *Neighbors*, organized by Professor Jerzy Jedlicki, was held at the Historical Institute of the Polish
Academy of Sciences on November 24, the day before Jan
T. Gross's polemical article was printed in *Gazeta Wyborcza*. I delivered the introductory remarks. After sketching the history of falsification and the road to the truth about Jedwabne, I shared four
observations with the audience of almost 150:

1) Thousands of articles and books have already been written about
the Holocaust. It might seem that we already know everything
about the subject. Professor Gross's *Neighbors* demonstrates that
this is not the case.

2) The existence of censorship until 1989 made it impossible for us
to speak the whole truth about our recent history. The fact that
books like *Neighbors* can appear in Poland is a sign that we have
recovered our freedom, become more normal, and jettisoned our
complexes.

3) There are thick volumes more or less deserving of the term
"great" that sink without a trace. There are also literary works,
including poems, articles, and essays, that become well known and
are constantly referred to in ongoing discussions. I am thinking

105

about Czesław Miłosz's *Campo di Fiori,** Zofia Nałkowska's *The Medallions,** Kazimierz Wyka's *A Pretense of Life,** Jan Błoński's article "Poor Poles Look at the Ghetto,"* or Krystyna Kersten's courageous declaration about the Kielce pogrom.* I believe that Jan T. Gross's book is set to take its place in this category of texts.

4) In the country where Gross has been living, but not only there, the view is sometimes expressed that Poles imbibe anti-Semitism along with their mothers' milk. I think that such generalizations are shown to be nonsense by the very fact that the original publication of *Neighbors* took place here in Poland, by the response to the book, by the size of the audience here in this room, and perhaps above all by the visible results of the publication of *Neighbors* in the form of the opening of a new investigation into the Jedwabne crime.

After listening to my introductory remarks, Professor Gross read the text of his polemic with me and Jacek Żakowski, which was published the next day in the weekend edition of *Gazeta Wyborcza.*

I participated in an earlier meeting held on May 19 in the Ministry of Foreign Affairs palace on Foksal street. There were a dozen or more people there, including Professors Jerzy Holzer, Tomasz Strzembosz, Jerzy Tomaszewski, and Feliks Tych. Almost all of them had something to say about the "Jedwabne affair." It is significant that, in his polemic with me, Gross summarizes only one set of remarks, those of Waldemar Monkiewicz, while passing over all the others in silence. I had already familiarized myself with *Neighbors.* I have in my hand the official minutes of that meeting. Those minutes contain a summary of my remarks: "The time has come to begin speaking openly about these events.... Professor Tomasz Szarota stated that the worst way for the Polish authorities and public opinion to react would be any possible attempt at undercutting in a basic way the credibility of the account presented in Professor Gross's book or at redirecting the discussion towards a search for alleged instigators or beneficiaries of an 'anti-Polish campaign.'"

The name of Waldemar Monkiewicz appears frequently in the polemic with me. This man has published several texts (I know of five) on the crime in Jedwabne. Gross says, "I did not come upon

Monkiewicz's texts before writing 'Neighbors'—not that I regret this." Whether Gross likes it or not, Monkiewicz's texts are part of the "literature" on the subject, and it is the duty of a researcher to become familiar with that literature first, and only then to pronounce his verdict, even if that verdict is one of disqualification. Monkiewicz consistently insists that the crime in Jedwabne was carried out by the Germans with only minimal involvement by the local Polish population. Gross, on the other hand, states that nothing certain can be said about German participation, rejecting any information about the presence there on that day of any more than a dozen or so ethnic Germans, and charges the conscience of the Polish population of Jedwabne with the crime. My position is completely unequivocal: I think that, in terms of the perpetrators, Gross is right, not Monkiewicz.

Gross writes, "Szarota should already have been aware that Monkiewicz had nothing to say about what happened in Jedwabne, and was only presenting his own deductions." Somewhat earlier, he chided me—deservedly so in this instance: "Szarota erroneously identifies Monkiewicz as the prosecutor at the 1949 Łomża trial." Indeed, I made a mistake. I repeated this information from an article titled "...Aby żyć" [To Survive], by Danuta and Aleksander Wroniszewski, in the Łomża weekly *Kontakty* (July 10, 1988).

The only reason that I refer to Monkiewicz is that he writes about the activities of the two [German] police battalions, no. 309 and no. 316, in the Białystok region, about the [German] *Kommando Białystok* that committed murder in the region, and about its commander, the Warsaw Gestapo functionary Wolfgang Birkner. Reserve Police Battalion no. 309 was commanded by Major Weiss. In Christopher R. Browning's book *Ordinary Men*, recently published in Poland, we learn that "After entering Białystok on June 27, Major Weiss ordered his battalion to comb the Jewish district and apprehend all the men.... The operation began like a pogrom. Jews were beaten and humiliated, their beards were set alight, and they were shot at as the police led them to the town square or the synagogue.... The pacification, which began as a pogrom, quickly turned into a more systematic mass execution. The Jews were crowded into the

107

town square and then forced to the park, lined up against a wall, and shot. The murdering went on until dusk. The entrance to the synagogue, in which at least 700 Jews were shut up, was doused with gasoline.... It is assumed that between 2,000 and 2,200 Jews died that day." There is not a word in Jan T. Gross's book about the crime committed by German hands in Białystok thirteen days before the crime in Jedwabne, although the analogy of burning Jews in a synagogue and in a barn (as in Jedwabne and Radziłów) ought to occur to a researcher.

*

Let us now take up Wolfgang Birkner. Although I gave his SS rank, *Hauptsturmführer* (the equivalent of captain) in the interview by Jacek Żakowski, he is still "someone called Birkner"—as if he were a figment of the imagination of Waldemar Monkiewicz—for my polemical adversary Gross. In *The Warsaw Ring of Death* Władysław Bartoszewski identifies Birkner as a functionary of the Warsaw Gestapo, assigned to Department IV A 4 (personal security), and also to Special Department IV N (information gathering). A few days ago, I learned that that same Wolfgang Birkner had responsibility within the Gestapo for overseeing the activities of one of the most mysterious Polish underground organizations, *Miecz i Pług* (The Sword and the Plow). It can therefore be assumed that he was an eminent specialist in the mounting of *agent provocateur* operations. Far be it from me to say that Birkner had anything certain to do with the events in Jedwabne and Radziłów. It is enough that he may have poked his finger in, even if he did not participate personally. He was a prime example of the "murderer from behind a desk."

Gross writes, *"I cannot understand why Szarota is 'not yet able, as a historian, to confirm the information provided by Monkiewicz.' All the more so, since Szarota met Monkiewicz personally."* My reply is simple: to date, Waldemar Monkiewicz has never revealed where he got his information about the participation of *Kommando Białystok* in the Jedwabne murder, where he came across the name of Wolfgang Birkner, or on what basis he states that trucks carrying 232

German police arrived in Jedwabne on July 10, 1941. I believe that I am not the only one who would want to know these things, and I cannot imagine how he can continue to remain silent on this subject.

*

Were Germans the instigators of the murder by Poles of their Jewish neighbors in Jedwabne on July 10, 1941? Today, in our present state of knowledge, this is a question we are unable to answer. Even if it turns out that it was the Germans who suggested the idea of burning the Jews in a barn and who ensured that the perpetrators would not be punished, this does not diminish the guilt of those who committed this savage crime. In such a case, however, the events in Jedwabne should be listed among the well-organized operations of the Nazi *Einsatzgruppen*, *Einsatzkommandos*, and *Sonderkommandos** referred to in the relevant orders as *Selbstreinigungsaktionen*, or "self-purification operations." In short, the idea was to provoke anti-Jewish pogroms in the occupied territory in the East "without leaving any traces" of German involvement. I describe this mechanism in detail with reference to the case of Kaunas in my book *U progu zagłady* (On the Threshold of Destruction). This does not mean that there were no instances of pogroms erupting spontaneously, before the Germans arrived. However, Jedwabne was already under German occupation on July 10, 1941.

Analogies may be sought between the course of events in Jedwabne and in Kaunas. Similarly, should any involvement of Wolfgang Birkner in the preparation of the Jedwabne crime be proven, this would indicate that German involvement was greater than Gross supposes. The responsibilities of a researcher also include checking out such leads.

In engaging in a discussion with Jacek Żakowski, I was not acting as a reviewer of Professor Jan T. Gross's book, despite the fact that, on several occasions, he refers to me as such in his polemical fervor. I was to write a long review of *Neighbors* for *Biuletyn ŻIH* (The

Bulletin of the Jewish Historical Institute*). However, I shall not be writing the review. In contrast to Professor Gross, I do not feel that we know today everything there is to know about the events in Jedwabne. He understands exactly what happened there, and why, on that nightmarish Thursday, July 10, 1941—but I do not! Not yet. I am waiting for confirmation of reports that persons freed from the prison in Łomża returned to Jedwabne before the pogrom. I am waiting for the results of archival searches that must be carried out in Ludwigsburg, Potsdam, and Berlin. Finally, I am waiting for the results—unfortunately delayed—of the investigation being conducted since September by the Institute of National Remembrance.*

P.S. I must candidly admit to the participants in the meeting at which Professor Gross was present at the Tadeusz Manteuffel Historical Institute, where I have worked for 38 years, that it was one of the most unpleasant experiences in my life. However, the meeting enriched my knowledge of human nature. In some, I discerned boastfulness, gall, the irresponsible use of words, bloody-mindedness, and deep-seated resentments, and in others a lack of loyalty and civil courage. I shall long remember this lesson.

Tomasz Szarota

Alicja Zielińska

In the Shadow of the Crime

"Kurier Poranny" December 1, 2000

In Jedwabne, no one doubts that a crime was committed against Jews in 1941.

The people are, however, troubled by the surrounding circumstances. They would like to know why it happened, what the actual participation of Poles was in this massacre, and whether they acted alone or under Germans compulsion. Jan T. Gross's statement that it was not the NKVD* or the UB* who killed the 1,600 Jews, but the "society" [in the Polish edition—trans.] of Jedwabne who acted in such a savage way, is received as an unjust accusation. The greater the number of descriptions of the events of 60 years ago that appear, the harder it becomes to discuss then with the locals.

"It's a small town, everybody knows each other, one's afraid of the next," explains a woman who lives at Wojska Polskiego Street. She does not want to talk. *"I don't have the strength. Those memories are too painful, and afterwards people pester you about it. I talked about it once, and they wouldn't give me peace, asking why I did it. It's best to explain that you don't remember anything. The only trouble is, how can you not remember?"* she asks in a tremulous voice.

"There aren't any of those who murdered the Jews here anymore. They moved away or died off," she adds. *"How many there were exactly*

and why they did it, nobody knows. Did the Germans force them, or did they do it of their own free will? We were only witnesses." She was 13 years old back then. She saw how the Jews were driven out of the whole neighborhood. They were led in the direction of the park. They walked in a group. There were many, many of them. Men, women and children. The Germans weren't much to be seen; they had surrounded the town. The locals were calling the tune. They did most of the instigating, they waved axes and clubs. A monument to Lenin stood in the park. They knocked down the statue, dragged a few young Jews out of the crowd and ordered them to carry Lenin on their backs, while others had to sing Russian songs. Then they had to dig a hole. First Lenin was thrown in, and then the Jews were pushed in and buried. Then they herded the crowd out of town, to the fields, to that barn where they burned everyone to death. The woman turns her head away and looks out the window for a long moment. *"I only saw the glow of the fire and heard a terrible cry. I can see that image before my eyes to this day."*

Did the town residents watch the crime? *"Whoever was bold went,"* she replies. *"There wasn't anyone to go from our house; the NKVD* took my father in 1939 and sent him to Siberia, and my brother was hiding from the Germans. But the men, I know that some of them poked around in the remnants of the blaze. They were looking for gold. They pulled off rings, earrings and necklaces."*

She also heard of mothers who jumped into the water with tiny babies, because they preferred to drown rather than die in the flames. She nods her head. *"That was at the pond. They hadn't started in on the group yet, but already there were a few of them that dragged those poor women out of the crowd and murdered them. It was Sodom...."*

*

The barn belonged to Bronisław Śleszyński. His daughter, who lives in the center of Jedwabne, does not want to talk about those events. She shows us out of her apartment. *"I wasn't there on the town square then. Believe me, I didn't see it, I didn't beat any Jews,"* she remarks in her agitation. *"A German came with Karolak* [the mayor—ed.], *ordered him to turn over the keys and that's it. So father gave them to him. What was he supposed to do? If he hadn't turned them over, he would have been killed himself, and the Jews would still have been burned. After all, they were destroying whole ghettos. Along the whole eastern border it was the same thing as in Jedwabne. I won't say a thing. In 1941, I was 17 years old. I will make a statement only before the prosecutor, and only if he's not a Jew or a communist."*

Because now it looks as if there's an attempt to whitewash the Germans and accuse the Poles.

*

The next address. The proprietress of the house, an older woman, remembers those events, but the daughter, who takes care of her, will not allow a conversation with her mother.

"She's over 80 years old. She takes it badly when she talks about it and can't sleep nights. Once I encouraged her to reminisce for a journalist from Kontakty, *and to this day she chides me for it. Mama had many friends among the Jews. The awareness that they died in such a tortuous way is still a great trauma for her."*

"It is painful for all the inhabitants of Jedwabne," she adds. *"If you hear on television or read in the paper that in Jedwabne there was a slaughter of Jews like nowhere else in all Poland, and if it turns out that Poles took part in it, which was documented, then indeed we wonder where all that evil in people, that led them to commit such horrible acts, came from. Even worse, because we know that in Jedwabne, just like in the rest of Poland, people were intimidated by the occupying army. Everyone was afraid. The Germans must have provoked the people of Jedwabne to do such a thing. Did they know when taking part in it what would happen to the Jews? Definitely not. The Nazis used them. People say that those people were given vodka earlier or some stimulants, because they were all worked up that day."*

*

A school, in the teachers' lounge. *"Whether you believe it or not— it's horrible, shameful. Nothing like that should ever happen,"* comes the answer at once. *"It's an undeniable fact. Jews were killed, but to what extent Poles were responsible—that issue hasn't been clarified. The community was definitely divided, as it is now. But something like that could have happened due to a defined group of residents who held grudges against the Jews. And they didn't do it of their own initiative. That's impossible,"* doubt the teachers. *"Round up 1,600 people and lead them to their death?"*

The secretary of the town and district office also has her doubts. Like most, she knows the events only from stories. According to her, it was the town riffraff who took part in the massacre, and not in any circumstances the society.

"My parents said that there was one guy who always walked around with a knife, and his wife had her whole backside poked full of holes he'd just as soon stab her as look at her. You never knew what he'd do next. There are a lot of questions to be answered. Even the number of murdered Jews. In Jedwabne the biggest building is the church, and there is no way that all the residents would fit in. So how did they stuff 1,600 people into a barn? Or the matter of the German gendarmerie. They must have been in the town. Even Wasersztajn testified that all Jedwabne was surrounded so that nobody could sneak out. And after all, 500 or a maximum of 600 Poles lived here then, including children and old folks. So they must have brought in German detachments. It's not all the same if the slaughter was committed only by residents taking advantage of permission from the local gendarmerie, or by a group of scum stirred up by the Germans who sent a battalion of police to purge the town of Jews," says the secretary.

It's difficult to hold conversations in Jedwabne. Those who earlier talked to reporters about these events now refuse to speak. One of the women can't forgive herself for talking with a Jewish journalist (as she assumes from the sound of her last name). She claims the journalist twisted her words and wrote that she confirmed in a stuttering voice that the Poles murdered the Jews. "I never said any such thing in my life. And do I stutter?!"

Like an echo, the theme of who was responsible for what happened resurfaces, including the Jews themselves. There is talk of revenge for their attitude [during the 1939–1941 Soviet occupation —ed.] toward the local people. That when the Russians came they didn't have to search out the Poles that could cause them trouble.

"They denounced many people to the NKVD, * and those people were then sent to Siberia. The Jews informed on people—where they lived, what they were doing," says one of the women. "My father was also denounced, I know exactly by whom. Father worked in a sawmill, a Jew was the owner. The Ruskies came to search for weapons. Father had some, they arrested him and sent him to Russia, to Archangel. I never saw him again. He joined Anders' army, * made it to England and never returned to Poland. And the UB* killed my brother, after the war. He survived the Ruskies, the Germans, but his own people finished him off. What a fate."

*

In Jedwabne there are two monuments commemorating the martyrdom of residents during World War II. A black stone obelisk stands near the Catholic cemetery. It was erected in recent times. On the base is a crowned eagle and the inscription: "To the memory of about 180 people including 2 priests who were murdered in the territory of Jedwabne district in the years 1939–56 by the NKVD, the Nazis and the UB. [Signed] Society."

A stone obelisk in the field where Śleszyński's barn once stood reminds us of the murder of the Jews. It was erected in the 1960s by the Łomża branch of ZBoWiD.* White, freshly painted posts, a blue metal fence, wreaths and candles. The inscription on the stone is still the same as years ago: "SITE OF THE SUFFERING OF THE JEWISH POPULATION. THE GESTAPO AND THE NAZI GENDARMERIE BURNED 1600 PEOPLE ALIVE JULY 10, 1941."

Alicja Zielińska

115

ADAM DOBROŃSKI

JEDWABNE STIGMATIZED

"KURIER PORANNY" DECEMBER 1, 2000

I am thinking back to a recent visit to Jedwabne to gather material for a television report. The town was living in fear. An invasion by journalists from all over the world was underway, and Jedwabne was consolidating a defense of its honor. Let me add that externally, the town could be any other town in this part of Poland, in other words: poor, with rising unemployment, and lost in everyday affairs.

The stories about the "good Jews" they knew in Jedwabne, the friends from school and from the playground, the outgoing salesmen in yarmulkes, and the honest craftsmen, sound authentic. Examples were cited of enduring repression together, mutual gestures of assistance, or at least sympathy. No doubt these are all authentic images; perhaps repeated many times over, certainly willingly displayed today and presented as evidence for the defense.

There is no doubt that until the war, and especially until 1937, life in Jedwabne was calm, which isn't to say by any means that identical values were respected, day and night, night and day, day in and day out, at open doors and windows.

Will the Jews not betray us?

I will hazard the opinion that the worst offender here was ordinary human envy, and not different speech, a different religion, different clothes or customs. Many Catholics were under the impression that the Jews had things better because they lived in greater harmony and prosperity, were more clever, and found it easier to stray from the straight and narrow to earn a few pennies. Jews more often left to seek their fortune in the wide world, and young Zionists left Poland for good, making no bones about the fact that, for them, Poland was but a temporary, makeshift homeland. So when dark clouds began gathering over Poland, supporters of the National Democracy* asked a question which had the force of a ticking time-bomb: Will the Jews not betray us? The inferred response was: yes, they will, you can't trust them. From one month to the next, there was growing suspicion. Meanwhile, the church in Łomża put up no resistance whatever to these trends, and yet so much depended on the attitude of the local priest. Now, before the television cameras, the inhabitants of Jedwabne admit that tragic things did happen in that July 1941, the handiwork of "no one knows who," but most probably of local and out-of-town riffraff and thugs with whom no decent resident of Jedwabne would associate.

Who was that thug?

No one remembers being present in the crowd that escorted the Jews to the site of the atrocity (the most they remember is watching from a distance). However, one hears of attempts to give water to the suffering Jews: "I tried to give someone a cup of water, but some thug hit me on the hand with a club...." Therefore, there were witnesses who knew virtually nothing. No one took part in the murder.

Reports on the conduct of Jews under the first Soviet occupation* and their deference to the NKVD* are more detailed. That is what happened in other Polish places "liberated" by the Red Army, when a considerable number of Jews, especially those who were younger,

117

poorer, and already under communist influence, severed their neigh-borly ties with the Poles for good. Today, no one in Jedwabne remembers anything about any persecution of the Jews by the NKVD, and it is not the done thing to name traitors from one's own Catholic circles.

The Germans watched...

Quiet insider discussions are in progress in Jedwabne, and the visitor can only hear fragments of these opinions, a few facts here and there, and only on the condition that he switches off his camera or tape recorder and seems trustworthy. Then, he hears the names of those who forgot their fear of God, were tempted by Jewish property, and allowed themselves to fall under Satan's power. For example, there is a story of a man who murdered a Jewish child; God later punished the man by taking away his own children. A horrible chill blows from these frugal sentences. How could anyone do such a thing to his fellow man? Germans, too, come up in these tales, because nothing could happen back then without their permission.

There are bound to have been Germans in the town, but how many? Certainly they approved of the atrocity, but to what extent? Was it all according to their plans, under their protection? I am quite sure that they were prepared to contribute to the atrocity and, if necessary, even finish it off.

What next?

A recurring question is about how the Jedwabne affair will end. The overwhelming majority of the Jedwabne residents do not re-member the Jews, though they must have heard about July 1941. One local schoolboy said that, if things carry on this way, everyone who was born in Jedwabne will be considered an heir to the atrocity and will be stigmatized because the blood of murderers flows in his veins. From a distance, from beyond the seven seas, and sometimes even from Warsaw, it is easy to hand down only righteous verdicts, apply-ing the principle of collective responsibility. But a local government official sweats over the inscription on the new memorial to the atrocity: "If we write that it was Poles who murdered the Jews, we will have to post a 24-hour watch over the monument. The Poles include my father, my mother and my grandparents."

Adam Dobroński

STANISŁAW KRAJEWSKI

A TIME OF PENANCE

"WPROST" DECEMBER 3, 2000

The case of Jedwabne weighs heavily on Poland. One day, fifty-nine years ago, residents of this locality murdered most of their Jewish neighbors. Half a century has elapsed and nothing has happened. Poland is celebrating a decade of independence, but the case of Jedwabne is still barely known.

This is a great moral challenge and a serious political problem. The distant story shows that Polish Christians did more than witness the Holocaust: in Jedwabne, they took part in it. Many will deny it, since the revelation undercuts the widely accepted image of the Poland of the time. "It is impossible," some will say. Others, refraining from denying the fact, will state that "there is no point in reviving a story which took place more than half a century ago." But it should be stressed that the truth will out, and it could have a far-from-salubrious effect on the world's image of Poland.

Let us recall: in July 1941, people from Jedwabne (with the participation of strangers) murdered most of their Jewish neighbors—over 1,600 people. Even though the murderers were acting under German eyes, there were no German orders. Unable to finish the bloodbath with axes and other primitive tools, the perpetrators herded Jews into a barn and burned them there.

Everybody in town knew about it; everybody could see it, hear it and smell it. It seems hard to believe that the things that happened then did not become the dominant subject of conversations. People must have been talking about it ever since. Yet the topic of Jedwabne has never been aired publicly. Not a word was uttered about it in the church; the local priests did not urge their congregations to reflect on it; historians remained silent. Is it not strange that not a single writer in Poland had sufficient courage to deal with this topic? The neighbors took over Jewish-owned houses. Has anyone ever tried to describe how it happened, or how the new occupants felt? Christians rescued a handful of Jews from the massacre. Polish neighbors did not thank them. Did the rescuers not deserve gratitude? What does the fact that the tragedy passed into oblivion indicate? Over the past fifty years, not even the smallest monument to the victims has been erected. The truth proved to be too horrifying to face.

Young people from Jedwabne surely have a difficult time dealing with the burden despite the fact that only some of those living at the time were perpetrators. Spiritual leaders today should help break the silence and overcome the fear of speaking about this shameful incident publicly. The younger generation, one way or another, is linked to the tragedy only indirectly—but could become accomplices by remaining silent. Years ago, it would certainly have been hard to stand up to the murderers, protected as they were by the town authorities. But afterwards? A few years later? Decades and decades later? Individuals involved in the Jedwabne massacre were brought before the court after World War Two—under communist rule, a fact which did not make it any easier to raise the issue. But even today, ten years after the fall of communist Poland, solidarity with the victims has not been expressed and there is no sense of disgrace.

Keeping the silence about the tragedy does Poland no good. The massacre in Jedwabne will soon be known worldwide. Its symbolic meaning may overshadow the meaning of the Kielce pogrom.* We all will be blamed unless we do something to convince the world that Poland does not treat the tragedy of Jedwabne lightly. Poles will be accused of being unable to wrestle with the sore spots in their history, blamed for making foreigners do their dirty work. Recently, some officials from the local and national governments have demonstrated their good will. A penitential service has been offered in Jedwabne, and historians participated in a meeting organized at the Ministry of Foreign Affairs. However, this is far too little. The truth has not reached the public and the fact that the Jedwabne [criminal—ed.] case is to be reopened by the Institute of National Remembrance* is as encouraging as it is worrying—for it may be perceived as an attempt to relieve us all from responsibility for hasty actions. By July 2001, the date marking the sixtieth anniversary of the massacre, Jan Gross's book will have been published in English and it will surely be followed by a series of reviews. The gravest accusations of Polish anti-Semitism will become more credible. This can be prevented only if Poland's most honorable representatives show that they are aware of the problem, deplore the tragedy, and are not shirking their responsibility.

What should be done? The residents of Jedwabne should be helped and prepared for bearing the burden of the tragedy and the prospect that their town's name will acquire a sinister meaning even outside Poland. There is a need for the official acknowledgment of the truth and for paying homage to the victims—publicly and openly. The ceremony should make worldwide headlincs and be broadcast by CNN. It should be made clear that the ceremony is organized on behalf of all of Poland, and it should be attended by the Polish leadership: the president, the primate of the Roman Catholic Church in Poland, and the prime minister. A successful ceremony will be tantamount to success in the Christian-Jewish dialogue. The Church's *teshuva* will bear fruit.

Stanisław Krajewski

These are fragments of a lecture delivered at the Literature House in Warsaw on October 5, 2000, during a session organized by the "Open Republic" Association, *Więź* monthly, and the Polish Pen-Club. The full text of the lecture was published by *Więź* in February 2000. The other speaker at the session was Archbishop Józef Życiński.

KRZYSZTOF JASIEWICZ

RESEARCH STILL NEEDED ON THESE NEIGHBORS

"GAZETA WYBORCZA" DECEMBER 9–10, 2000

The Soviet authorities elevated Jedwabne to the rank of regional [*raion*] capital. On January 15, 1940 the Jedwabne region, officially known as *raion jedwabinsky*, in the Białystok district, was proclaimed. Its area encompassed 550 square kilometers; from the north to the south it stretched for 40 km, from the west to the east for 25 km.

There, at the forks of the rivers Narew and Biebrza close to the Ławki marshes, a tragic murder of Jews by Poles took place on July 10, 1941, right after the German invasion. For a long time yet there will certainly be extensive controversy over this dramatic incident, which professor Jan T. Gross describes in his book *Neighbors*.

A shocking event, it raises various emotions, some of which are dangerous. As a sociologist, Gross must have taken this into consideration. All the more so should we expect reliable and comprehensive documentation covering a wide range of sources. Many of these sources would have strengthened the argument of his book. However, as he admits himself, Gross moved too hastily into print. He decided not to research the source materials. His "new approach to sources" (the title of a chapter in *Neighbors*) doesn't always advance the cause.

It should be noted that the roots of the Jedwabne pogrom exist in various epochs, including the 1939–1941 Soviet occupation.

Soviet documents regarding the northwest territories of Poland that were incorporated into the part of the Belorussian Soviet Socialist Republic known as "Western Belorussia" and including the Białystok area and therefore Jedwabne, can be found in thousands of files in more than a dozen archives. It is surprising that professor Gross completely passed over this Soviet material, even though he knew that it was already accessible, at least from the work of Michał Gnatowski *W radzieckich okowach 1939–1941* [In Soviet Chains] (Łomża, 1997), which Gross cites in *Neighbors*.

How many victims could there have been?

Eight years before the outbreak of the war, there were 1,263,300 people in the Białystok Province [of Poland—ed.], including 153,500 Jews who made up 12.1% of the population (38.3% in towns). Gross quotes these very facts from the general census of 1931. In the Soviet records, however—which also took into account so called *bezhency**, that is escapees from the German occupied zone—there were 1,507,617 inhabitants in April 1940, with Jews representing 11.8 percent in the Białystok district (smaller than the pre-war province). Subsequent [Soviet—ed.] statistics from February 1941 put the Białystok district population as 1,309,440, with 9.7% of them being Jewish—the Jewish share in the population was declining.

The Jedwabne region population statistics from the NKVD* materials are more detailed. The head of the regional division of the NKVD, State Security Lt. Kostrow, noted in a secret report titled "Information on the political-economic position of the Jedwabne region in the Białystok district on September 16, 1940" that the region's population was 38,885—by ethnic background, 37,300 Poles, 1,400 Jews, and 185 Belorussians.

We may assume that the decided majority of these Jews lived in the town of Jedwabne. In my opinion, confirmed by research on areas lying immediately east of the Białystok district, there seem to have been many more Jews departing from than arriving in this small town in the nine months from September 1940 to June 1941 (and thus up to the eve of the German-Soviet war).

After May 1940, the border between the General Government* and Soviet-occupied Poland was very secure, with little hope of illegally crossing the border. The number of arrests had been rising by the month since the beginning of Soviet occupation. Arrest depended first of all on an individual's being a "danger to society" or, in the vocabulary of the NKVD/KGB, a *"sotsyalnoopastniy element"*, as covered by Article. 74 of the [Soviet—ed.] criminal code. According to the Soviets, the "socially dangerous element" could be an artisan, someone engaged in commerce, or owner of a house or shop—in short, practically anyone. Many Jews were arrested in this category. They were also among those who allowed themselves to be recruited for voluntary work in the depths of Russia. The *raion jedwabinsky* was one of the most economically backward parts of the Białystok district.

Several questions beg for answers. How is the count of 1,400 Jews recorded in Soviet documents from September 1940 to be reconciled with that of 1,600 in Jedwabne who were chased into the barn and burnt alive by Poles in July of the following year? Is it possible that the author of *Neighbors* inflated the number of victims? Is it really possible that Gross failed to notice the appendix in Gnatowski's book containing NKVD Lt. Kostrow's report? Why did he ignore such a document?

Anti-Semitism and hostility to the Soviet Union

In the reports of regional NKVD division heads, we are informed that there is anti-Semitism in the Białystok district. For these functionaries, anti-Soviet attitudes are often identical with anti-Semitic ones. The following are some examples connected with the elections.

Thus in the Lubeszczyńskie village, Bielski region, in the ballot box for delegates to the Supreme Council of the Soviet Union and Soviet Belorussia (March 1940), a note was found with the following text: "Long Live Poland! Jan Turlejski [one of the candidates] is a bandit. Get out! Otherwise we'll hang you on the first tree we find

—may you rot and die, whore, Jew-face [...]. Down with communists!" In Białystok, the NKVD* made note of a flyer distributed during the elections for local government (December 1940): "To all Jews! By grace of God may you not make it to election day, may you all rot. You came to Poland dirty as swine and you'll leave just the same [...] Hey, you wives of Tatars and dirty Jew-faces, we are all going to vote because we're forced to. [...] Remember, Jew, you're in Poland, your wanderer's fate brought you here but your face will not disappear from my memory, it'll smash your hook nose." Col. Misiuriew, chief of the district NKVD, refrained from quoting further from the flyer because of its "offensive language." Another flyer proclaims: "We want the true Christian faith, not cant and lies imposed by Jews and Stalin."

In the opinion of the NKVD, the regions of Jedwabne, Zambrów and Czyżew were anti-Semitic. In the latter of these in 1939, during the two-week Nazi occupation, Poles and Germans looted Jewish property.

Lt. Kostrov, NKVD chief in Jedwabne, in assessing the "economic-political situation of the region," writes of a bitter Polish-Jewish conflict. He refers to pogroms in 1934–35 and notes that, in the township of Radziłów not far away, four people died in a related matter.

In this regard, it is striking that the Jedwabne region, as reported in other Soviet documents, had the lowest percentage of Jews in the Białystok district, some 3.6%. Considerably more Jews lived in the following regions: Kolno (15%), Czyżew (12.7%), Zambrów (10.5%), Ciechanowiec (9.5%) and Białystok city (37.7%).

Why did the murder in the barn occur there, where there were the fewest Jewish neighbors? This is one detail from a historical point of view, but a reliable researcher ought to know the facts and at least try to explain them. Why did the greatest repressive measures before the outbreak of the German-Soviet war affect this particular region? It is known that on the night of June 19, 1941, close to 12,000 people in the Białystok district were arrested and deported, which is four times more than in neighboring regions. It transpires from NKVD documents found in Minsk that, in the area around Jedwabne, the

Polish underground numbered 1,500 people (representing 4% of Poles in the region, not counting their families). Did this have any connection with the drama in the barn at Jedwabne? Did the hatred for the Soviet system, whose symbol were the Jews, express a specifically interpretation of the patriotic mindset?

We do not find out from Gross's book.

As seen from the Gulag

The author of *Neighbors* demonstrates a reluctance not only for Soviet sources. He also steps around Polish ones, despite knowing them well. This concerns accounts by people who joined Anders's army.* The Documents Office of the Second Corps collected these with care and they are stored, along with the entire Second Corps collection, in the archives of the Hoover Institution in California.

These accounts speak volumes about the Soviet occupation of the eastern marches* of Poland in 1939–41. In almost all these accounts, it is possible to learn about the participation of Jews in anti-Polish activities. Jews are in the groups welcoming the Red Army, in *ad hoc* revolutionary committees and quasi-militias. We see them at "meetings" both among the audience and on the speakers' platforms, among members of the election committees, and among the commissars, apparatchiks and various imported Soviet activists that arrived there. In these accounts, Jews denounce others and are disloyal to their Polish neighbors and the Polish state. The Jews reduce the eastern marches to poverty and economic death throes. They play the part of *sledovateli** and NKVD officers; they torture people in the prisons and deport Polish civilians to Siberia.

I have looked through thousands of accounts (amongst others, those of the Eastern Archives in Warsaw and the Sikorski Institute in London, as well as copies of the Hoover Archives). There are also (with similar frequency, at times as background, like the Jewish problem) notes on the drunks and dregs of society, criminals, thieves, and farmhands—often Belorussians—who, in the first weeks of the occupation, took to robbery, murder, rape, denunciation and organized raids on country estates and smaller units of the Polish army.

Besides, numerous Soviet documents attest to the anti-Polish attitude of part of the Belorussian population.

A reading of this literature leaves the impression that the Jews who collaborate with Soviet authorities are responsible for the entire misfortune of the Poles in the eastern borders. The strength of this conviction surely indicates the state of public opinion at the time, as well as the anti-Semitism ingrained in Polish tradition.

It is odd, therefore, that professor Gross does not include such accounts in his account of the anti-Semitic nature of the events in Jedwabne, as part of the threshold of the Holocaust. On the other hand, if we were to accept Gross's "new approach to sources" (which relies on the change from "*a priori* critical to in principle affirmative" in the appraisal of relation to "all fragments of information at our disposal," then it would also be necessary to consider whether the accounts of those survivors of the camps and prisons of the "Gulag Archipelago" should be treated in a similar manner.

Anti-Jewish delusions

One important matter is that the Soviet documents do not confirm the suppositions of massive Jewish collaboration with the Soviet occupation authorities.

In the mid 1930s, of course, Jews made up over 38 percent of the central NKVD* staff (data from July 1934, published in Moscow a year ago). After the great purge in the central apparatus, however, Jews accounted for not quite four percent, with ethnic Russians dominating (over 66 percent). This remained so until the outbreak of war with Germany. Yet the myth of the ubiquitous "Jewish communist"* persisted.

Over 30,000 Soviet personnel, known as the *Vostochniks* arrived in occupied northeast Poland between 1939 and 41. Most of them came from Soviet Belorussia. An analysis of Soviet administrative apparatus personnel questionnaires allows us to maintain that the entire Soviet activist cadre was made up of outsiders, from party secretaries down through the subordinate party, police, administrative and economic apparatus. In these ranks, Belorussians clearly dominate. There are many ethnic Russians (most in NKVD structures) and there are also Jews (between 10 and 20 percent).

Out of 403 people in management positions (Secretaries and Directors of departments) in the Białystok district in January 1941, there are 298 Belorussians (74%), 37 ethnic Russians, 56 Jews (13.9%), eight Poles, two Ukrainians and one Lithuanian and one German. In the upper party echelons in the district, the participation of Jews is greater (18.4%).

Nor was there any "Jewish invasion" in the Jedwabne region. In October 1940, a mere 13 Jews sent from the Soviet Union worked in the region. We know the personal data of the party leadership in Jedwabne. All matters in the region were under its jurisdiction.

The first secretary of the Regional Committee of the Belorussian Communist Party (Bolshevik) was Mark Rydachenko, born 1901, a Belorussian, member of the BCP(b)* since 1926, educated in secondary and higher party schools, a member of the apparatus since 1934. The second secretary was Dmitriy Ustilovskiy, also a Belorussian, born 1904, BCP(b) member since 1926, incomplete elementary and secondary party-school education, in the apparatus since 1939. The third secretary for personnel is a Russian, Pietr Bystrov, born 1898, BCP(b) member since 1919, incomplete elementary and incomplete elementary party-school education, in the apparatus since 1938.

In the ranks of the party, ethnic Poles are few and far between; all of them came from the USSR. In party documents, there are constant laments that so few locals have been recruited.

According to Lt. Kostrov's report in September 1940, the NKVD had 130 informers and agents in Jedwabne. Their nationality is unknown, but through January 1941, it is recorded that 25 informers were recruited among a hundred Polish partisans who gave up the underground struggle.

In the fall of 1940, nearly 5,500 people were openly collaborating with the Soviet authorities in facade organizations in the Białystok region. The largest number of careerist collaborators, 2,773, is found

129

among ethnic Poles—that is, 51 percent! Next come 1,425 Belorussians (26%) and 1,050 Jews (19%).

In the Jedwabne region however, there are 126 Poles (70%), 45 Jews (25%), four Belorussians, three Russians, and three "others" among 181 careerist collaborators. Upwardly mobile individuals from working-class backgrounds dominate, with the remainder being mainly farmhands and provincial intelligentsia.

In the region, 3.2% of the Jews are careerist collaborators, as contrasted with only 0.34% of the Poles, a proportion that is ten times lower. The statistics, as we see, show there were clearly more Polish collaborators. However, the Jews must have stood out more and caused more resentment.

This false perception of reality by the Jedwabne neighbors, however, is not reflected in Gross's book.

Gross's first text about Jedwabne appeared at the beginning of the year in *Europa nieprowincjonalna* [Non-provincial Europe]. As research editor of that volume, I thought that the press would take up the theme of Jedwabne. Andrzej Kaczyński from the newspaper *Rzeczpospolita* did so. The magazine *Myśl Polska** did so as well, in its June 2000 issue: "Nor is there any lack [in *Europa nieprowincjonalna*] of controversial historians, such as Grzegorz Motyka, Jan Tomasz Gross or Jerzy Holzer, whose tendencies for national self-castigation provoke numerous protests.... Amongst some it is possible, unfortunately, to sense hidden anti-Polish complexes, to find stereotypes that are injurious to us."

Neither self-castigation nor complexes is the issue. The issue is that of truth, an appalling truth, which the historian must honestly and comprehensively examine, and which the public must find out about. Even if this truth hurts and outrages us. Even if we refer to this act of genocide in Jedwabne as an instance of the Holocaust.

Krzysztof Jasiewicz

DAWID WARSZAWSKI

RESPONSIBILITY AND THE LACK OF RESPONSIBILITY

"GAZETA WYBORCZA" DECEMBER 9–10, 2000

"I would be lying if I said that this book does not fill me with fear," writes Jacek Żakowski at the beginning of his essay "Every Neighbor Has a Name" [*Gazeta Wyborcza*, November 18/19, 2000]. The subject of Żakowski's essay, and of his interview with the historian Tomasz Szarota that precedes the essay in the same issue of the newspaper, is Jan Tomasz Gross's book *Neighbors*. Gross's book is about the murder of 1,600 Jewish citizens by the Polish residents of the town of Jedwabne in July 1941, shortly after the arrival of the German army in a part of eastern Poland that was previously occupied by the Soviets.

"This fear has three sources," Żakowski continues. "First, there are the facts" described by Gross, which unequivocally document the full horror of a massacre that lasted for several days and was perpetrated by the "neighbors" of the title, before the eyes of everyone. "Whatever it was that impelled them to that crime may still lie somewhere deep within them (within us? within me?)," writes Żakowski. Without a hint of equivocation or leniency, he analyzes the terrifying consequences of that reflection. The third reason for his fear is that "all of us share the responsibility for whether or not such things ever happen again"—and there is no guarantee that the future will not be equally murderous. "After Bosnia and Rwanda," writes Żakowski, "it is hard for us to be shocked by human cruelty." Reflecting on the individual evil that may well lurk within each of us, or reminding us that this evil may again reveal itself in all its murderous might in the future, Żakowski shows himself to be fully conscious of the challenge that the Jedwabne crime poses to our good feelings about ourselves.

The language of ethnic war?

However, the most important thread in the essay consists of Żakowski's reflections upon the second of the fears aroused in him by the reading of Gross's book. Here, the source of the fear is neither the events presented in the book nor the ever-present threat that they could recur in the future. Żakowski's second fear stems from the fact that "in appealing to the language of ethnic quantifiers, Gross runs the risk of causing or contributing to further misfortunes"—to new crimes like the one in Jedwabne. It is, in fact, not clear who could murder whom after reading *Neighbors*, but we all know that language can indeed lead to crimes. This is what makes it so important to use language in a responsible way.

The thesis that Gross "clearly pushes us in the direction of such language" appears repeatedly in the essay. What sort of language is this? Żakowski answers this question without ambivalence. "This is the language of ethnic war, of genocide." Żakowski cautions us that "In Europe, we were reminded of the danger of such [nationalistic —D.W.] quantifiers when we saw what happened in Bosnia." Żakowski concludes: "I am all the more astonished at Jan Gross—who himself once heard that language in Poland [Gross emigrated after March 1968*—D.W.], for now being ready to call it forth again and to run the risk of nourishing ghosts that are on their way to extinction." If we were to take Żakowski's rhetoric seriously, we would have to place *Neighbors* on the same bookshelf as the collected speeches of General Moczar* and Radovan Karadzic. However, there is no question of treating Gross's book that way, because Żakowski's charges are just as empty as they are serious. Nevertheless, they cannot be passed over indifferently. Żakowski is a respected journalist, and his text is the first important voice raised in *Gazeta Wyborcza* on the subject of *Neighbors*. It is not my intention to write about the Jedwabne crime here. Gross has written almost everything about the facts themselves in his book, and the rest is up to the historians. On the other hand, it is too early for a debate on the meaning of Jedwabne, since instead of debate there has rather been silence broken only by the excellent articles in *Rzeczpospolita* several months ago, and the easily predictable attacks from the Catholic-nationalist press. Clearly, it is not the details of the Jedwabne crime—the worst known Polish crime against the Jews—that are most important to Żakowski, either. Nor the first revelation of this crime to the public. Nor an analysis of the circumstances that led to it, or of those that led to its being covered in silence. Nor the failure to pose questions about the consequences of this silence in terms of the accuracy of the image of the German occupation that still functions in the minds of the Polish public. Nor even certain factual shortcomings in Gross's book, as properly pointed out by both interlocutors in Żakowski's interview with Szarota.

"The greater guilt" and "the deeper hurt"

Żakowski builds his whole accusation on three quotations from Gross's book. Someone might say that three quotations are too little to serve as the basis for a charge of "pushing in the direction of the language of genocide." Nevertheless, it is also the case that a few words can suffice to doom even a work of many volumes. Let us therefore examine Żakowski's evidence. Here are the incriminating passages:

> "*[T]he 1,600 Jedwabne Jews were killed neither by the Nazis, nor by the NKVD,* nor by the UB,* but by society....' Might there not lie concealed here an important part of the answer to a question that haunts Polish public opinion: Why do the Jews have such an ingrained resentment towards the Poles, seemingly even more deeply rooted than their resentment towards the Germans themselves who, after all, were the*

inventors, initiators, and principal perpetrators of the Holocaust? And if, in collective Jewish memory, their Polish neighbors in numerous localities murdered them of their own free will—not on orders or as part of an organized, uniformed formation (and therefore, at least on the level of appearances, acting under compulsion)—then are the Poles not somehow, in the perceptions of the victims, particularly responsible for those acts? After all, a man in uniform who kills us is at least to a degree a state functionary; a civilian in that role is nothing more than a murderer.... [In thinking] about the national pride and sense of identity rooted in the historical experience of many generations, we are not equally responsible for the shameful deeds of our forebears and countrymen?"[1]

Żakowski deals briefly and decisively with these theses of Gross. In his opinion, the assertion that the Jedwabne Jews were killed by "society" [the term used in the Polish edition, rather than the "neighbors" of the American edition—trans.]—the Polish society of the town of Jedwabne—is "a lie." He does not, indeed, justify this assessment in his essay, but, in the accompanying interview with Szarota, Żakowski asks, "So who is guilty in your opinion: the Germans, the dregs of local society, members of the anti-Soviet underground out for revenge [for alleged Jewish collaboration with the Soviets—D.W.], or the anti-Semitic society of Jedwabne? I have the impression that Gross accepts too easily the view that the crime was the work of the whole town." Szarota replies that indeed "the account... would rather indicate that a relatively small group supported by the Germans terrorized the rest of the inhabitants and committed the massacre that later covered all of Jedwabne with shame.... But just think how much courage would have been needed under such circumstances to stand up to them."

---

[1] Thus runs the Polish edition, which differs from the American edition of *Neighbors* precisely in these points. For a comparison with text of the same passages in the American edition, see the notes to Żakowski's article, pp. 76–90 (translator's note).

In other words, Szarota does not agree with Gross's interpretation of the sources, as far as the universality of the involvement of the Jedwabne Poles in the massacre is concerned. This admissible difference in the evaluation of historical material suffices (even though Szarota does not provide any justification for his position) for Żakowski to pronounce judgment in categorical terms: since the involvement of all the Polish inhabitants of Jedwabne in the massacre has not been proved beyond all doubt, then the thesis that "society killed" the Jedwabne Jews is a lie [once again, this is the wording of the Polish edition—trans.].What about the responsibility of those who did not oppose the massacre? Szarota correctly points out that doing so required great courage. However, while this may at best explain passivity in the face of the crime, it cannot justify such passivity. Nevertheless, Żakowski forges ahead: he points out that not only Poles, but also Jews failed to protest. This is not a slip of the tongue. The emphasis on the lack of Jewish protest returns three times in his questions to Szarota. In a word, if passivity is to burden the consciences of the Poles, then it should burden the consciences of the Jews in the same way, for they, too, failed to protest. This formulation is even more astounding than the previous one. Yet this is not all. In order to confront Gross's second thesis that the experience of murder at Polish hands may have caused Jews to feel a resentment towards the Poles "seemingly even more deeply rooted than their resentment towards the Germans," Żakowski simply replaces it with another. "Previously, the thesis that 'Jews blame the Poles more than the Germans for the Holocaust' was something that I came across mainly in anti-Semitic hate literature," notes Żakowski, and says: "I reject the language in which such views can be expressed." Yet the view that Żakowski so categorically rejects is one that Gross never even expressed. It is true that such formulations occur, very rarely, in statements by some Jewish authors. Such statements are just as representative of Jewish opinion as a view sometimes expressed in the pages of silly hate literature—that wealthy Jews from the West made use of Hitler to kill off the poor Jews from the East—is representative of Polish opinion. Jewish authors, after all, have no doubt that the Germans, in Gross's words as quoted by Żakowski himself, "were the inventors, initiators, and principal perpetrators of the Holocaust." There is, however, a certain difference between "blaming more" and "having a more deeply rooted resentment" (and note that Gross qualifies this with the word "seemingly"). It is puzzling that Żakowski seems not to notice the difference. Would such resentment not be understandable, furthermore, if it happened often enough during the war that Polish neighbors took upon themselves the role of helpers in the German work of the Holocaust, and then kept silent about it for half a century? And if, when the truth finally began to come out, those who revealed it were accused of "pushing us in the direction of the language of genocide"?

The Jedwabne affair has made it impossible for us to go on rejecting the possibility that Poles may have committed the mass murder of Jews in some other places, as well. At present, we know about such a massacre only in nearby Radziłów. This is too little to categorically assert the memory by Jews of Polish complicity, which is why Gross himself puts it in the grammatical conditional. But what we already know is enough for us to pose such a qualified thesis. What is more, posing such a thesis is, in the light of the facts, both a scholarly and a moral imperative. Żakowski's polemic completely evades precisely this aspect. First, Żakowski groundlessly imputes to Gross a thesis about the supposed attribution by the Jews of greater responsibility for the Holocaust to the Poles than to the Germans, then he rejects this thesis in outrage, and finally denies the possibility of attributing responsibility for anything to anyone except the direct perpetrators. Here, his polemic with the second thesis passes over noiselessly into a polemic with the third. "There is no responsibility for grandfathers and great-grandfathers," he writes, "because those not yet born had no way of restraining them... Jan Tomasz Gross is responsible for himself, and I am responsible for myself. Neither of us has the right to complain to the other about his countrymen or forebears."

National guilt and the reconciliation of nations

Żakowski is right. We are not free to keep reproaching others about their countrymen or forebears. Like him, everyone can demand that the deeds of others not be charged to their account. "I am irritated by the language of large-scale quantifiers," he writes, "which attempts to implicate me in culpability for a crime committed half a century ago only because I am a Pole." Żakowski has the right to demand that he not be implicated in anything else having to do with Poles, blameworthy or praiseworthy, only because he is a Pole. We all make up our personal identity at will, the things that shame us as well as the things we are proud of, from among the elements of the collective identity. Żakowski is aware of this. "I am ready to surrender even my pride in Tischner* or Copernicus, and in Plato as well, for the sake of such an understanding [of the question of implication in culpability—D.W.]," he writes. Aside from the somewhat problematical Polishness of Plato, such a standpoint is clear.

However, it should be equally clear to Żakowski that his individual opting out of the community of the implicated does not cancel out the existence of that community. To the same degree that I identify with some collective, I bear consciously and by choice a responsibility for the things it has done, good and evil, now and in the past. As opposed to the furnishing of the individual identity according to one's choice, responsibility is a package deal. No one can opt out of Polish responsibility for the crime of Jedwabne, let us say, while at the same time remaining entitled to forgive anyone in the name of the Poles for crimes committed against Poles, no matter who committed them. Żakowski's recipe has already been applied in practice, although this may be the first time it has been formulated in print. In Russia, as in Poland, there is no sense of collective responsibility for crimes committed by Russians. One of the reasons for this is that the Russians—again, like the Poles—have more often been victims than perpetrators. In such a situation it is hard to be surprised by a disinclination to look into the darker pages of their own history. But it is also hard not to notice the results of such an attitude, not only in connection with the relations between today's

137

Russians and the descendants of the victims of Russian crimes, but also in reference to their own fate. A society that tolerates silence about its own crimes does not know how to unequivocally condemn the crimes committed against it. If the fact that some Poles were murdered in Katyn* is nothing to worry about, then there is no way to feel outrage at the fact that some Russians (not to mention Poles, as well) were murdered in Kolyma.* In such a society, the party of the builders of the Gulag can go on being a leading political force.

The Germans did otherwise. They did not apply Żakowski's recipe—for they did not have the option. The crimes committed against Germans in the final phase of the war can hardly be compared with the limitless evil that the Germans did in Europe. The acceptance of collective responsibility for those crimes and its transfer to the following generations not only made it possible for the Germans to find reconciliation with the descendants of their victims. It also turned Germany into a state that is profoundly democratic, ruled according to law, and sensitive to wrongdoing. Clearly, Jedwabne is not Katyn or Treblinka. Nor is there any responsibility on the part of the Polish state for crimes committed when Poland was under occupation. Nevertheless, it is worth comparing the experience of those who applied Żakowski's recipe in practice, and those who rejected it.

Żakowski does not want to assume responsibility for crimes that he did not commit himself. He is within his rights in this, and need in no way justify his decision. He did so nevertheless, and the justification deserves separate treatment. In his opinion, "tribal" language—which he says Gross resorts to in speaking of the responsibility of the Jedwabne society for the murder of Jews or the resentment of Jews against Poles—is "the language of misfortune." "It is the language, we must remember, of ethnic war, of genocide." This is why Żakowski is so firmly opposed to Gross's use of "large-scale quantifiers," such as speaking about "all" Poles or Jews.

Never mind that Gross never even comes close to resorting to large-scale quantifiers. In the flood of totally groundless accusations that Żakowski unleashes on him, this additional one makes little difference. The thing is, however, that Żakowski is obviously right in his criticism of "the language of large-scale quantifiers," especially when applied to guilt for crimes committed in the past. He is right —with one important exception.

Without the use of this language of "large-scale quantifiers" it is, as Żakowski correctly notes, impossible to incite hatred—but it is also impossible to lay it to rest. Crime is impossible, but so is reconciliation. Genocide, but also brotherhood. German-Jewish (but also German-Polish) reconciliation would have been impossible without Willy Brandt's gesture at the Warsaw monument to the Heroes of the Ghetto. When he knelt there, the German chancellor acknowledged past crimes in the name of all Germans—and asked that those crimes be forgiven. He was credible when he did so because, as chancellor, he had the right to represent all Germans.

Willy Brandt could have said that he did not wish to be "implicated in the crimes of a quarter of a century before," and his biography would have given him a particular right to say so. Yet he did not do so. Although he was innocent of it, he took upon himself the burden of the past. By doing so, he overcame it. If he had repudiated that burden, he could not have done so. *Mutatis mutandis*, Lech Wałęsa did something similar in the Knesset when he asked forgiveness for the wrong done to Jews by Poles. Only by speaking in a credible way and in the name of their collectives could Brandt and Wałęsa overcome the past.

The point here is not only bringing closure to the past, but also taking responsibility for the future, and this is the reason for the third of Żakowski's fears. Throughout the existence of socialist Yugoslavia, no one ever appeared in the name of the Croatian nation to ask the Serbs for forgiveness of the crime of genocide committed against them during the Second World War. No such person appeared because Tito and his successors, out of concern for the endurance of their regime, took pains to prevent anyone from acquiring a mandate to speak in the name of the Croatians. It was therefore impossible for a Croatian Willy Brandt to appear—which was nevertheless proof to the Serbs that the Croatians did not feel guilty for their crimes, and could therefore repeat them, and that this needed therefore to be prevented. We know the bloody sequel.

Books like *Neighbors*, the pioneering studies of the postwar fate of the Germans in the north and west [of Poland], and the studies of the violence-soaked history of Polish-Ukrainian relations are vitally necessary in Poland. They are no less necessary than works documenting the crimes to which Poles fell victim, so that we might know where we wronged others, and where we were wronged. And also so that, having asked forgiveness in the former cases and having forgiven in the latter, we can all finally arrive at the sort of moral order in which it will no longer be possible for anyone "to be implicated in culpability for a crime" from half a century ago only because he is a Pole (or a Russian, or a German, or a Ukrainian, or...).

Dawid Warszawski

Jacek Kurczewski

Ritual Murder

"Wprost" December 10, 2000

The Polish Republic may be guilty of disbanding whole ethnically Ukrainian and Belorussian villages, and even Polish ones, but its conscience is free of mass slaughter and the organizing of pogroms or extermination camps.

1. *"Wiśniewski pointed to a massacred cadaver of a young man of Mosaic persuasion, about twenty-two years old, whose name was Lewin, and said to me, Look, mister, we killed this SOB with stones…. They took healthier men and chased them to the cemetery and ordered them to dig a pit, and after it was dug out, Jews were killed every which way, one with iron, another with a knife, still another with a club…. Władysław… drowned two Jewish blacksmiths… Gitele Nadolny (Nadolnik), the youngest daughter of the* melamed*… had her head cut off, and the murderers, we are told, later kicked it around…. Szelawa took away one Jew. His tongue was cut off…. I started pleading to spare my barn, to which they agreed and left my barn in peace, only told me to help them chase the Jews to Bronisław Śleszyński's barn… When Jews broke the statue* [of Lenin], *they were told to put its various pieces on some boards and carry it around, and the rabbi was told to walk in front with his hat on a stick, and all had to sing, 'The war is because of us, the war is for us.' While carrying the statue all the Jews were chased toward the barn,*

and the barn was doused with gasoline and lit, and in this manner fifteen hundred Jewish people perished."

2. Those were the Poles of *Neighbors*—a book by Jan T. Gross describing mass carnage committed in the Podlasie region of Poland. This was previously a Soviet-occupied zone. But in the short interim after the Soviets fled before the approaching German army, the local Polish-ethnic group carried out ethnic cleansing. The polemics over the book which recently unfolded in the Polish daily *Gazeta Wyborcza* have proved how difficult it is for Poles to recognize this fact out of their past. Professor Szarota has charged Professor Gross with writing "the sociology" and not "the history" of the event. Meanwhile, the author has scored a number of unquestionable successes in research on the history of that eastern part of Poland under Soviet occupation. So long as he wrote about Soviet terror he remained an historian, but has he now ceased to be one? Reaching for the work of Hannah Arendt and Jerzy Jedlicki to support his claim, Żakowski has confessed that it never occurred to him that Poles were capable of doing what they did. Both quote the Jews' sympathy for the Soviet authorities, as if that alone would constitute a justification for the actions of the mob and the reaction of the parish priest, who call —only once—for calm and for leaving things up to the Germans.

The Polish intelligentsia—as with every elite of this sort—nurtures the myth of their own nation's uniqueness. In fact, a unique nation we are not. When I was a student at the university, I had to persuade my excellent teacher Witek Jedlicki that there was anti-Semitism in Poland simply because there always has been. People still living in the Podlasie region kept telling me that the best times had been the Nazi times, and when a colleague of mine, Klaudiusz, joined our research team in the villages and learnt from the locals what they could do to a Jew, he took the first boat to New York, where, eating Polish ham, he prefers to keep as far away from Poland as possible. Jedlicki (Witold) emigrated to Israel; another of my teachers, Benek Tejkowski, still lives in the country, but has now acquired a new name Bolesław and such anti-Jewish phobia that he puts the Polish Primate, Cardinal Glemp—and myself, too, of course, on his list of anti-Polish Jews.

3. People here used to say that Polish anti-Semitism was of the traditional variety. But what does that mean? Superstition cultivated by the Polish Catholic Church that reminds people over and over again about the story of the blood-sucking Jewish innkeeper who refused to sell vodka on credit, and who had been brought in by the Polish Catholic landlord to collect money because he was a member of the tribe of Christ's enemies (i.e. the Jews)? Urban mobs held pogroms from time to time, but Jewish religious communities could avoid them by paying an additional special "tax." On July 10, 1941, the Germans let the Poles of Jedwabne take their revenge in an act of traditional anti-Semitism that rivalled the massacres committed by the Cossacks—and the Germans filmed it. The Poles themselves burnt their Jews alive. The survivors who were placed under protection when the Germans restored order in the village were then sent for orderly extermination—with the application of modern methods —in the appropriate death camps.

The temptation is to say that it was a primitive village mob that carried out the massacre. However, urban residents were not free of anti-Semitism where Polish Poles and Polish Jews lived side by side. The development of democratic practices and of the national consciousness exacerbated mutual relations—something like the Palestine of today. Further, the contagion infected the intelligentsia as well—which is something else that we remain silent about. If we searched the History Museum of Warsaw University, we could read about the Respublica student fraternity, which refused entry to students of Jewish origin "regardless of their creed" (ah, those little racists, I wonder how many of them died later from bullets fired by Adolf's soldiers?). We would also find there a picture of one Professor Czarnowski who strongly opposed anti-Semitism. However, we would find nothing about the racist orders issued by the University authorities or about the infamous stamping of students' identity booklets with the letter "Ż" [standing for the word *Żyd*—Jew]. Should our compatriots from Jedwabne then cause us any consternation? They were no different from the others, except that they killed their Jews as a scapegoat for all their real and imaginary sufferings. It was ritual murder.

4. One party remains innocent of that horrible tragedy, namely the Polish state. Had Poland accepted the conditions of Hitler's ultimatum, Polish losses would have been much, much smaller. Who knows, perhaps it would have been possible to conquer the Soviet Union. The West would not have been dragged into the war against Germany, and the attack [by Germany against the Soviet Union in 1941— ed.] would have been conducted not from the countryside near the town of Łomża, but from the outskirts of Minsk [and thus, starting closer to Moscow, would presumably have had a greater chance of success—ed.]. The resistance put up by Poland saved the Soviet Union. Therefore, all the more ignominy falls upon Stalin and Molotov for treacherously stabbing Poland in the back. Polish resistance saved the lives of those Jews who survived, even if they survived in Siberia.

Thus the honor of Poland was also saved, since the Polish state never had to cooperate with Hitler in ethnic cleansing, as did Pétain's France or Tiso's Slovakia. Some say: the state did not co-operate because it did not exist. But the sequence of events is quite the opposite: the Polish state ceased to exist because it refused to go along with Hitler. The Polish Republic may be guilty of disbanding whole ethnically Ukrainian and Belorussian villages, and even Polish ones, but its conscience is free of mass slaughter and the organizing of pogroms or extermination camps.

5. Professor Gross asks what inscription should be put on the monument in Jedwabne. For me it is obvious: FROM THE POLISH STATE IN REMEMBRANCE OF ITS JEWISH CITIZENS MURDERED BY THEIR NEIGHBORS IN FRATRICIDAL RAGE.

Jacek Kurczewski

PAWEŁ MACHCEWICZ

IN THE SHADOW OF JEDWABNE

"RZECZPOSPOLITA" DECEMBER 11, 2000

There is no doubt that Jan T. Gross' book and the discussion it has aroused is one of the most important events in recent years in the Polish debate about the past. *Neighbors* and Gross's *Upiorna dekada* [The Ghastly Decade;* Cracow, 1998], published two years ago (and virtually unnoticed), concern the most important issues for Poles, issues which shape our image of ourselves on such important topics as the German and Soviet occupation, Polish attitudes towards the Germans and Jews, and the attitudes of Poles towards the Holocaust.

No wonder these issues still cause white-hot emotions despite the passage of several decades. This could be seen at a recent meeting of the Historical Institute of the Polish Academy of Sciences, devoted to Gross' book and attended by several dozen people. This was an exceptional meeting mainly because of the high temperature of the debate, towards the end of which the participants were either shouting at each other or weeping.

Therefore, is there an opportunity to talk calmly about Gross's books and consider arguments other than one's own?

PAWEŁ MACHCEWICZ

Facts and questions

Let us try to reconstruct the most important facts and questions to which there are no answers yet.

On July 10, 1941, the entire Jewish population of the small town of Jedwabne, with almost 3,000 inhabitants, located a few kilometers from Łomża, was murdered. The number of victims fluctuates between 900 and some 1,500 to 1,600 people; Gross assumes the highest possible figure. The Jews were killed by their neighbors, the Poles. Not by all the Poles, of course. On the basis of investigative and court records from 1949, the author identifies several dozen of the most zealous murderers.

These facts are questioned by virtually no one, but there are doubts as to the role of the Germans. The event was certainly not spontaneous. It was recorded by a German film crew who appeared in Jedwabne that morning. The records contain information on conversations between the Germans and the town's leaders over the preceding few days. In order to understand the context of the Jedwabne incident, one should also bear in mind the fact that, several days earlier, two German police battalions had murdered 2,000 Jews in Białystok, burning many of them in the synagogue.

There is a striking similarity between the methods used at both locations, because in Jedwabne at least several hundred Jews were burned in a barn. Gross does not pay too much attention to these issues (or to other versions of the story according to which somewhere between several dozen and more than two hundred German functionaries were there). He considers the Germans to be of no crucial significance in establishing a picture of what happened on that 10th of July.

What were the motives?

Historians also point to other circumstances which Jan T. Gross either ignores altogether or does not consider to a sufficient degree. A key question is the motives that led to almost the entire Jewish community of a small town being massacred by its Polish neighbors in a single day. One of the motives was certainly anti-Semitism (that part of Poland was the only one where the National-Radical Camp* had strong rural influence), or it could have been simple greed—a desire to grab the victims' possessions. But that is probably not all.

According to descriptions of what happened on that day, an important motive might have been a desire to wreak vengeance on the Jews for their (factual or alleged—we are not yet able to determine this) collaboration with the Soviet occupation forces between September 1939 and June 1941. Gross claims there is no reason to believe that the Jews of Jedwabne collaborated with the NKVD* to a greater extent than the Poles did, or that the Jews helped hunt down and eliminate a partisan unit in the neighborhood. Yet we know that, before they died, young Jews were forced to remove the statute of Lenin which the Soviet occupants had placed in the town, and that on their way to their deaths they were forced to sing "The war is because of us, the war is for us."

Professor Tomasz Szarota has pointed out that some of the chief murderers, the Laudański brothers, had previously lost a sister, who was arrested and murdered by the NKVD. Another important piece of information (absent in *Neighbors*) is that, a few days before the pogrom, a group of prisoners, former members of the anti-Soviet resistance who had been released by the advancing Germans, arrived in Jedwabne.

The above details provide no ready replies, but they suggest that collective opinions about the co-responsibility of Jews for Soviet atrocities, even if far from the truth, might be to blame for the massacre.

Of course this does not change the moral assessment of what happened in Jedwabne, nor does it excuse the murderers. Whether or not the atrocity was inspired by the Germans or fuelled by a desire to wreak vengeance on the Jews for their alleged collaboration with the Soviets, the fact remains that the Jews died at the hands of their Polish neighbors. The same thing happened in Kielce* on July 4, 1946: even if the Kielce pogrom was the result of provocation by the UB* (there are reasons to suppose it was), there were Poles who were quite prepared to take up knives and crow-bars and march to

7, Planty Street in order to kill Jews. A historian, however, cannot stop at a moral assessment, but has a duty to sift through even trivial circumstances if these can help in understanding the meaning of events.

That is why it is worth listening to Gross' critics, who accuse him of playing down facts and presenting interpretations that do not comply with the ideas contained in *Neighbors*. These accusations are not caused by a desire to play down Polish responsibility for the atrocity (this opinion was to be heard during the above mentioned debate at the Historical Institute), but by a desire to get as close to the truth as possible, and by a certain humility towards historical matter which seems to be more confused and less certain than the author of *Neighbors* cares to admit.

A single event, a general thesis

The debate on the integrity with which Jan T. Gross reconstructs the background to and sequence of events in Jedwabne covers up the most important and controversial aspects of *Neighbors* (as well as *The Ghastly Decade**). Out of a study devoted to a single town, the author makes very sweeping statements about Polish-Jewish relations, Polish co-responsibility for the Holocaust, and collaboration with the Germans.

The *leitmotif* is that *"Jedwabne—though perhaps one of the most excessive... of all murderous assaults by Poles against the Jews—was not an isolated incident,"* and that *"in collective Jewish memory this phenomenon is ingrained—that local Polish people killed the Jews because they wanted to, not because they had to."* In *The Ghastly Decade*, Gross claims that *"in the overwhelming majority of cases, the Poles neither offered help nor accorded sympathy to their murdered fellow citizens, and all too often took part in the Holocaust."* He also argues that it would have been possible to rescue far more Jews: *"...no police force is capable of enforcing rules that are universally broken. If one Pole in five or one in ten—instead of one in a hundred or two hundred—had helped a Jew, the Gestapo would have been*

*powerless. Brutal repression is applied most easily on a small commu-
nity of people that is isolated within its own society."*

India and the General Government

These are exceedingly strong words, and one should ask to what extent they are justified. Let us begin by agreeing with Gross that numerous reports and memoirs confirm the indifference of Poles towards the fate of Jews; even worse, they confirm cases in which *szmalcownicy** blackmailed Jews or—in rural areas—cases where Polish peasants captured Jews who were in hiding (of course it is impossible to venture at making a precise determination of the scale of these phenomena). But considering Germany's policy of extermination *vis-à-vis* the Poles, the very idea that widespread help for the Jews would have kept the hands of the Gestapo tied and would have protected the Jews against repression seems to be a piece of historical science fiction. Such an idea is more in keeping with Gandhi's struggle by means of civil disobedience against British rule in India than with the historical reality in the General Government.* In any case, harboring Jews put the entire Polish family under threat of death, and the most that can be expected of people is a sense of decency, but not heroism.

However, the most important thing is that, at present, we have abundant information on only one event—the massacre by Poles of the entire Jewish population of Jedwabne. There is reason to believe that a similar episode occurred in the neighboring town of Radziłów. Perhaps other cases we know nothing about will come to light, but for now Gross's categorical statements have no justification. Anyone engaged in research into such a sensitive issue is obliged to formulate his ideas with precision, and to be responsible for every word. These elements are often lacking in Gross's books.

Let us cite yet another issue concerning collaboration with the Germans by Poles and Jews. If Gross rejects the idea of Jewish collaboration with the invading Russians in 1939, he has a totally opposite view of Polish attitudes towards the Germans after the outbreak of the German-Soviet war. He writes in *Neighbors*: "*To put it simply, enthusiastic Jewish response to entering Red Army units was not a widespread phenomenon at all, and it is impossible to identify some innate, unique characteristics of Jewish collaboration with the Soviets during the period 1939–1941. On the other hand, it is manifest that the local non-Jewish population enthusiastically greeted entering Wehrmacht units in 1941 and broadly engaged in collaboration with the Germans, up to and including participation in the exterminatory war against the Jews."*

How else can one describe these views than the replacement of one stereotype—"Jewish communist"* sympathizers with another stereotype, this time about Polish attitudes in support of the occupation?

The need for research

Gross' book is very much needed. It stirs our consciences, striking at the heroic image of the German occupation, in which there was generally no room for *szmalcownicy*,* peasants baiting Jews escaped from the ghettos, and Polish participants in pogroms directed against the Jews. Let us hope that this will spark off a debate on the most painful topics of our past. Most of all, however, we need academic research in the true sense of the term, which will verify the views set forth in *The Ghastly Decade** and *Neighbors*.

Such research (based, among other things, on the underground press and the records of postwar trials of *szmalcownicy* and collaborators) is due to be undertaken—eleven years too late—by the Institute of National Remembrance.* The failure of historians to engage in research that could have been, and should have been, undertaken after 1989 is going to cause irreparable harm. Jan T. Gross's book will appear in the United States and Germany in a few months' time, and it is this book—not source-based scholarly works which have not been written yet—that will shape the views of a major part of world opinion on Polish-Jewish relations during World War II.

I pay my respect to Jan T. Gross for his courage in tackling such a difficult subject, but at the same time I have a serious suspicion that his numerous oversimplifications and very risky generalizations will make Polish-Jewish dialogue and a readiness by Poles to confess their own guilt more difficult, rather than easier.

Paweł Machcewicz

Michał Głowiński

A Pogrom and General Matters

"Nowe Książki" January 2001

Not being a historian, I can add nothing to the facts presented by Jan T. Gross; nor can I confirm them or question them. This noteworthy book, which recounts events so dreadful they seem unbelievable, goes beyond what happened in early July of 1941 in the small town of Jedwabne, situated in the vicinity of Łomża. Its message is much broader and—at the same time—immeasurably important. This must be seen as the reason for the reverberations that the book has caused, as well as for the debates that it has stirred up.

I would rather not go into a debate on whether the murder of Jedwabne's Jews was an old-fashioned pogrom or one of the crimes that go to make up the Holocaust. Most pogroms were not staged by outsiders. Rather, they were perpetrated by neighbors and acquaintances, even if the initiative came from the outside. And to be murdered by the people one knows, people who in more peaceful times walked the same streets, people whom one saw regularly or perhaps shared a classroom bench with, is a far cry from being killed by invaders with whom one has nothing in common. I do not know whether the distinction between familiars and outsiders can be applied here in the strict sense. Still, I believe that the Jedwabne criminals who murdered the Jedwabne Jews fit into a different category, for their victims, than the Gestapo—if for no other reason than the fact that the killers were not anonymous. The victims died at the hands of a Stasiek or a Jurek they had known since childhood.

There is no question that being murdered by one's neighbors is a particular situation. Gross shows us the terrifying extent of these events and how they explain, at least indirectly, the resentment felt by a certain number of Jewish Holocaust survivors toward Polish society. After all, we see here the questioning of the most elementary expectations one has of the people with whom one has so far coexisted, or with whom one has at least not been in a state of war. This, too, is a significant message contained in this important book.

Another component is the question of how it was possible, of what factors made the Polish inhabitants of this small town run amok set about the merciless slaughter of their Jewish neighbors. I would say that this is a matter of the etiology of a crime. It is not explained by the simplest of motives, such as greed or revenge (for some offense that, as Gross shows, was not committed on the scale of the town's community). The scale was surely tipped by irrational considerations, such as the conviction that the person to be destroyed belonged to an inferior species, unworthy of walking the earth. Or to put it differently: the conviction that the life of a Jew, in contrast to the life of any other person, had ceased to have any worth and that the only reasonable thing to do was to bring it to the quickest possible conclusion.

The primitive residents of Jedwabne and the vicinity certainly did not engage in any such deliberations. They knew what they knew; after all, they had all heard about "Jewish communism"* and the murder of children in order to obtain the Christian blood necessary for baking matzo. The hatred that pushed them into crime was not some sudden plunge or murderous epiphany; it had its roots and it was fixed. These people not only lived in hate, they were brought up to hate. Here, it seems to me, we arrive at one of the most important questions in Gross' book, one that defines its message: did the inhabitants of Jedwabne succumb to such a powerful influence of Nazi ideology that they no longer felt any qualms about murdering their neighbors—or was it something that happened earlier that decided their actions?

Gross writes that the crime would never have happened had Hitler never invaded Poland, which makes Hitler responsible for Jedwabne, too. Of course, there is no denying the truth of this statement, but it does not exhaust the matter. Nor does it provide an excuse. The fact that the Jedwabne massacre was perpetrated almost immediately after the German invasion (Jedwabne had been within the Soviet occupied zone) makes such an explanation all the less exhaustive. Nor can it offer any sort of solace to anyone's self-regard, to even a minimal degree. It must be said that even if the organizers of the pogrom were acting under the influence of incitement and sudden emotions, they had been well prepared for what they did, and they had been taught to hate. They had not been taught in the first weeks of German rule but, in fact, all their lives. Even before the Germans arrived, the organizers of the pogrom had been taught about various Jewish iniquities, including their objective of ruling over the world. The organizers had already been taught that a Jew was no different from the devil and, in fact, was the devil.

The Jedwabne tragedy must also be viewed from another perspective. It was, to a greater or lesser degree, a result of what happened in the period between the First and Second World Wars, a consequence of intensified propaganda, and a result of what a simple man, deprived of scruples and inhibitions in a time of madness, could hear from the pulpit and from nationalist extremists. The patterns at work were perhaps the mob psychology skillfully described by Gustave Le Bon in the late nineteenth century. The Jedwabne mob was not only equipped with pitchforks and axes (baseball bats were still unknown); not only did it lose control of its emotions—it also had an ideology. This same ideology was familiar to those who, while not participating in the crime, did nothing to stop it. Since Jews were communists—Gross quotes the opinion of a local clergyman—there was no reason to defend them.

This book is about the Jedwabne crime, but its message—let me repeat—is broader. Its main element is a largely implicit polemic against silence, or in fact with a particular way of thinking and presenting one's own history that is concealed by that silence. It is a universally acknowledged truth that no community enjoys being reminded of shameful acts committed by its members, even if the figures in question were as primitive, uneducated, and even savage as the actors behind horrifying events in the obscure backwater town called Jedwabne. They do not like such things, even when there is no possibility of any talk about collective responsibility. Gross's book is an appeal for a multi-faceted concept of history that is in accord with the facts, and therefore not only for an end to the silence, but also for a renunciation of the self-satisfaction that results from the conviction that all the right, including the moral right, is on our side. The residents of Jedwabne were unquestionably members of the Polish people, and yet they participated in the Nazi system of crime. The question of how this was possible is not the only question that organizes the book's narrative. Another question appears, even though it is never directly formulated. Its sense is best captured in the words of Mickiewicz:* "Why is it that you do not wish to write about this, gentlemen?"

Gross' book is, after all, a contribution to a debate about what history should be and how it should be written in order to avoid silences, stereotypes, and simplified differentiating dichotomies: the history of Polish-Jewish relations, the occupation years, and the postwar period, as well. I would say that the distinctive rhetoric of the book and its style of argumentation are a more or less concealed polemic with the dominant mode of writing history, a mode that has general roots but that is also connected with the practices that were obligatory in communist Poland. From at least the mid–1960s onward, the falsification of history, in fact, did not consist only in passing over in silence whatever failed to agree with a suggested or imposed view of the world, or only in directly following the ideological line, but also in attempting in some way to cater to commonly held convictions and opinions so as to create, in consequence, a smoothed-over (and falsified) version of history. This tendency was hardly a specialty of the communist period in Poland; it has its adherents and practitioners to this day. And even if their purpose is not simply to raise public morale, they do not want to be depressing, to pose vexing questions, to sow anxiety or self-critical reflections.

Jan Tomasz Gross's shocking book is a protest against this mode of historical writing.

The book should be seen from both Jewish and Polish perspectives. I think that, for Jewish readers, it will become one more document of the destruction, one more tale of misfortune, and perhaps also—unfortunately—a confirmation of opinions that are widespread in certain circles, but are none the less idiotic, about inherent Polish anti-Semitism. It is truly important, however, for Polish readers, and it is to them that it is addressed. It is important because it insists on fundamental questions about the behavior of Polish society in a terrible time. It insists on a questioning of the stereotypes that prettify historical truth. It insists on self-critical reflection. It insists on the renunciation of the self-satisfaction that lulls moral vigilance.

Michał Głowiński

Jan Nowak-Jeziorański

A Need for Compensation

"Rzeczpospolita" January 26, 2001

The discussion around Jan Tomasz Gross's book *Neighbors* goes on. The book, after 60 years, threw a shaft of light and recovered from oblivion the bestial murder during the war of the Jews of the small village of Jedwabne. Unfortunately, the debate is beginning to move in the wrong direction.

It is not easy for any nation to acknowledge things that cover it with shame. It is human nature that wc are inclined to remember the wrongs done to us, and that we do not want to remember the wrongs what we have unto others. Instinctive self-defense compels us to call into question even indisputably proven facts, to seek mitigating circumstances, to clear our own conscience while blaming others.

Pride and shame

The question is not whether 1,500 or 900 Jews were murdered in Jedwabne. The most essential thing is not whether the motive for the murderers was greed or revenge for the collaboration of Jews with the Soviet occupation regime. And whether Professor Jan T. Gross skipped over an important source, omitted a sentence in a document he cited, or failed to consider the testimony of a particular witness are not the most important issues.

In the light of not one or two, but several testimonies and accounts, not only of witnesses and victims, but also of the perpetrators, it is an undeniable fact that old people and children, men and women, were murdered in Jedwabne in an unbelievably brutal manner at the hands of Poles. Attempts to undermine this fundamental assertion are, in the light of the evidence presented, nothing but a denial of the truth. From the documentation presented by the author, it is clear that the Germans were the instigators of the pogrom. In the introduction itself we find out from Gross that on that fatal day German cameras and film crews were waiting and that there was a meeting of the Gestapo with the village authorities. The pogrom was therefore not spontaneous.

It is also clear from Gross that, without German encouragement, permission, and support, the massacre would not have been possible. This does not in the least change the fact that, acting of their own free, unforced will, Poles tortured and killed their victims. None of the Polish murderers was in uniform and no one can hide behind the argument that he had to obey orders or perish himself. Nor is it possible to explain the mass murder as revenge for the collaboration of Jews with the Soviet occupation regime and for their participation in the persecution of Poles. Gross cites the written accounts of the ringleaders of the massacre who, before communist Polish judicial authorities, pled their cooperation with the NKVD* during the Soviet occupation as a mitigating circumstance.

Even were it true that not a single Pole embraced the protective red banner during the Soviet occupation and that all Jews without exception collaborated with the Soviets, nothing can justify the killing of people like animals—the stoning, the butchering with knives, the decapitation, the stabbing with sharpened stakes, the wholesale murder of women and men, of the old and the young herded to the Jewish cemetery, the burying alive of still-breathing victims, the drowning of women with their children in the pond, and, at the end, the forcing of the remaining victims into the barn where they were burned alive.

Since we share national pride in our victories, in our laudable actions and in the contributions made by Polish artists to the common treasury of human values, then we must also bring ourselves to feel national shame for shameful actions. As a nation nearly entirely Christian, we must beat our breasts, acknowledging the sins and transgressions of each Polish Cain who violated the commandment "Thou shalt not kill!" If we expect from others redress for crimes committed against Poland and against Poles, we must also demonstrate the will to redress the evil committed by us to our neighbors.

In the footsteps of the Germans

No one ever performed a greater service for the Germans than Chancellor Willy Brandt when, before the eyes of the entire world, he fell to his knees before the monument to the heroes of the Warsaw ghetto. This was a symbolic act of atonement for the German crime of genocide, and it was performed by a person who had nothing to do with that genocide. The strong sense of collective guilt shown until today by the majority of Germans has caused the world, not excluding Poland, to more easily pardon them their terrible crimes, and to place the onus on "the Nazis," rather than the German people.

For many years, we protested against the mendacity of the Russian inscription in the Katyn* forest, an inscription stating German fascists murdered Polish prisoners of war there in 1941. In Jedwabne, similar falsehoods are inscribed on two monuments. On the one erected during the Polish communist period, the inscription speaking about the execution of Jewish people burned by the German Gestapo and *gendarmerie*. Not a word about the Poles. The other monument was erected recently, after 1989, "to honor the memory of 180 persons, including two priests, who were murdered in the territory of the Jedwabne district... by the NKVD,* the Nazis, and the UB*." This marker is signed, "society." Not a word about the Jews. As I write these words, both monuments are still standing.

Rabbi Baker's appeal

The effacement of this shameful blot demands at least a symbolic act acknowledging guilt and atonement. This could be the fulfillment of the imploring request by a Rabbi from Jedwabne, Jacob Baker. Invoking John Paul II's request to Jews for forgiveness for the suffering that Jews endured at the hands of Christians, Rabbi Baker asks for the dignified burial of the bones of the murdered, their interment in a Jewish cemetery, and the commemoration of the place where the synagogue stood.

A ceremonial remembrance of the victims of the bloody pogrom at Jedwabne, with the motto "Thou shalt not kill," and with the participation of the primate of Poland, bishops, and representatives of the highest state and civil authorities and of Jewish organizations, could be the symbolic act of atonement that is so necessary.

Only in this way can we cure the nation of the ethnic or class hatred that led in the past to the most terrible crimes in human history. Kosovo is a contemporary example.

A shared examination of conscience

The six centuries of the presence of the Jews in Poland is today a closed book. To close the book with dignity, a mutual and straightforward accounting is necessary. Not everything in the mutual relations between Poles and Jews was bad. In the centuries before the rebirth of Israel, Poland was a refuge for Jews persecuted and expelled from both the East and the West. A dignified, final accord would be the realization of an idea raised in the press, the publication of a great book by Polish and Jewish historians. It would consist of two parts. The first would present what was good in the life they shared. The second would be a straightforward accounting of the wrongs committed.

This mutual and shared examination of conscience would certainly be rejected with fury by the extremist elements on both sides, but it would have great significance for all those who feel an attachment to the common values based on the Ten Commandments and the Gospels.

The question of the mass murder in Jedwabne has not only a moral dimension that is an internal Polish affair. It could also strike a fatal blow to the good name of the Poland that belongs to the

159

civilized world. Jan Gross's book will be published in English in New York on April 1. Simultaneously, the influential *New York Times* will publish excerpts in its book review section, which is widely read by the western intellectual elite. Since we demanded that the Russians acknowledge the Katyn* atrocities and reveal the instigators and the circumstances of the murder of unarmed Polish prisoners of war in the Katyn forest and elsewhere, we cannot feel resentful to the author of *Neighbors* because, sixty years later, he revealed and documented the mass murder committed by Poles in Jedwabne, a murder that we would prefer not to know about and not to remember.

Preventive action

Historians have the right to carefully verify the documents and accounts provided by Gross. Some of his conclusions are polemical in character and also stirred my reservations. However, we do not have time to wait for the moment when each item has been placed under the researcher's microscope, tested, corrected or filled in. Fundamental Polish interests demand the initiation of immediate preventive action to limit the damage caused to Poland by the world reaction to the news of the massacre in Jedwabne.

Within the Jewish Diaspora, especially in America, there are—just as in Polish society—extremist, chauvinistic elements as well as others who believe that the cultivation of hatred and demands for revenge can be a dangerous boomerang. On the basis of my own personal experience, I am convinced that we have both friends and relentless enemies among the American Jews. The oldest and most influential Jewish organization in the United States, the American Jewish Committee headed by David Harris, supported the efforts to bring Poland into NATO in the most effective of ways.

At the other extreme, there are Jewish counterparts of belligerent Polish anti-Semites. They see Poles, all Poles, as the most anti-Semitic nation in the world. They seem not to perceive the symptoms of this social disease in Russia, Germany and other countries of our region. The danger exists that Gross's book will be exploited in ways not intended by the author, to promote the thesis that "every Pole sucked anti-Semitism with his mother's milk." I took these words of Shamir as an insult to the memory of my mother, who was deeply religious and who taught her sons from childhood that displaying contempt to another person because of his origin, religion, or race is a mortal sin that violates the injunction to love one's neighbor. Those Poles who have fought racial prejudices their entire life must also take Shamir's words the same way.

Accusing the Polish nation of collaboration with the Nazis and participation in the Holocaust is the same type of slander as the "Auschwitz lie" that denies the existence of extermination camps and gas chambers.

Against defamation

I spent the war in Poland, and I wandered all over the country. In the first year of the occupation, it was not only my Jewish friends and schoolmates whom I met. Supporting myself as a salesman, I often visited the small town of Konstantynów in Podlasie, which was populated in the majority by Hasidic Jews. They lived in deathly fear of the Germans, but did not fear the Poles. In the first year of the occupation, commercial relations with the Polish population enabled Jews to avoid hunger and to survive. Only later did *szmalcownicy** become a terror for Jews who were trying to conceal their origins. From documents in the Jewish Historical Institute* in Warsaw, it appears that the pogrom in Jedwabne was not an isolated incident. There were others. It is worth noting, however, that they occurred in Lithuania, in the Białystok region, and in Eastern Galicia immediately after the flight of the Soviet occupier. Jedwabne was not a common phenomenon throughout Poland.

To conclude from the 1941 pogroms that the Holocaust was the common work of Poles and Germans is a libel. All who feel themselves to be Polish have the responsibility to defend themselves against such slander. The majority of Polish society might be charged with having an attitude of indifference to the extermination of the Jews—if not for the fact that the entire civilized world reacted to the

161

fact of genocide with indifference and passivity. The difference is that Poles were eyewitnesses, defenseless witnesses living in constant fear for their lives and the lives of their families.

Adam Michnik* correctly, and in my presence, warned Jews gathered at a New York synagogue that the defamation of Poland could provoke a secondary wave of anti-Semitism among people who had spent their entire lives fighting racial prejudices.

It is worth adding that any eruption of neo-anti-Semitism in Poland would cause terrible harm not to Jews—there are barely a few thousand of them in Poland—but to the position and the good name of Poland in the world. Certainly this was not Gross's intention when he revealed the crimes committed by the Jedwabne Poles. In order to avert this secondary anti-Semitism, it is necessary to place the tragedy of the Jews on the agenda of the Polish—Jewish dialogue, especially in the United States, now. Jan T. Gross ought to be involved on the Polish side, for a great deal depends on how he himself presents *Neighbors* to western readers.

Jan Nowak-Jeziorański

Tomasz Strzembosz

Covered-up Collaboration

"Rzeczpospolita" 27 January 2001

I had not intended to lend my voice to the discussion that ensued after the appearance of Professor Jan T. Gross's book *Neighbors*, pertaining to the murder of Jews carried out in July 1941 in the little town of Jedwabne in the Podlasie region.[1] Mainly because the discussion conducted to date, whilst raising many essential themes, had ignored the most crucial fact: what had occurred in Jedwabne after the German army had entered the area, i.e. who committed the mass murder of the Jewish population of Jedwabne, when, and under what circumstances.

That is what should be written about first and foremost, the more so since Gross's theses, in the light of certain sources, do not appear entirely true. On the other hand, the documentation in my possession still does not authorize me to speak out publicly on precisely that key issue.

Nevertheless, both in Gross's book as well as in Andrzej Żbikowski's article recently published in *Rzeczpospolita* (January 4, 2001), such shocking statements were articulated that they cannot be

---

[1] By Podlasie, I understand here the territory of the eastern part of historical Mazovia, the inhabitants of which include the Mazovian minor gentry and Belorussians and Jews, far less numerous here. (At the request of Prof. Strzembosz, we include footnotes that were omitted in the original publication by *Rzeczpospolita*—ed.)

passed over in silence. They concern both the attitudes of the Polish and Jewish population in the lands first occupied and subsequently annexed by the Soviet Union, as well as the evaluation of those attitudes.

Before I address the subject proper, I feel I must clearly state several things at the very outset. Murders carried out on any group of civilians cannot be justified. Nothing justifies the killing of men, women or children simply because they represent some social class, nation [i.e., ethnic group—ed.] or religion, because the meting-out of justice must be done on an individual basis. Such crimes cannot be justified by one's own convictions, nor by the orders of one's superior, nor "historical necessity" nor the welfare of some other nation, class, religion or social group, nor the good of any organization, military or civilian, overt or clandestine.

I should like those who read this text to be aware of the fact that such is my basic position. I am also fundamentally opposed to murdering the soldiers of any military or police formation simply because they are serving therein, especially when they are unarmed or surrender. Whoever carries out such a murder, regardless of whom he represents, is to me nothing more than a murderer.

General horror

Before evaluating the attitudes and behavior of different social and national groups in the lands occupied by the Red Worker-Peasant Army (RWPA), one should recall some basic facts, for without an awareness of the realities of that period it would be impossible to understand the people living there and those swept in by the storm of war.

The German incursion into Podlasie horrified the general population, which received the German forces with easily discernible hostility. The locals supported units of the Polish Army that were being driven to the east. With regard to unmobilized reservists and youth of pre-conscription age, many of them traveled eastward in search of a unit willing to accept and arm them. Hence, a number of men from that region (including unmobilized ones) ended up taking part in the defense of Grodno and the Sopoćkinie region—against the Red Army.

The population of Podlasie, especially after the Battle of Andrzejów fought by the 18th Polish Infantry Division, supported the small partisan detachments emerging in the area of Czerwony Bór and the Biebrza Marshes, which saved them from destruction. The anti-German attitudes of the locals were uniform and resolute.

The period following the incursion of the Red Army into the eastern regions of the Republic of Poland may be broken down into three sub-periods. The first, referred to by Prof. Ryszard Szawłowski (and not only by him!) as the Polish-Soviet war, lasted two weeks, up till the start of October 1939, when organized resistance by larger combat units of the Polish Army ceased, although individual sub-units continued partisan-type actions. The second was the conquest of the area, combined with a socio-political and economic "revolution," pre-planned and carried out with the aid of the Soviet troops and special services. That is why I have chosen to call it "a marionette revolution." That was when the first arrests took place. This period ended in November 1939 with the incorporation of the north-eastern lands of the Republic of Poland into the Belorussian Soviet Socialist Republic and of the south-eastern lands into the Ukrainian Soviet Socialist Republic.

In actuality, that period lasted another two months, when the Soviet administrative system (republic, *oblast'*, *raion*) was finally introduced in the annexed areas.[2] The third sub-period, early 1940 to June 1941, was marked on the one hand by unification with the USSR's socio-economic system (forced collectivization of agriculture, strengthening of state farms,[3] completion of the nationalization of industry, trade, the banking system and the like). On the other hand, it witnessed a violent increase in reprisals, especially in the first

---

[2] The formal incorporation of the Polish eastern lands into the Soviet Union occurred at the beginning of November 1939, but the division into *oblast'* and *raion* was not completed until January 1940.

[3] The collective farm, or *kolkhoz*, was an agrarian production cooperative, and the state farm, the *sovkhoz*, was set up as soon as the RWPA entered, when vast landed estates immediately became state property and others were parceled up.

half of 1940, in the form of mass arrests and deportations, which in the area of so-call Western Belorussia lasted to the end and involved some 150,000 people. I wish to dwell a bit on the latter development. Many do not realize that those actions were carried out in accordance with the principle of collective responsibility.

A time of deportations

The first deportation on February 9–10, 1940 encompassed military and civilian settlers and foresters together with their families. The second, on 13 April 1940, involved those whose family members (heads of households, brothers, sons) had been captured as Polish soldiers, policemen and the like, or had fled abroad, gone into hiding or been arrested as conspirators or "enemies of the people," i.e. as a socially dangerous element (SOE). The third, carried out on June 29, 1940, mainly involved towns and encompassed so called *bezhency*,* including many Jews,[4] notably those who had registered to return to the part of Poland under German occupation. That fact partially explodes the myth of Polish Jews joyfully welcoming the Red Army solely due to their fear of the Germans. The last deportation began on June 14, 1941 in the Wilno region (taken over when the Republic of Lithuania was liquidated in June 1940), and in the lands of the Belorussian Republic on June 20. It was interrupted when the Germans launched their aggression.

As we can see, all these acts of violence were undertaken on the basis of collective responsibility. An entire family was held responsible for a father who had been a soldier, for a brother who had fled. All those who had lived in a forester's house were considered guilty. Blows were struck at the "nest." In Warsaw, for instance, the Germans retaliated for armed street attacks by shooting all the inhabi-

---

[4] According to the Soviet documents, there were 72,896 refugees in the area known as Western Belorussia at the beginning of 1940. Only 25,621 had jobs; the rest shared the miserable lot of the unemployed. In ethnic terms, there were 4,290 Poles, 65,786 Jews, 1,703 Belorussians, 577 Russians, and 169 Ukrainians. On June 29, 1940, a total of 18,650 people were deported; according to Albin Głowacki, 84% of them were Jewish.

tants of the nearest building, although they had no links to the resistance fighters, or by killing prisoners in Pawiak prison, or the people of a village near which a military train had been blown up. That collective responsibility encompassed children, women and the elderly. It was the weakest who paid with their lives during transport or exile—in Siberia or "the starvation steppes" of Kazakhstan.

Betrayal during the days of defeat

Who carried out the terror? The NKVD* and in the early period also the RWPA, which had under its command *Chekha*-type operational groups that followed the army "to clear the area," just as *Einsatzgruppen** followed the *Wehrmacht*. What about the militia (police)? Few people know that, in the years from 1939 to 1941, there were three different kinds of militia.

The first were the various emerging "red guards" and "red militias," consisting of locals armed with clubs, sawed-off shotguns, axes and revolvers, though sometimes also machine guns, who backed up the RWPA in its "liberation march" and implemented the "class anger" of social groups oppressed by "feudal Poland." They generally appeared shortly after September 17, 1939 (or on the that very day—a rather telling fact), and most often acted with bloodthirsty savagery, not only behind the lines of the Polish Army but also after the incursion of the Red Army, which gave local "revolutionary elements" several days of grace to settle past scores and exercise class revenge.

Later, those "militias" were replaced by the Workers' Guard, set up in the occupied territories in accordance with an order issued by the commander of the Belorussian Front on September 16, 1939, and by the Citizens' Militia, established on the strength of a similar order of September 21, 1939. Subsequently, after Western Belorussia had been incorporated into the Belorussian Soviet Socialist Republic, they were replaced by the NKVD-linked Worker-Peasant Militia (WPM), initially comprising only newcomers (so-called "easterners") [i.e., from the Soviet Union proper—ed.], later supplemented by locals.

Apart from a small group of communists in the towns and even smaller ones in the countryside, the Polish population responded to the USSR's aggression and the Soviet system being created there the same way it had reacted to the German aggression. There are thousands of diverse testimonies attesting to this. Participation by Polish peasants in what were called *selsovets** (rural and commune soviets) was no indication of anything, because those were bodies of only a decorative nature. The executive committees and—even more important—the party and police apparatuses controlling them were what mattered. It was the latter who were frequently involved in the looting of the gentry manor houses and palaces left behind by their owners.[5]

By contrast, the Jewish population, especially youths and the town-dwelling poor, staged a mass welcome for the invading army and took part in introducing the new order, some with weapons in hand. This, too has been attested to by thousands of Polish, Jewish and Soviet testimonies. There were also the reports of the chief commander of the Armed Combat Union,* Gen. Stefan Grot-Ro-wecki, there was the report of the emissary Jan Karski,*[6] and there were accounts written down both during the war as well as years later. This has also been reported in the works of Jan T. Gross himself who—while citing Polish accounts above all, of which thousands are found in the archives of the Hoover Institution in the US—arrived at conclusions which he expressed clearly and unequivocally.

---

[5] It is significant that we find no reports of Polish peasants looting the manor houses in "Western Belorussia," while such attacks were committed frequently by Belorussian peasants.

[6] It may be worth quoting a fragment of this report, which is omitted by Gross in *The Ghastly Decade.** It reads: "Things are worse when [the Jews] inform on Poles, students of Polish nationality, and Polish political figures, and when they sit at desks and direct the work of the Bolshevik police, or are members of this police, or when they untruthfully slander the way things were in the former Poland. It must un-fortunately be stated that these incidents are quite widespread, far more frequent than cases indicating their loyalty to the Poles or their sympathy for Poland" (Artur Eisenbach, "Raport Jana Karskiego o sytuacji Żydów na okupowanych ziemiach polskich na początku 1940 r." [Jan Karski's Report on the Situation of the Jews in Occupied Poland at the beginning of 1940], *Dzieje Najnowsze,* 2 (1989), p. 179.

The Soviet army was enthusiastically welcomed not only in areas formerly occupied by the *Wehrmacht*, but also in border areas that the Germans had never entered. Moreover, those "guards" and "militias," spouting up like mushrooms after a rainfall in the wake of the Soviet aggression, consisted largely of Jews. And not only that. Jews launched acts of rebellion against the Polish state by occupying localities, setting up revolutionary committees there, arresting and executing representatives of Polish state authorities, and attacking smaller and even quite large units of the Polish Army (as in Grodno).

Dr Marek Wierzbicki, who has been for several years researching Polish-Belorussian relations in what was called Western Belarus in 1939–1941, has also taken note of Polish-Jewish relations. In a lengthy, as-yet-unpublished article, he writes about the three-day battle between Jewish rebels in Grodno and the Polish Army and police (September 18, before the arrival of RWPA units), two-day clashes over nearby Skidel, and Jewish revolts in Jeziory, Łunna, Wiercieliszki, Wielka Brzostowica, Ostryń, Dubno, Dereczyn, Zelwa, Motol, Wołpa, Janów Poleski, Wołkowysk, Horodec and Drohiczyn Poleski. Not a single German had been seen in any of those localities—the revolts were directed against the Polish state.

This was armed collaboration, siding with the enemy, treason committed during days of defeat. How large was the group of people who took part in it? We shall most likely never be able to present any figures. At any rate, that phenomenon encompassed the entire area in which the Belorussian Front of the RWPA was deployed.

New arrangements in public offices

Another matter was co-operation with organs of repression, above all the NKVD.* First the "militias," "red guards" and revolutionary committees, and later the workers' guards and citizens' militias undertook such co-operation. In towns, they consisted mainly of Polish Jews. Subsequently, when the Worker-Peasant Militias took control of the situation, Jews—as Soviet documents have indicated—were considerably over-represented in them. Polish Jews in civilian dress, wearing red arm-bands and armed with rifles, were numerous participants in the arrests and deportations. That was the most extreme example, but for Polish society the most glaring thing was the large number of Jews in all Soviet public offices and institutions. The more so since Poles had been the dominant group there before the war!

On September 20, 1940, at a conference in Minsk, the capital of the Belorussian Soviet Socialist Republic, the head of the municipal NKVD office in Łomża stated: "Such a practice has taken root here. The Jews have supported us and only they were always visible. It has become fashionable for the director of every institution to boast that he no longer has even a single Pole working for him. Many of us were simply afraid of the Poles." At the same time, at party meetings in Białystok *oblast'*, "complaints" multiplied that one heard only Russian and Yiddish spoken in Soviet offices, that Poles felt discriminated against, and that a cleaning woman in one Białystok office was harshly rebuked for singing Polish songs while she worked. That was in accordance with the truth and the then obligatory "party line," for at that time at the top Soviet leadership level a "new policy" towards Poles had been agreed.

In the afore-mentioned article, Marek Wierzbicki thus synthetically presented the situation of that period: "The bloated Soviet administrative structures gave masses of unemployed Jews an opportunity to find jobs. That was of no mean importance to them, since the industrially impoverished towns of the eastern borderlands had provided few job opportunities. Being considerably better educated than the Belorussian community, the Jewish population provided numerous clerks, teachers and functionaries of the security apparatus. That undoubtedly influenced Polish-Jewish relations, since Jews most frequently took the place of previous clerks and teachers of Polish nationality.... Moreover, between September and December 1939, there were many arrests of representatives of the Polish community who had held more senior posts in the administration and political authorities of the Polish state before the war or had been engaged in public affairs. Local Jews—members of the interim administration or militia—were very helpful to the Soviet authorities in tracking down and detaining them."

He continued, this time citing none other than Jan T. Gross: "It also occurred that representatives of the Jewish population ridiculed Poles, emphasizing the sudden change of fate that had befallen both communities. Often directed to Poles were such malicious remarks as 'You wanted a Poland without Jews, now you have Jews without Poland' or 'Your times have ended.'"[7]

Hence the participation of Jews in the Soviet apparatus, including the militia, is documented in Polish accounts (especially in those on which Jan T. Gross has been basing his books and articles for a quarter of a century), accounts written down during the war and preserved at the Hoover Institution in the USA, as well as in documents of the Soviet and party authorities of the former USSR that are now being analyzed, and in (Polish) Armed Combat Union* reports published long ago in the work *Armia Krajowa w dokumentach* [The Home Army* in Documents] (vol. I, London 1970).

Professor Gross therefore lacks justification when he states in *Neighbors* that, *"To put it simply, enthusiastic Jewish response to entering Red Army units was not a widespread phenomenon at all, and it is impossible to identify some innate, unique characteristics of Jewish collaboration with the Soviets during the period 1939–1941."*[8]

A false equation

The second part of that statement, this time pertaining to Poles, runs as follows: *"On the other hand, it is manifest that the local non-Jewish population enthusiastically greeted entering Wehrmacht units in 1941 and broadly engaged in collaboration with the Germans,*

---

[7] J.T. Gross, "Introduction" to: *W czterdziestym nas matko na Sybir zesłali* [In 1940, Mother, They Sent Us to Siberia], Warsaw 1989, p. 29.

[8] One question begs to be asked: Why is it that the accounts in the archives of the Hoover Institution, which were reliable enough to serve as the basis for the description of the most complicated issues connected with the Soviet occupation, become unreliable and cease to be "sources" wherever they have anything to do with the Polish Jews? We should add that each of these accounts is corroborated by dozens of others published in a free Poland since 1990, as well as by documents to be found in the archives of Belarus, Ukraine, and Russia.

up to and including participation in the extermination campaign against the Jews.... The testimony by Finkelsztajn concerning how Radziłów's local Polish population received the Germans reads like a mirror image of widely circulating stories about Galician Jews receiving the Bolsheviks in 1939."[9]

Without going into the merits of the issue, I should first like to call attention to the methods. Hundreds of surviving accounts, the reports of Underground Poland, including that of Jan Karski,* who was favorably disposed towards the Jews, do not justify such generalizations. And perhaps rightly so. One must study the situation in various localities rather than relying on even the most widespread general opinions. And yet Finkelsztajn's account and several accounts by peasants from surrounding villages have justified passing judgment not on the attitude of individual people, but on the entire local population (with the exception of Jews). The same is the case with the thesis that the Polish population of the several-thousand-strong town of Jedwabne murdered their Jewish neighbors, based on the testimony of Jews who had escaped and managed to survive, as well as on UB* materials, obtained as a result of (undoubtedly cruel) interrogations in 1949 and 1953, at a time when Polish bishops were being sentenced for betraying the Polish nation and spying for "the imperialists."

I shall now move on to what has been referred to as Polish collaboration. Andrzej Żbikowski has presented it more extensively than Prof. Gross has. It supposedly involved the murder of Jews by Polish "gangs," composed primarily of people recently released by the Germans from Soviet jails, as well as attacks on "retreating smaller Soviet army groups," also carried out by such gangs. A plain and simple equation: 1939 equals 1941.

But, in the name of God, joyfully greeting Germans who arrive right in the middle of a horrible deportation and thereby make it possible for hundreds of people to leave their grim places of torture—the jails of places like Brześć, Łomża, Białystok and Jedwabne—is one thing, attacking Red Army soldiers who had been occu-

---

[9] *Neighbors*, p. 155.

pation troops only the day before is another, and killing soldiers of the Polish Army is something else again. Indeed, Jews may not have had things too good in pre-war Poland, and there was undoubtedly "a balance-sheet of wrongs,"* to quote Broniewski's poem. However, Jews were not deported to Siberia, they were not shot or sent to concentration camps, they were not killed through starvation and hard labor. If they did not regard Poland as their homeland, they did not have to treat it as an occupation regime and join its mortal enemy in killing Polish soldiers and murdering Polish civilians feeling to the east. They also did not have to take part in fingering their neighbors for deportations, those heinous acts of collective responsibility.

There were no red flags on only three houses

Let us now move from general matters to the situation in the town of Jedwabne and the surrounding rural community. Jan Gross is right in saying there were not many testimonies regarding the town itself, but they are not that few. In fact, there are considerably more than those on which he based his account of the burning of Jews on July 10, 1941. The "New approach to sources" which he is promoting with regards to Jewish accounts could be applied in this particular case. These, after all, were accounts provided by persecuted individuals who were saved from annihilation only thanks to the Sikorski–Maisky agreement* of July 1941. These are the voices of eyewitness survivors of a crime. In their accounts, they touch on "the Jewish problem" spontaneously and "from the heart," even though no one encouraged them to do.

Did Jedwabne Jews, like others, cordially welcome the Red Army incursion? The accounts recorded during the war as well as those I obtained at the start of the 1990s indicate that this was indeed the case.

First, accounts submitted to the army of Gen. Anders* and archived in the Hoover Institution, and now also available at the Eastern Archives in Warsaw.

Account No. 8356, recorded by cart maker Józef Rybicki from the town of Jedwabne: *"The Red Army was received by Jews who built arches. They removed the old authorities and introduced new ones from amongst the local population (Jews and communists). The police and teachers were arrested...."*

Account No. 10708, recorded by a municipal government employee in Jedwabne, Tadeusz Kiełczewski: *"Right after the encroachment by the Soviet Army, a municipal committee was spontaneously set up, composed of Polish communists (the chairman was the Pole, Czesław Krytowczyk, and the members were Jews). The militia also consisted of communist Jews. At first there were no reprisals, because they did not know the population. The arrests started only after local communists had provided the necessary information. Local militiamen searched the homes of people they felt were concealing weapons. The main arrests by the Soviet authorities only started after the first elections."*

Account No. 8455, recorded by a locksmith-mechanic from Jedwabne, Marian Łojewski: *"Following the incursion of the red army, first an order was issued for all the weapons owned by the local population to be turned in. Anyone who held back would face the death penalty. Next, searches were conducted in various houses, and that as a result of accusation by Jewish shopkeepers who accused Poles of stealing different goods from them in their absence.[10] The arrests took place of many people against whom local Jews had held grudges over having been prosecuted by the Polish State and over their persecution."*

Account No. 2675, recorded by wood sorter Aleksander Kotowski of Jedwabne: *"I was not present when the red army entered. Admitted to the authorities were Jews and Polish communists who had done time in prison for communist activities. They led the NKVD* to apartments and houses and the denounced patriotic Polish citizens."*

And finally, the account given by Łucja Chojnowska, née Chołowińska, on May 9, 1991. Mrs. Chołowińska, the sister of Jadwiga, whose married name was Laudańska, found herself in the spring of 1940 in a partisan camp at the Kobielno forest range, situated amidst

---

[10] As can be imagined, Jews left their homes and went into hiding during the short lived German occupation of Podlasie [in September 1939—ed.], and this may have led to theft.

the Biebrza Marshes. During a battle between Polish partisans and the Soviet army on June 23, 1940, she was captured. Our conversation, which took place in Jedwabne, pertained to that battle, not the situation in the town both women had formerly lived in. Nevertheless, in the course of the conversation, Łucja Chołowińska-Chojnowska said: "In Jedwabne, inhabited mostly by Jews, there were only three houses that had not displayed red flags when the Russians marched in. Our house was among them. Before the first deportation, a Jewish woman, a neighbor lady (we had got along with the Jews very well) ran over and warned us we were on the deportation list. Then my sister Jadwiga, her child (a four-year-old girl), and I fled to Orlików, taking along only some clothing." Let us note that the Jewish neighbor lady knew who was on the deportation list, even though that was the most closely guarded of secrets. So much for starters.

The arrests begin

Here are more questions. Who made up the militia in Jedwabne and what was their attitude towards townsfolk regarded as being too closely linked to the Polish state, as unfavorably disposed towards the new system, or as enemies? Did terror also take place in Jedwabne? If so, how did it come about, and was it implemented only through the agency of the Soviet citizens known as "easterners"? Or was it bolstered by "former" Polish citizens, inhabitants of Jedwabne and the surrounding countryside? Let us look for the answers in what historians call "personal documents" created during the war and later.

Account No. 1559 was given by Kazimierz Sokołowski, a worker from Jedwabne: *"Soviet authorities were set up a militia, mainly from communist Jews, and the arrests of farmers and workers on whom the militia had informed began. They imposed heavy taxes on the population, they imposed taxes on the churches and arrested a priest. Mass searches began in the homes of unfavorably disposed people, enemies of the people.... The local populace in the main avoided voting [on October 22, 1939—T.S.]. All day, the militia led them by force and at gunpoint to the polling station. Shortly after the vote, they staged a night-time raid, arrested entire families and deported them to the USSR."*

Account No. 1394, written down by Jedwabne worker Stanisław Gruba: *"Homes were raided in search of weapons, anti-communist literature, etc. Suspects were immediately arrested, as were the families of priests, and put in prison so an investigation could be held."*

Account No. 2589, recorded by a farmer from the rural Jedwabne area, Józef Karwowski: *"In October 1939, the NKVD* ordered pre-election meetings and rallies. People were forcibly herded to them by the NKVD and militia. Whoever resisted was immediately arrested and never heard from again."*

Account No. 2545 was provided by Józef Makowski, a farmer from the rural Jedwabne area: *"They arrested people, tied their hands, threw them into cellars and pig-sties, starved them, didn't give them any water to drink, and brutally beat them to force them to confess to belonging to Polish organizations. I myself was beaten unconscious during NKVD interrogations in Jedwabne, Łomża and Minsk."*

Account No. 8356 was written down by Józef Rybicki of Jedwabne (whom we have already met): *"Searches were conducted in the homes of better-off farmers, whose furniture, clothing and valuables they took away. A few days later, they came at night and arrested them. They took people to meetings by force. Anyone that resisted was called a* vreditel ["wrecker" or "troublemaker"—tansl.] *and arrested. The village mayor drew up lists, going from house to house and writing down the names of many people and the year they were born. The commission[11] comprised soldiers and Jews and local communists. Candidates to the assembly were imposed from above—those were Jews who had come from the USSR and local communists."*

They donned red arm-bands

Let us now move on to the post-war accounts I received while preparing a story on the battle of the Kobielno forest range.

---

[11] The conscription commission. Young men were first drafted into the Red Army in September 1940.

Jerzy Tarnacki, a partisan from Kobielno, wrote in a letter of October 24, 1991: *"A patrol comprising a Pole named Kurpiewski and a Jew called Czapnik came for me and my brother Antek. During the arrests we managed to flee from our own back yard. I went into hiding in the village of Kajtanowo [Kajetanowo—T.S.] at the place of a friend, Wacław Mierzejewski. From him I learnt of the existence of a Polish partisan unit on the other side of the River Biebrza. I was in hiding from January to mid-April 1940."*

Stefan Boczkowski of Jedwabne wrote in his letter of January 14,1995: *"The local Jews of Jedwabne donned red arm-bands and helped the militia arrest 'enemies of the people,' 'spies,' etc."*

Dr. Kazimierz Odyniec, a physician, the son of sergeant Antoni Odyniec, who was killed in action at Kobielno on June 23, 1940, wrote in his letter of June 20, 1991: *"Towards the end of April 1940, a local Jew came to our home in the uniform of a Russian militiaman and told my father to report to the NKVD.... My father told us good-bye, but first had my mother follow that militiaman and see where else he would go, because he had a dozen-odd names on his list. As it later turned out, my father did not go to the NKVD. The next day the NKVD arrested my mother, demanding that she tell them where my father had hidden."* In a letter written to me after Jan Gross's book came out, Dr Odyniec noted: *"Gross emphasizes the cruelty of the Polish side without saying a word about the behavior of a sizeable group of Jews who openly co-operated with the Soviets and were the people who showed the Soviets who should be arrested or deported. I can give you an example close to home."* Here he repeated the above account. *"I also remember that the corpses of Polish partisans after the fighting in Kobielno were transported by the Jew Całko, my Uncle Władek Łojewski's neighbor"* (Letter of October 25, 2000).

Roman Sadowski, a Home Army officer, the husband of Kazimierz Odyniec's sister Halina, who had been deported on June 20, 1941, into the depths of the USSR, wrote me on November 10, 2000: *"During the Soviet occupation Jews were the 'masters' of this region. They entirely co-operated with the Soviet authorities. According to the accounts of my wife's cousins, it was Jews together with the NKVD that compiled lists of those to be interned (deported)."*

Although I had not conducted a systematic, nor sufficiently early search for documents pertaining to the attitudes of Jews from Jedwabne and its environs, it can be seen that a considerable number of spontaneous and unsolicited testimonies have accumulated. I cannot say, as Gross did, that *"I found only one statement providing specific information about the kind of reception that the entering Soviet army received from the population of Jedwabne in September 1939—as we know, this was the moment when the memory of Jewish disloyalty was fixed for many Poles—and it is none too reliable, for it was written more than fifty years after the events it describes"* [Strzembosz is quoting from the Polish edition of *Neighbors*; the corresponding passage in the American edition breaks off after "in September 1939"—ed.]. Gross then goes on to tell about the information obtained by Agnieszka Arnold during her work on a film on the burning of Jews in Jedwabne.

Not being a specialist in those problems, I have cited the five accounts above, which were mainly recorded before 1945 and concerning the attitudes of Jedwabne Jews towards the Soviet authorities who were then in the process of installing themselves. I have also quoted nine accounts on the activities of the militia, comprising mainly Jedwabne Jews, although their commandant was a Pole, Czesław Kurpiewski, a well-known pre-war communist.

To that should be added an extremely characteristic piece of information, independently repeated in two separate accounts: apart from Jewish militiamen, Jews in civilian clothing, with red arm-bands and armed with rifles, also took part in the arrests.

Trzcianne: a characteristic incident

The same documents from the archives of the Hoover Institution, which, after all, Jan Gross was quite familiar with, provide a list of towns and smaller localities in which Jews enthusiastically welcomed the Red Army and later manned militia posts. Those towns are Zambrów, Łomża and Stawiski and the villages are Wizna, Szumowo (the militia commander there was a Jew named Jabłonka), Rakowo-Boginie, Bredki, Zabiele, Wądołki Stare, and Drozdowo.

Also known is a characteristic incident that occurred in the Jewish town of Trzcianne, situated opposite Jedwabne across the River Biebrza. According to the account (of August 16, 1987) by Czesław Borowski, who lived in the village of Zubole adjacent to Trzcianne, the incident occurred as follows: *"Somewhere towards the end of September, perhaps at the start of October 1939, the Germans had withdrawn from the area but the Russians still hadn't arrived, so a kind of neutral zone arose. In Czerwony Bór there was still fighting going on. In Trzcianne, Jews were preparing to welcome the encroaching Red Army. Patrols of Jewish militia went out ahead as far as Okrągłe (a bend in the road and bus stop) in the direction of Mońki. Seeing a cloud of dust in the distance and believing that to be the Red Army, they moved back to the welcome arch built at the head of the village [town—T.S.]. But those were not Soviet soldiers, but rather 10 to 15 Polish uhlans [cavalrymen] moving through that neutral zone. There they saw the welcome arch and a welcoming rabbi with bread and salt. The uhlans charged the crowd, destroyed the triumphal arch, struck out with the flat of their sabres, smashed up a few Jewish shops and wanted to burn down the town, but that did not occur. The rabbi's daughter died of a heart attack. The uhlans rode off. The Jews of Trzcianne had weapons ...."*

That account, recorded by me nearly 50 years after the event occurred, has been verified by Russian sources. According to the latter, at the end of September 1939 "a band of Polish soldiers" commanded by two landowners, Henryk Klimaszewski and Józef Nieczecki, attacked the town, where they engaged in "plunder and a pogrom of the Jewish population." During that action, Henryk Klimaszewski was said to have called for settling scores with the Bolsheviks and Jews, saying: "Beat the Jews for Grodno and Skidel, the time to settle accounts has come, down with communists; we'll butcher every last Jew."

The Germans saved hundreds of inhabitants

Apart from the Hoover Institution collection, with which Prof. Gross is familiar, and aside from the accounts I obtained, there are other testimonies to the behavior of Jews from Jedwabne in 1939––1941. In their article "To Survive" (published by *Kontakty* on July

179

19, 1988), Danuta and Aleksander Wroniszewski noted the account of a Jedwabne inhabitant: "I remember how the Russians loaded the Poles onto carriages to be taken to Siberia. On top of each carriage was a Jew armed with a rifle. Mothers, wives and children knelt before the carriages, begging for mercy and help. The last time this happened was June 20, 1941."

Did the Polish inhabitants of Jedwabne and the surrounding villages enthusiastically welcome the Germans as saviors? Yes, they did! If someone pulls me out of a blazing house in which I could burn to a crisp in seconds, I will embrace and thank that person. Even if the next day I regard him as yet another mortal enemy. At that time, the Germans rescued hundreds of local villagers (perhaps also Jedwabne residents?) who had for days been hiding in the fields or the brush-covered slopes of the Biebrza. They saved them from being sent to their death in the wastelands of Kazakhstan or the Siberian taiga. Everyone already knew by then what such exile meant: letters and other signals from the *spetsposoleks** had been getting through. The deportations were accompanied by a simultaneous wave of arrests, often not identified by historians, of suspects who ended up in prison camps or in the prisons for long sentences that they often failed to survive.

Let us not wonder at their joy nor at those "bands," as Andrzej Żbikowski calls them, for attacking groups of Soviet soldiers leaving the area. Until only yesterday their persecutors represented one of the cruelest systems known to mankind.

A horrible day for Poles

Not long ago, a very specific and very credible source was published: *The Chronicle of the Benedictine Sisters of Holy Trinity Abbey in Łomża (1939–1954)*. Published in Łomża in 1995, it was compiled by Sister Alojza Piesiewiczówna. Let us quote the fragments dealing with the June 20–22, 1941:

"June 20. The Feast of the Sacred Heart of Jesus. A horrible day for Poles under Soviet subjugation. Massive deportations to Russia. From early morning carts full of Polish families rolled through town to the railway station. Better-off Polish families, the families of nationalists,

Polish patriots, the intelligentsia, and the families of those in Soviet prisons were taken away. It was difficult even to comprehend what categories of people were being deported. In Polish souls there was weeping, moaning and terrible despair. But the Jews and Soviets, on the other hand, were triumphant. It is impossible to describe what Poles are going through. A hopeless situation. But the Jews and Soviets are demonstratively overjoyed, threatening soon to deport every last Pole. And that could well have been expected because on June 20 and on the following day, the twenty-first, they carted people to the station without interruption.... And God truly saw our tears and blood.

June 22. In the early morning there was the droning sound of airplanes and every so often the blast of bombs exploding over the town.... Several German bombs fell on the more important Soviet outposts. An incredible panic broke out among the Soviets. They began fleeing in disarray. Poles were very happy. The sound of each exploding bomb filled their souls with inexpressible joy. Within a few hours there wasn't a single Soviet left in town, and the Jews were hiding somewhere in basements and cellars. Before noon, prisoners left their jail cells. People on the streets embraced one another and wept for joy. The Soviets had withdrawn without their weapons, and they did not fire a single shot in response to the approaching Germans.

That evening there wasn't a single Soviet in Łomża. But the situation remained unclear—the Soviets had fled, but the Germans had not entered. The next day, June 23, the town was just as empty. The civilian population began looting. All Soviet stores, bases and shops were smashed and robbed. In the evening of June 23, several Germans entered the town—the people breathed a sigh of relief."

During those days there could have been no other reaction. Several weeks later the Armed Combat Union* hastily rebuilt the underground network broken up by the Soviets. Weapons left by the fleeing Russians were extensively gathered up and the "interregnum" was used to prepare for a struggle against the next occupation regime. There are also numerous testimonies to that, as well as to such facts as robberies, retaliation and pogroms. As usual, the reality is far more complex than we are able to imagine.

Tomasz Strzembosz

181

HALINA BORTNOWSKA

WHEN A NEIGHBOR HAS NO NAME

"GAZETA WYBORCZA" JANUARY 27–28, 2001

The book by Jan Gross, *Neighbors*, calls into question a view I had so far held, and which could be put in a nutshell as follows: in Poland, anti-Semitism has existed and was commonly accepted; however, it has nothing to do with the extermination of Jews under Nazi occupation. This belief represented a paradigm, that is, a basic, unquestionable tenet of my understanding of Polish-Jewish relations and modern history. Now, this paradigm of innocence has crumbled. This is typical of paradigms: irrefutable facts, which are contradictory to paradigms, make the overwhelming assumptions disappear, and their sudden negation makes us wake up in a completely different world. Nobody likes it. Imagine what a problem, an Englishman would have if he realized that he was not living on an island! It would be better for us if we did not make such discoveries.

Not only *szmalcownicy*

The paradigm of innocence is very deeply rooted in the Polish vision of history. In particular, we have grown accustomed to believing that we are innocent of the extermination of the Jews—all of us, including "our anti-Semitics," who rescued Jews despite the fact that they did not like them, which made it all the more admirable. It is more difficult to make sacrifices for people one dislikes…. I know that there were such humanitarian anti-Semites, as depicted in the Władysław Bartoszewski's book *Ten jest z Ojczyzny mojej* [This One is From My Homeland]. That's the point—the ones who rescued others were from my homeland. We cross the *szmalcownicy** off the list. They are hyenas, only ostensibly our fellow Poles—in fact, they are foreigners. This was still possible.

Reading Gross's book, I cannot classify the perpetrators of the Jedwabne pogrom in this way. It was surely a pogrom carried out on license from the Nazi occupation authorities, an authorized pogrom inspired within the framework of the larger, pre-planned Shoah. As such, in fact, it represented participation in the Shoah. This pogrom could never have happened without the underpinnings of classical anti-Semitism, which is similar to the anti-Semitism that still crops up left and right in today's Poland.

In my opinion, one of the most important insights in the present debate on Gross's book, and one that makes things all the more terrifying, comes from Professor Krystyna Skarżyńska. She writes that "in the light of psychological knowledge, it is almost certain that, among the Jedwabne population, there would not have been so many people willing to kill their neighbors had they been certain that their countrymen would condemn them for doing so. Even if they acted under strong Nazi pressure. People always assess the social costs and benefits resulting from their actions. It is very likely that those who murdered their Jewish neighbors felt that they had the support of what they assumed were like-minded Polish neighbors and opinion makers." If this is so, then the paradigm of innocence that I also believed in no longer exists. Luckily for me, I have someone to teach me how to live without this paradigm. The method was invented years ago by German friends from the movement *Aktion Sühnen-zeichen** [Signs of Repentance Action]. I learned about this as we sifted side by side in silence through the soil of death at Birkenau or in the ruins of a carpet-bombed hospital in Dresden.

HALINA BORTNOWSKA

Removing the bandages

It's going to be difficult. Even some Polish Jews are attached to the paradigm of Polish innocence. Who wants to join in the sort of long-overdue repentance that is defined as self-flagellation? The *Signs of Repentance Action* model is probably obsolete. Flagellation is better done privately, only in the eyes of God, just as fasting and praying are done discreetly. What is needed in public is truth. Not self-flagellation, but the removal of the bandages from old wounds —and this is said to be painful—in order to see what is underneath: only a scar, or the return of the cancer?

Many years ago, a young Polish Jew said while talking about the memory of the Holocaust that she wanted to have children, but only if they were daughters. A son must be circumcised, she said, and wondered whether she had the courage to mark him that way, perhaps for death. Her words stunned us. Yet we did not stop defending our collective innocence. She may have been worried about a future child because an inherited injury from the past was fixed in her memory. Now, after Gross's book, I think things are different—and worse. That reasons for fear are also provided by today's anti-Semitic slogans and games, which are not unrelated to what happened back then. That something is still smoldering, which makes us realize that another conflagration is not to be ruled out. What Professor Skarżyńska wrote about Jedwabne is still relevant.

Having supported Professor Skarżyńska's arguments, let me return to Jacek Żakowski's remarks against the acknowledgement of collective responsibility. For Żakowski, the paradigm of collective innocence is superfluous, for each neighbor, each other, has a name of his or her own. Guilt is attributed to unique individuals, and individuals must be recognized as innocent if they do not join in the crime. Each neighbor has a name. However, I might not know that name, or I might have forgotten it. And the other, that neighbor, may also forget my name—my personhood—or may negate it. And thus, in such a case, one neighbor may somehow suspend or annul the moral imperatives that apply to relations with others. We know from Gross's accounts that the neighbors' names were used in Jedwabne when people pleaded for rescue. Rarely did it do any good. When a pogrom breaks out, names no longer count. Nor are there neighbors any longer. So it was—not far away, but in a certain place and in certain circumstances, in Poland.

How to live without the paradigm of innocence

What Skarżyńska suggested is still relevant: the responsibility of each and of all to remember the personhood of others, and the responsibility to preserve memory as a warning—the memory that is opposed to the large-scale quantifiers that dehumanize. Work by historians is needed on Jedwabne and other places where we already know that things were similar, or where we do not know and need to check. When the paradigm of innocence was removed, the fear arises that there may be far more such places than we previously thought.

Aside from historical revelations, there is also a need for action addressed to those people who are vulnerable to anti-Semitism. What kind of action? Professor Skarżyńska indicates the general direction. They must know that the poison they bear makes them unwanted. The fact that the specter of anti-Semitism haunts the whole world, or almost the whole world, is no excuse. The point is our own, Polish anti-Semitism, especially the kind that appears among the people who accent their Polishness, rather than their own name.

Halina Bortnowska

BOHDAN SKARADZIŃSKI

JEDWABNE—CRIME AND REPENTANCE

"WIĘŹ" FEBRUARY 2001

On the edge of the town, silhouetted by the church, there is still a stone obelisk with the inscription: SITE OF THE SUFFERING OF THE JEWISH POPULATION. THE GESTAPO AND THE NAZI GENDARMERIE BURNED 1600 PEOPLE ALIVE JULY 10, 1941. However, we now know that only the first part of the inscription is true. There is a debate in progress on how to carry out an unprecedented rehabilitation of the Germans without completely destroying the self-esteem of the local Polish population, or rather the self-esteem of the population of Mazovia and Podlasie. However, as far as the world at large is concerned, this concerns the self-esteem of the Poles in general, for who is going to go into details about our geography and history?

I was moved by the public disclosure, from distant New York, of the criminal secret of Jedwabne, all the more so because I was born in these parts and my forefathers are buried here. There is no point in proving that I personally had nothing to do with the event, or my father or grandfather. But neither is there any point in saying that I feel totally free of responsibility.

Jedwabne should not come as such a surprise to me. I am well-versed in the history of Polish warfare. It contained episodes of relentlessness and cruelty, directed at times against innocent and defenseless people. But in this case, I was surprised. I did not expect Polish-Jewish antagonism could have such abysmal depths. In particular, I never dreamed that such a thing could happen in my "parish."

Serious and somber moods

I had an opportunity to observe the Jewish Holocaust at close range, since I was near the Warsaw ghetto. And I remember how, shortly before the elimination of the ghetto, the Germans removed the Polish police (the "blue police"*) and replaced them with Lithuanians, Ukrainians, Latvians... No one liked the "blue police," yet nevertheless they were Poles, and this vote of no confidence, as it were, by the occupation regime was well received by public opinion. Let no Polish hand be close to that atrocity! Warsaw public opinion reacted positively—no doubt with exaggeration—to any form of help for the martyrs of the ghetto. It was unthinkable that the population of the capital, though far from perfect, felt like summoning up its anti-Semitic feelings at that moment. Why should the Polish provinces behave any differently? Unfortunately, various things happened and, unfortunately, the little town of Jedwabne became the same kind of symbol of the Mazovia-Podlasie Holocaust as Treblinka or the ghetto in Białystok, as if there were not enough human complexes and historical "burdens" in this area!

Moods are serious and somber. That is a good sign, for there have been no attempts to ignore empirical facts or pin the blame on someone else, for example the Turks or the Chinese. Everyone knows that the Jewish population preferred Russia to Poland. Judging from a distance in time, is there any wonder that this was so? No one tries to use Jewish-Polish animosity, which really existed in Jedwabne, as an excuse for our atrocity, a collective atrocity aimed at the Jewish population of Jedwabne regardless of age and sex and in a manner that was brutal even for those bestial days. Attempts to implement justice under the "reds" did not go beyond the facades that were typical of that system, and the entire event was concealed from public opinion in Podlasie and Poland. Was that solely the fault of the communists? What about the handing down of information within families, often so effective on the subject of the public "secrets" of the liberation from the east in 1939 and 1944? And what about the Church, starting with the Jedwabne parish? And then there was the "first *Solidarność*" period [i.e., 1980–1981—ed.], and ten years or so of various forms of liberty and democracy!

Finally, the local press is not conducting a cover-up, and is not seeking mitigating circumstances, which amounts to a statement that there is no use trying to justify the crime. Nor can postwar conspiracies of silence be appealed to. Honest information prevails. However, reports by a survivor have also been published, and there has been an overexcited letter from a reader who hails from Białystok who now lives in Australia.

"The truth is naked and dirty. Keeping silent after such an atrocity means the same as taking part in it," we read in Białystok regional daily *Kurier Poranny*. "Accepting the perpetrators of the massacre in our society is the same as having taken part in that massacre. We literally drank vodka over the graves of the people... and in our memories they were as distant as the ancient Romans or Vikings.... How is it that we, born in a country still wet with blood, knew nothing about this?... What I have read makes me sick. It's not that I have delusions about what kind of people my fellow countrymen are, it's just that as a result of these events, my view of what constitutes the lower limit has sunk even lower."

Elsewhere, the editors of *Kurier Poranny* say that they have not received a single official statement about Jedwabne, "not a single letter from either the local authorities or the central authorities of Podlasie Province." That is typical. As we know, the authorities in Poland do not serve fundamental interests, but are concerned purely with budgets and elections.... The paper carries without comment a suggestion by Professor Jacek Kurczewski about altering the inscription on the monument in Jedwabne to read: *FROM THE POLISH STATE IN REMEMBERANCE OF ITS JEWISH CITIZENS MURDERED BY THEIR NEIGHBORS IN FRATRICIDAL RAGE*. Personally, I would keep our unfortunate Polish state out of it. It has already suffered enough from a lack of sovereignty, so it is a matter of decency to leave it alone. Our state has had a good ten years to show what it is capable of. Well, it was a "rule-of-law" state, whose duty was only to seek out "crimes against the Polish nation"—which does not include the Jews!

The Jews were considered insufferable by the Catholic and Orthodox population of Podlasie, but they also lent a bit of life to this backwater during the First and Second Republics,* especially to its towns... and most of all to the "capital" of the area, Białystok. In 1939, the Jews comprised over half the population of Białystok, which had slightly more than 100,000 inhabitants. Synagogues and prayer houses of the various currents of Judaism were much more in evidence than all the churches combined.

At this point, may I be allowed to make a digression. In Jerusalem, in a cafe I happened into near the Jaffa Gate, the Hasidic owner heard me speaking Polish. He showed me a book of photographs in which he was collecting autographs of people from Poland—especially people from the Białystok area. There is nothing strange about that. The book in question, by Tomasz Wiśniewski and Jarosław Wojtach, bears the title *Synagogues of the Białystok Region*, and is bilingual and suitably subtitled *Heartland of the Jewish Life*. The authors boldly say that "it is not without reason that the Białystok area is called the 'heartland of European Jewry.'" Synagogues were not just places of worship, but also centers of community self-government, education and culture. "It is thanks to them that the Jewish people was able to survive hundreds of years. Without these small and often modest houses of prayer, there would be no state of Israel today," we read.

The worst forces in history

The annihilation of the Jewish population of Podlasie was the result of a veritable volcanic eruption of the worst forces in history—Nazism, which was given a boost at the start by communism. A symbol of Podlasie was the great synagogue in Białystok, in which the encroaching Germans burnt about 1,000 Jews in 1941, before blowing it up in the aftermath of the uprising in the Jewish ghetto in the city. This disaster put an end to long centuries of co-existence, with the additional historical twist, particularly gloomy for Polish self-esteem, that we contributed to that disaster without any procrastination on our part.

What can we do now? There is no doubt that the worst thing is to do nothing. It is the worst thing from a moral point of view, for, when a crime occurs that is not subject to a statute of limitations, there should be a suitable punishment, or at least penance. It is also the worst thing from the educational point of view: we cannot build our collective attitudes towards the dawning century and millennium on false self-awareness. The devil has made beneath our skins a home for himself no worse than among other nations. Except that this home of his is a peculiar kind of home....

An atmospheric tavern, even with the modish appellation "pub," is the best place to meditate on the Leninist slogan *shto dielat* [what should be done?]. Its official name, *Magnat* [the Magnate], is meant to refer to time-honored Polish traditions, and especially local ones. It is located in a beautiful old cellar recently cleared of rubble in the very heart of the city. Of course, these were once Jewish-owned storehouses: reality, even historical reality, is not to be cheated. All of downtown Białystok was built atop the ruins and charred rubble of Jewish property.

If yet another monument will not make the problem go away, then things are not going to be easy. We are in a state of complex social depression in Poland—and we have a multitude of problems among ourselves. It is difficult for people to tackle anything that is not directly linked to grim reality, which is onerous and thankless for most. Should an additional subconscious layer of guilt be added to this mixture? Penance—underlain by uncertainty over unresolved legal and property issues! Only crumbs remain of the formerly Jewish-owned property, yet the real estate itself—usually in the center of Podlasie towns—possesses considerable value. All our sense of repentance would evaporate if people had to pay compensation. Then it would be impossible to leave things in the domain of half-sentences and rumors.

The fundamental condition is the renunciation by Poles in general of their lamentable attitude towards Judaism and the Jews—in relation to matters past, present, and to come, once and for all and with no ifs, ands, or buts. On a community-wide scale and in serious terms, there is nothing to argue about because of the total lack of knowledge in Poland about the phenomenon of Israel. Nor do we know anything about the fortunes of that people, with their unique religion, who survived thousands of years under the most difficult conditions, scattered around the world and persecuted to the point of physical extermination. It is more than odd that not even centuries of coexistence with Jewish Diaspora communities have provided us with any deeper familiarity with these people, with their real talents and their real faults and weaknesses. Take, as an example, the way the Poles sneered at the Jewish martial virtues. That was taken for granted in Polish barracks, and spread from there around the country. And what did the wars with the Arabs in the mid-century demonstrate? What about the fact that has Israel endured all this time in a constant state of semi-mobilization? Soldiering never boiled down to mere personal courage and physical fitness, although their current adversaries will hardly deny the Israelis these qualities. It was also a matter of planning, intelligence, organization and discipline, training and education, technology and logistics. And how are the Jews coping with all this in their third generation? And what happened to all those stupid jokes told in Poland?

The same applies to our image of Jewish agricultural talents. Barely a hundred years ago, Palestine was mainly a desert littered with rocks or interspersed with malaria-infested marshes. Today, Israel sustains a greatly enlarged population, and exports fruit, vegetables and even wine to cater to the pampered palates of Western Europe. With its prosperity, it beats its Arab neighbors, hands-down, despite having started from an identical position and, in addition, despite not having oil. In terms of prosperity, Israel leaves Poland, and even that the Czechs and Hungarians, far behind. Nor can we turn up our noses at the standards of medicine in the Jewish state, or of education, physics, chemistry, literature, music, sports, social welfare....

191

Perhaps there would be some way to get today's Poles, so hungry for the modernity and money, interested in all this. Bad stereotypes and old prejudices—let them try and defend themselves against the reality of Israel! If any lessons seep through to Polish brains from this, so much the better. It would be a side effect, but a beneficial one.

The measure of the twenty-first century

The point is, would it be possible to gather together in Białystok a handful of resourceful and energetic people, convinced of the need to rebuild relations between Israel and Podlasie on the banks of the Narew and Jordan rivers, in a manner that befitting the twenty-first century? It is pointless to suggest a detailed program for such reconstruction. Anything that can arouse human curiosity in the Jewish phenomenon is good—interest in the pioneering spirit of the Jews of Białystok, the culture and sport of modern Israel, Jewish relations in the world, the relationship between Judaism and Christianity, the militancy connected with Jerusalem, banking and the diamond trade... even the truths and myths about "Jewish communism,"* should the Poles be interested in this subject.

I personally see the best hope in direct, personal contacts. Warsaw has a small but vibrant Jewish community. It would be a good idea to search for scattered groups of Podlasie Jews in Israel, beginning with a reconnaissance of their "pilgrimages" to Treblinka and Tykocin. There are also some sort of pilgrimages from Podlasie to the Holy Land. Could they not be enriched with the subject of the reconciliation of Poles and Jews? Our Pope, John Paul II, apologized to the Jews before the Wailing Wall, and our Primate publicly presented a Polish "examination of the conscience," so no religious harm would be done.

As far as work on the scale of the century is concerned, it must be targeted at young people, starting with secondary-school students but aimed mainly at the University of Białystok. One can easily imagine a center for Jewish studies, which does not exist anywhere in Poland, and certainly nowhere east of the Bug river. It might involve research into the current sociological realities of Israel—a phenomenon on a world scale, and also include Hebrew studies, the geopolitics of the Middle East, the history of the Jewish Diaspora, and biblical archaeology. The university would be an ideal place for passionate enthusiasts. There would be opportunities for cooperation with Jewish colleges and college communities all over the world. Global scale! The intellectual potential of the subject might well be more appealing to the young than other global topics!

Those are the various thoughts that run through our minds while we sit in the formerly Jewish-owned cellars of the today's *Magnat* bar in Białystok. The old walls seem to tell us: if we are to perform penance, then let this take the form of a practical deed so that, while enriching the memory of the Jews of Podlasie, may enrich us ourselves—spiritually, certainly, and there is a host of other possibilities. In Cana in Israel, I saw crates of wine bottles commemorating the miraculous turning of water into wine. Labels inform and encourage us. Today, this wine flows to the entire Christian world. Would these ancient cellars in Białystok not serve a more worthy function if they reminded us of sunny Galilee while, at the same time, helping to perpetuate the memory of the Jews?

*

In this article I have omitted to mention that it is not just the population of Podlasie which owes something to the Jews. The whole of eastern Europe—from Samogitia by way of Slovakia to Bessarabia, all the way to the "beautiful blue Danube," has something to think about and something to regret. I did not mention this because I did not wish to make it look like an attempt to whitewash the events in Podlasie or absolve that area of its co-responsibility. But I must admit that if the case of Jedwabne, Tykocin and Białystok, and other such places could also inspire kindred places elsewhere in eastern Europe to undertake suitable action in their own front yards, then the nationalism of the undersigned would be pleasantly tickled.

Bohdan Skaradziński

BOGDAN MUSIAŁ
INTERVIEWED BY PAWEŁ PALIWODA

WE CANNOT BE AFRAID

"ŻYCIE" FEBRUARY 2, 2001

Paweł Paliwoda: There is a view that the book Neighbors, *by Jan Gross—while not free of flaws in research—fully presents the nature of events in Jedwabne. What is your response to this?*
Bogdan Musiał: Gross falls short of this in many respects. He shows those events in a specific way, using a narrow base of sources. I am surprised how he managed to reach his conclusions.

I agree that Gross has made Poles more sensitive to an issue about which little was and is known. He did so through provocation and very emotional language. There is no fundamental analysis, however—that is, on the issue of historical context. The author presents the situation in Jedwabne between 1939 and 1941 as if nothing was happening during this period.

— *Gross and his supporters maintain that mention of a context for these events is a search for an alibi for the perpetrators of the crime, motivated by anti-Semitism.*

— Suspecting from the outset that this is about anti-Semitism is nonsense. A fundamental condition of discussing past events properly is to determine their historical context. We can't present historical facts from the view point of the year 2001. We must reconstruct the background of events, their genesis. The historian must sensitize

194

himself to a past context. There is no sense in a position like: I've had plenty to eat, live in New York or Warsaw, never had anything to do with facts of this kind, and now I will take some document and evaluate it from a moral point of view. That is arrogance. This isn't about an alibi for criminals—they should be condemned categorically. If Gross had written that X or Y was responsible for these crimes, that would be acceptable. However, he makes the society of Jedwabne, Polish society, responsible for this crime. First, he ought to prove this thesis.

— *What type of facts could make for a better understanding of the drama in Jedwabne?*

— Can you explain to me why this didn't occur in Jedwabne in September 1939? Why it didn't happen until 1941? Suddenly, 2 years after the Red Army invaded these territories, so much had changed. Why? Why doesn't Gross pose this question at all? We know from history that similar incidents occurred at this time in the eastern strip running from Latvia to the territory of present day Moldavia shortly after the Soviet occupation forces left this area. An explosion of anti-Semitism occurred in all these places. Poles were not everywhere. There were Rumanians and Jews, Latvians and Jews, Ukrainians and Jews, Belorussians and Jews. If we look at what went on in the territories of present day Moldavia, the events in Jedwabne pale in comparison. Yet there weren't any Germans or Poles there. The inter-ethnic conflicts that arose were strictly related to the Soviet occupation of these territories. Gross omits this issue.

— *What is the relation between the Soviet occupation and anti-Semitism?*

— The Soviets, on entering these territories, destroyed the old bourgeois, capitalist system together with its representatives. They didn't however have much knowledge in personnel matters and thus had to rely on local sources. Who did this involve? In Poland before the war, there were tensions between Poles and Jews which were begging for conflicts. One part of the Jewish population, which had a leaning to the left, especially young people, did in fact collaborate with the Soviets. In this way, Poles began to see Jews as traitors, allies of the Soviets. It is widely believed that the Siberian forced labor deportation lists were prepared by Jewish communists. In part this is true.

We can take, for example Michael Mielnicki's account. He was the son of Chaim Mielnicki from Wasilków (the account is contained in the book *Białystok to Birkenau,* which came out in Toronto in 2000). He recalls that NKVD* functionaries came to them and that his father helped them fill out lists of those who were to be sent to Siberia. He describes Poles using the terms "traitor," *"Volksdeutsche,"** and "fascists"—the language of the Soviet occupation regime. He quotes his father as saying, "We must get rid of these Polish fascists for they are our enemies." Except that, amongst these fascists and traitors, there were also children and babies. Despite so many Poles being deported with the help of his father, Michael Mielnicki expresses great surprise that there were suddenly so many anti-Semites among these Poles after the Germans invaded.

— *Tomasz Strzembosz makes a similar argument to yours.*

— I totally agree with the central arguments of Professor Strzembosz, as contained in the text published recently in *Rzeczpospolita* (January 27–28, 2001). I presented this issue comprehensively in the book *"Kontrrevolutionäre Elemente sind zu erschiessen." Die Brutalisierung des deutsch-sowjetischen Kriegs im Sommer 1941* ["Counterrevolutionary Elements Must Be Shot." The Brutalization of the German-Soviet War in Summer 1941]. I based this book primarily on Jewish accounts from the period 1941–42. This doesn't mean that all Jews collaborated with the NKVD. They were, however, perceived as doing so by many Poles who did not see Jews being arrested and persecuted by the NKVD, but did see Jewish policemen every day for two years.

— *The opinion that the Soviet army invading Poland was greeted with ovations by a significant part of the Jewish population is often presented as another anti-Semitic stereotype.*

— There is no doubt about this. It is also confirmed by Jewish historians. In the work of Ben-Cion Pinchuk, as for example in *Shtetl Jews under Soviet Rule: Eastern Poland on the Eve of the Holocaust.* His main sources were accounts by people who survived the Holocaust in these territories. Pinchuk comes to completely different conclusions than Gross, as he has an incomparably more professional base of source material. Pinchuk writes of the greeting of the Soviets and Jewish involvement, especially in the first phase of the building of the Soviet system. In the cities, Jews who were adherents of communism played a large role in sustaining Soviet authority. They created revolutionary committees, militias and so forth. Pinchuk establishes all of this on the basis of accounts not by Poles or anti-Semites, but by those of Jews, as preserved at Yad Vashem [the Memorial Institute in Jerusalem—ed.]

Gross quoted this monograph only once. Its thesis does not suit him as it is very inconvenient. He should, nevertheless, be able to say why Pinchuk comes to conclusions different from his own, despite knowing the facts that Gross writes about. This is why Gross makes a wide circle around the work of Pinchuk and many others.

— *I understand that Poles tainted with anti-Semitic crimes did not so much suckle hatred towards Jews with their mother's milk, as to arrive at their anti-Semitism by seeing some part of the Jewish population collaborating with the communists. This does not change the moral assessment of the Jedwabne atrocity, but it overturns the core argument of the adherents of the anti-Polish view who see "spontaneous and disinterested anti-Semites" in Poland, "the most anti-Semitic country in the world."*

— It is absolutely certain that Poles are not anti-Semites by nature. This is an absurd thesis. Polish anti-Semitism has, of course, certain local traits but—just like the anti-Semitism of the Germans or Lithuanians—it was conditioned in a historical context, in an extraordinary period. I fully agree, however, that this does not lessen the moral blame of those responsible for the Jedwabne murder.

In regard to Gross's book there is naturally no statement of the sort that we find in Pinchuk that those Jews who were responsible for communist crimes, those who were engaged in the communist party, in the Komsomol [communist youth movement—ed.] or police, were the first to flee the areas left by the Soviets. I have many very interesting accounts, including some from Tarnopol, which indicate that before the German invasion there was already an awareness among Jews working in the Soviet apparatus that it could come to anti-Semitic pogroms. Those Jews who stayed became scapegoats.

— *What is the degree of awareness in the West of the flaws in the book by Gross? Are, for example the owners of the* New York Times, *one of the main promoters of this book in USA, aware of this?*

— I don't think so, because in the USA there is a specific perspective in understanding the dramas of World War Two. Jews were victims, certainly, but Poles were the helpers of the perpetrators or passive witnesses to extermination. The Gross's book precisely confirms these prejudices, and reinforces stereotypes. There is no awareness of its shortcomings.

— *What is the cause of this state of affairs?*

— There is still no historian in the USA who would concern himself with the theme of war crimes, in an ethnic context, in that time and place. What there is instead in the USA is the literature of Holocaust survivors' memoirs. These are subjective accounts that often contain a large emotional charge, and one that is anti-Polish. If such a person who hid somewhere was persecuted by Polish *szmalcownicy,* * then I am not surprised by a prejudice against Poles. The only problem is that this person then assesses all of Polish society from this perspective—and this is a mistake.

— *What does the American stereotype of the Polish anti-Semite consist of?*

— There is a widespread belief that the death camps were built in Poland because the Germans could count on Polish anti-Semitism and therefore had the appropriate emotional backing. This is a stereotype spread by people such as Claude Lanzmann or Elie Wiesel, people who are great opinion makers, as are newspapers like the *New York Times*. This assessment of history is an exact inversion of the anti-Semitic stereotype. This is anti-Polish chauvinism.

— *The Holocaust has become a subject that is taken up with singular frequency in recent years in USA. Where does this sudden American interest in history come from?*

— I would say that we are dealing with the expropriation of the Holocaust in American culture. In the 1950s, it wasn't in reality an issue for general public opinion; no one was particularly interested.

Even for those who survived and migrated to the USA, it was recommended that they not talk about the past. People said, "Let's look to the future." Only in the 1960s did the process begin of discovering the extermination of the Jews, and this took on momentum in the 1970s. At that time, the film *Holocaust* was screened, which nearly 100 million Americans watched. This film was a dramatization of factual events, but it had an immense impact on public opinion. Today, the Holocaust plays an enormous role in the USA. Norman G. Finkelstein writes about this "industry" in his book *The Holocaust Industry. Reflections on the Exploitation of Jewish Suffering.*

— *Does this mean that the memory of the extermination of the Jews is being commercialized?*

— Let me give you an explanatory example. In America, specialists in the Holocaust have the easiest time finding university or museum jobs. It is a subject which is easy to sell. It attracts people. If there is interest, then there must be something on offer to meet the demand. Such an offering could be an article, a film or a book. If you wish to publish a book in the States, then write about the Holocaust, and it is best to do so in such a way as not to trouble the reader, that is, in accordance with the prevailing stereotypes.

— *Has the history of the Holocaust then become pulp fiction?*

— American as well as Israeli historians and sociologists have repeatedly pointed out the exploitation of the Holocaust in America, where it has become an element of mass culture. They criticize this in strong terms, speaking of Americanization and mystification. Americans feel superior to Europeans, and therefore it would be a little awkward to talk, for instance, about the extermination of the Indians. Better to speak of the Holocaust, with which they have nothing in common. Germans and Poles are responsible for this—we [Americans—ed.] are not. At the same time, a moralistic phraseology and paternalist rhetoric are applied, which make a mockery of the facts.

— *In America, the extermination of the Jews is also instrumentalized in other ways, as a "religion of the Holocaust." What is the basis of this phenomenon?*

— The Holocaust, for part of the Jewish elite, is becoming a "surrogate religion," an instrument of integration. It is a means of countering the loosening of traditional relations that maintain the Jewish community, which is slowly melting into American society. Memory of the Holocaust and injustices committed, a common fate, is to become a means of rebuilding collective identity. The state of Israel could have become a similar point of reference for many Americans of Jewish origin. The policy of Israel in the Middle East does not suit many people. The Holocaust lends itself ideally as a touchstone of common fate.

— *Aren't the superficial and stereotypical concepts in the book by Gross most convenient for those who instrumentalize the Holocaust? Could the religion of the Holocaust survive without Poles as born anti-Semites?*

— Poles, as at best passive witnesses of the Holocaust, is an unquestionable dogma in America, a typical element of the Holocaust and its Americanization. It is unusually difficult to enter into a discussion with this dogma. There are various traps of political correctness lying in wait for revisionists. At every turn it's possible to fall foul of the accusation: you want to learn the context of the crime, and that means you are a closet anti-Semite.

— *How then can investigative historiography be conducted in such circumstances? Doesn't it require great courage?*

— It does. It is similar to my experience with the exhibition *Crimes of the Wehrmacht*. Before I approached it, I took a long time making up my mind. This exhibition was dogma. In a period of three years, it became practically a religious cult. Criticism of the exhibition was blasphemy. I thought to myself: "Oh my God, I'll start to criticize it and they'll eat me alive." Frankly speaking, to take on such a subject, it's necessary to have more than just research skills. Tactical and strategic skills are needed. Even more, a specific sort of intuition is required. This becomes very complicated.

— *It is said that the truth, regardless of what it is, has a liberating force. From what you say, however, it transpires that the truth itself is not always sufficient in relations between nations. How then ought the process of the normalization of Polish-Jewish relations look?*

— In spite of everything, it's necessary to cast fear aside and ruthlessly seek out the truth. Poles ought to say openly: of course, there were *szmalcownicy.** It is then necessary to investigate how many there were, what sort of influence this had on the fate of the whole Jewish population, where they came from, whether or not there were attempts by the underground state to counteract them, and so forth. In my opinion, this is very important. Nothing should be kept hidden. This will result in a growth of trust in the Polish side. We should remember that there are many responsible Jewish historians. Not all practice history the way Daniel Goldhagen or Jan Gross do.

A wonderful example of reliability is Peter Novick and his book, *The Holocaust in American Life.* He gives, for example, an analysis of the passive witness concept and asks critics: Would you be able to prevent the extermination of the Jews if this represented a danger to you and your family?

Naturally, on both sides there are those acting against reconciliation. The best means of neutralizing their influence is the spectacular disclosure of their mistakes.

— *Wouldn't the carrying out of such a spectacular action, such as your intervention in the case of* The Crimes of the Wehrmacht, *by a Polish author in relation to a Jewish one, inflame Polish-Jewish relations?*

— I don't think so. Of course newspapers like *The New York Times* would certainly throw themselves upon such a person with malicious glee—after all, there are people who are incorrigible. We cannot be afraid, however. This mustn't discourage us from honest investigation.

— *You propose reconciliation through getting to know one another. In the meantime, the majority of leaders on the Jewish side and the majority of the intellectual elite in Poland rather speak only of the need for Poles to admit to guilt. Everything is already known, and now the time has come for Polish expiation.*

— As a historian, I must first know what happened. Only then can I draw conclusions. I don't doubt that a certain significant group in Polish society either supported the Holocaust or were happy about it. However, and I continually repeat this, we should determine the context of these dramatic events. I don't believe that in a democratic state, in conditions of peace, this sort of incident would be possible. Why should the Polish nation be responsible as a whole for the deeds of the *szmalcownicy**?

Let's reach for another example: the year 1981.* There were *Zomowcy** and people were beaten up by them. Who should ask for forgiveness now and who should be made responsible for the crimes of martial law at that time? Does the entire Polish nation have to apologize, or does a specific group of people, have to apologize for similar atrocities at the Wujek coal mine? It would be equally inappropriate for Poles to apologize for the communist system on behalf of the entire nation, for the events of 1968 or 1970. This is an attempt to stretch personal responsibility into collective responsibility.

— *In other words, I would apologize on behalf of both of us for the fact that…*

— …for the fact that, having absolutely authority, you beat me up. This position is an absurdity. It is the identification of the whole of society with one of its specific groups. This is a manipulation that most often allows some group involved in a situation to avoid responsibility.

— *Isn't the thesis of Jews themselves being anti-Semites during the Holocaust equally absurd?*

— Sometimes it is, sometimes it isn't. It isn't when the "fervor of the converted" is considered. Such situations are known. Here we have a subsequent example of the activity of certain elements on the basis of which it isn't possible to assess all of society. I remember such a characteristic example from the Kielce Province, where the Mayor of one of the towns there, who was half-Jewish, turned out to be a fanatical anti-Semite.

Similarly, all deportations from ghettos occurred with the participation of the Jewish Police and ghetto administration. But was anti-Semitism the determining element here? Nonsense. It is possible to condemn these people morally, but necessary to understand the circumstances in which they had to act. We have to become familiar with and understand the context of this situation. What other alternative did they have?

— *If this administration and police were made up not of Jews but of Poles, there would be a ready argument that...*

— ...that this was anti-Semitism. There were instances where Polish firemen were used in deportations. There is one such account, and now it is treated as anti-Semitism. Except that the fact is that these same firemen were previously deployed in roundups of Polish workers for slave labor. Now comes the question: Were these firemen also anti-Polish?

— *In the columns of Gazeta Wyborcza, Ryszard Bugaj has formulated the supposition that maintaining the anti-Semitic-Poland thesis serves to justify the property claims of American Jews against Poland. Isn't Gross's book one of the elements of such propaganda?*

— I perceive a certain similarity between the situation of Poland and that of Switzerland. I don't think that Gross wrote particularly his book with this aim, although there always exists the possibility of exploiting this type of emotional writing. In the case of Switzerland, a great campaign was waged. There was continual talk about banks in the press and television, about the gold of murdered Jews and about the money that's in these accounts. In this regard it was forgotten, of course, that there were American banks that did exactly the same. There were also banks in Jewish hands that did exactly the same. There was silence about this, however, and the campaign was focused on Switzerland.

— *Is it possible to say anything positive about Jan Gross's book?*

— What Gross had to say has stirred an interest in this subject in Poland. I see, in fact, that what Tomasz Strzembosz wrote is a very interesting analysis. Others will follow. Up to now, there has existed a fear of seeking out the complete truth about Polish-Jewish relations. A fear of being accused of anti-Semitism and a fear of touching upon certain painful places in the history of Poland has predominated. Gross wanted to provoke Poles, to tell them how terrible they are, but at the same time he has forced them into debate. This can represent a great breakthrough in Polish historiography, which up to now hasn't had much to say on these issues, and has in the main confined itself to journalistic platitudes. Each source, every account, must be investigated regardless of its ethnic or social undertones. The historian cannot confine himself to statements about moral rightness. Gross and his followers actually end up confining themselves to this, and demand that we do the same. Knowing Jewish and other sources however, it is possible to reduce the majority of arguments by Gross to absurdity. Using methods like his, it is possible to prove anything. He has spurred investigation here, this is a fact—but he has not shown how the research should be done.

ANTONI MACIEREWICZ

THE REVOLUTION OF NIHILISM

"GŁOS" FEBRUARY 3, 2001

It is difficult today to pinpoint with entire certainty when this all began. Perhaps it was when the Jedwabne Jews published *Yedwabne: History and Memorial Book*, containing a description of the tragedy of their hometown, or perhaps it was when Prof. Jan T. Gross received a grant to study the 1939–1941 Bolshevik occupation of Poland's eastern marches* and was given access to materials kept at the Hoover Institution.

For Gross himself, the important date was 1998, when Agnieszka Arnold, at work on a documentary film, showed him footage from Jedwabne. Prof. Andrzej Paczkowski also played an essential role, by giving Gross access to documents from the Main Commission for the Investigation of Crimes against the Polish Nation*, although they were off-limits to other researchers at the time, for which Gross especially thanks him.

The campaign

It is certain, however, that the beginning was not the court case of 1949, when 15 men indicted for the murder of the Jedwabne Jews (seven other suspects could not be located). The basis of the trial was the account (or rather the accounts) by Szmul Wasersztajn. Twelve Poles were sentenced in a pseudo-trial that lasted barely a day (there are obvious parallels with the procedure followed in Kielce* in 1946), but it did not occur to anyone back then to accuse the Polish nation of playing a part in the Holocaust. This comes as little surprise considering that Wasersztajn's account clearly stated that the slaughter was carried out on orders issued by the German Gestapo on July 10, 1941, and under German supervision. The indictment also confirms this: "at the behest of the German state authorities, they took part in the apprehension of about 1,200 people of Jewish nationality, who were then burned to death en masse by the Germans..."

It would be difficult to assume that the authorities of the UB* and the Stalinist courts consciously aimed to clear the Poles and to falsely cast responsibility onto the Germans. Anti-Semitism was rather being sniffed out everywhere at the time and used eagerly as a pretext for repression. In this case, however, the evidence pointed primarily in the direction of the Germans. Gross initially treated Wasersztajn's report similarly. It was only later, as he writes, that he *"watched raw footage for [a documentary film by Agnieszka Arnold and]... realized that Wasersztajn has to be taken literally."* That was in 1998.

Two years later, Jewish and liberal circles were swept by a hysterical urge to prove that the Poles were responsible for the crime of genocide committed against the Jews by the Germans, for the Holocaust. This campaign was accompanied by lies that would have been difficult to imagine just a short time ago, such as the following statement of Gross's: *"nobody was forced to kill the Jews... the so-called local population involved in killings of Jews did so of its own free will,"* or that *"it was in no one's interest in Stalinist Poland to underscore Jewish wartime suffering at the hands of the Poles,"* or that strikes in Łódź in 1946 after the "Kielce pogrom" are *"perfectly understandable as a sign of frustration that one could no longer properly defend innocent Polish children threatened by the murderous designs of the Jews."* Poles who harbored Jews *"continued to hide this fact from their neighbors—all of them were not hated or feared as crypto-communists but rather as embarrassing witnesses to crimes... [and] to the illicit benefits that many continued to enjoy...."* Gross is thus undertaking a hate campaign directed at Poles and Poland, declaring a journalistic and propaganda war on us. Why?

Jedwabne for Kielce?

Perhaps a better reference point for understanding Gross's book is the political mechanism connected with the Kielce affair. For years, the so-called "Kielce pogrom" and later the "Kielce provocation" served as a key argument against Poland and Poles. In recent years it was proved beyond a shadow of a doubt that the so-called "Kielce pogrom" was in essence a crime against Poles, committed by the NKVD* and the UB. An essential, but still incompletely explained role was played by Jewish communists, especially Luna Bristigerowa, who was then in charge of a UB department and was the superior of the UB officer, Sobczyński, who supervised the unfolding of the "pogrom." Jewish refugees suffered then, and their deaths served as a pretext to persecute Poles fighting for independence and to unleash hysteria that induced Jews to emigrate to Palestine. These goals were achieved, but in the 1990s knowledge about this crime, committed by the Bolshevik occupation authorities, began to penetrate to public awareness, despite the resistance of the Commission for the Investigation of Crimes against the Polish Nation* and of judicial bodies that cancelled legal proceedings in the matter, calculating that the truth would never surface.

Hence when the myth of Polish anti-Semitism—previously fueled by stories about the "Kielce pogrom"—ceased to be useful, it was decided to find a replacement. Is the tragedy of the Jedwabne Jews to become such a tool? Is the hubbub surrounding Jedwabne intended to eclipse the responsibility of Jews for communism and the Soviet occupation of Poland? The creation of the Institute of National Remembrance* and access to previously unknown sources could soon reveal the horrifying scale of anti-Polish activities. Perhaps, then, this is all about blocking that process or giving it an "ideologically correct" form. And perhaps the goals are even more prosaic—perhaps it is simply a matter of creating prerequisites for the recovery of the property that belonged to the Jewish community murdered by the Germans on Polish soil?

Poles are guilty of the Holocaust and the communist occupation!

The first publication on this subject appeared in the newspaper *Rzeczpospolita* in May 2000, when, on the basis of the *Memorial Book* and the Wasersztajn account, Andrzej Kaczyński lay the responsibility for the murder of nearly 1,500 Jews at the feet of the Jedwabne Poles, accusing them of participation in the Holocaust. Protests from right-wing Catholic quarters were of no avail, the community of professional historians remained silent, and so the hate campaign spread even further. The position of the Polish government is not clear to this day. In any case, several historians met on May 19, 2000, at the initiative of the Ministry of Foreign Affairs, in the ministry's palace on Foksal street in Warsaw. Their task was to formulate an official position on this issue. As the newspaper *Nasz Dziennik* * wrote, "from the statements that were quoted in the press after that meeting, one could arrive at the conclusion that the worst possible reaction on the part of the Polish authorities and public opinion in this matter would be any possible attempt to fundamentally undermine the credibility of the accounts presented in Gross's book or to steer the discussion toward a search for the alleged instigators and beneficiaries of an 'anti-Polish campaign.'"

There was not long to wait for the results of such a position. First Jewish circles, and then liberal ones, began calling loudly for the punishment of the Polish nation for its crimes against the Jews. Stanisław Krajewski demands on behalf of the Jewish community in Poland that the president, prime minister and Roman Catholic primate publicly admit the "truth" about responsibility for the slaughter in Jedwabne. Jan Nowak-Jeziorański advanced a similar view on the pages of *Rzeczpospolita*, demanding an act of repentance from the Episcopate, the primate, and the prime minister in the name of the entire nation, just as Chancellor Brandt did before the Ghetto monument in Warsaw in the name of the German nation. Nowak equated the responsibility of Poles for Jedwabne to the responsibility of the Russians for Katyn*, thus adding identification with the Bolshevik NKVD to the identification of the Poles with the Nazis. This wasn't anything particularly new, because Jan Tomasz Gross, the author of the anti-Polish accusation himself, closed his book with a hypothesis that the true origin of communism in Poland should be sought in the activities of Polish anti-Semites, who collectively supported the Soviet occupation after 1945!

The propaganda of lies

Such a profusion of libelous accusations and absurdities would seem impossible in a country that regained independence after 50 years of occupation directed by communists of Jewish origin supporting Russian Bolshevism. It turns out not only that it is possible, but even that these libelous accusations and absurdities are being propagated by most of the media and, at a minimum, tolerated by the country's authorities. The only exception turned out to be Professor Radoń, head of the Administrative Body of the Institute of National Remembrance,* who voiced a shy reminder that Professor Gross's book is more of a political newspaper column than a historical work, if only because Gross disavowed in advance any search for sources that could undermine his thesis about the principal responsibility of the Poles.

Hence Gross relies exclusively on reports of the Jedwabne Jews who were saved from the Holocaust (thanks to Poles, after all) while omitting or downplaying any information about the presence and decisive role of German military units. He performs similar contortions in trying to convince his readers that the Jewish population in eastern Poland was not involved in any particular way in support for the Soviet occupation authorities in 1939–41.

The third fundamental instance of Gross's dishonesty as a researcher is his thesis that the origins of communism on Polish soil after 1944 should be sought in the anti-Semitism of the Poles. It is obvious to any historian that Professor Gross's book does not hold up to criticism in terms of methodology. Even Professor Tomasz

209

Szarota alluded to this in *Gazeta Wyborcza*, but that has not hindered these circles in the continuation of their anti-Polish campaign.

A revolution in historical sources

In order to prop up his accusation, Gross proposes a true revolution in the historical sciences. Up until now, historians were bound by strict critical rules in regard to their sources. Thus there was an obligation to take a critical approach to each account, to mutually corroborate the information obtained, and, first and foremost, there was an obligation to take all known sources into account. This means that an author cannot freely pick and choose from among existing reports those that suit his thesis better, but rather has the obligation to take into consideration all the information whose existence is known at a given time. Failing to exhaust the accessible sources disqualifies a study as a work of history, and demotes it to the rank of historical or political journalism. That is precisely the case here. Gross may not be aware of this, since he is a physicist and sociologist by training and took up history thanks to the grants he received from the Guggenheim and Rockefeller Foundations. Just to be on the safe side, Gross announces in his book the need for a "new approach to sources": "the starting premise in appraisal of [survivors'] evidentiary contribution [should change]," he writes, "from *a priori* critical to in principle affirmative." In short, when studying the history of the Holocaust, the point of departure in analysis of reports by surviving witnesses should be to trust their accounts, and not to seek to corroborate their description of events. Given such a premise, in fact, the entire existing historical oeuvre becomes useless and the events of the recent past can be written anew. And then it won't be hard to prove the theses that Gross's book forwards: the Poles are responsible for the Holocaust; the operation of the Nazi genocidal machine was underpinned by traditional, Polish, backward, atavistic anti-Semitism; the Jews were in no special way helpful to the Soviet occupation either in 1939 or in 1945 and, quite the contrary, were its main victims; and the Soviet army and communist regime were supported by peasant and small-town anti-Semitic masses who collaborated with every occupying authority—with the Germans, the Russians, the communists—in short, THE POLES ARE GUILTY. Despite appearances, Gross is not the originator either of this "methodology" or of these theses. They have long been spread on a large scale by political commentaries in *Gazeta Wyborcza* and the circle of historians connected with the paper. Among these historians we must name Andrzej Paczkowski, thanks to whose kindness Gross had access to materials revealing, for example, the names of communist agents, many of them still alive to this day. Paczkowski has long spread precisely such a vision of communism: "Not everything, rather very little can be explained by statements about 'outsiders,' 'the Jews,' 'NKVD* agents,' 'mercenaries' or 'traitors.' Poles appeared in the role of victim and persecutor.... And it is truly difficult today to say with full certainty on which side there were more of them." Krystyna Kersten and Jerzy Holzer write similar articles. This is precisely what the "Polish historical school" looks like today. Part of it willingly erects the edifice of anti-Polish "historiosophy" while the rest remain timorously silent.

What was it really like?

Only recently, on the pages of *Rzeczpospolita*, did there appear a lengthy article by Professor Tomasz Strzembosz, a distinguished researcher of recent Polish history and especially the period 1939– –54. Strzembosz's article demonstrates the actual role of the Jewish population in eastern Poland in the years of the first Soviet occupation.* The discussion to date, declares Strzembosz, "overlooks the most important fact: what happened in Jedwabne after the German army entered the area, i.e. who, when and in what circumstances carried out the mass murder of the Jewish population of Jedwabne." Strzembosz analyzes in depth the behavior of the Polish and Jewish populations in the years 1939–41, especially the initial and final periods of the first Soviet occupation. "The Jewish population," writes Strzembosz, "especially the young and the urban poor, participated en masse in greeting the entering [Soviet] army and in introducing the new order, even with guns in their hands. There are also thousands of testimonies to this: Polish, Jewish and Soviet, there are the reports of the Armed Combat Union* commander-in-chief, Gen. Stefan Grot-Rowiecki, there is the report of courier Jan Karski,* there are accounts recorded during the war and in the postwar years... What is more, the "guards" and "militias" springing up like mushrooms right after the Soviet attack were in large part made up of Jews. Nor is this all. Jews committed acts of revolt against the Polish state, taking over towns and setting up revolutionary committees there, arresting and shooting representatives of the Polish state authorities, attacking smaller or even fairly large units of the Polish Army (as in Grodno). ... It was armed collaboration, taking the side of the enemy, betrayal in the days of defeat."

Organizers of the red terror

So it was in the first period, when the Polish state was still defending itself, when our army units were fighting and it seemed that not all was lost. The Jews then played the role of a "fifth column." Later, things became much worse. Strzembosz cites the conclusions of Dr. Marek Wierzbicki as to who implemented the Bolshevik terror—of course the NKVD* and, before that, the Red Army, but the miscellaneous guard formations and militias played a decisive role on an everyday basis. And their ranks were primarily filled with Jews. "Polish Jews in civilian clothes, with red bands on their arms and armed with guns also play large part in arrests and deportations. That was the most drastic thing, but for the Polish community another glaring fact was the large number of Jews in all the Soviet agencies and institutions. ... in the period September-December 1939, numerous arrests took place of those representatives of the Polish population who before the war filled high functions in the administration and political structures of the Polish state or who were very involved in community work. The local Jews, members of the temporary administration or militia, provided extensive assistance to the Soviet authorities in tracking down and arresting them."

Why did this happen? What were the roots of this terrible hatred toward Poland and the cruel revenge on Poles? "It is true," writes

Strzembosz, "things were not going very well for the Jews in Poland... but still, Jews were not being deported to Siberia, shot, sent to concentration camps, or killed by hunger and slave labor. If they did not consider Poland to be their homeland, they still did not have to treat it as an invader and join its mortal enemy in killing Polish soldiers and murdering Polish civilians fleeing to the east. Nor did they have to take part in designating their neighbors for deportation."

Torture in Jedwabne

Strzembosz proves beyond a shadow of a doubt that events took precisely the same course in Jedwabne itself. Here is one account from a resident of Jedwabne, Józef Rybicki, summing up what happened in the town after it fell to the Soviets: "Jews who had put up an archway greeted the Red Army. They changed the old town government and proposed a new one drawn from the local population (Jews and communists). They arrested the police, the teachers.... They led the NKVD to apartments and houses and denounced Polish patriots."

The description of the tortures inflicted upon Polish conspirators by the NKVD in Jedwabne is shocking. The following is an account by Corporal Antoni B., a member of the anti-Soviet underground who was turned in to the NKVD by Jews:

"they took me for interrogation, the investigating judge and the NKVD commander and one torturer came, and they sat me on a stool next to a brick wall, then I look over and one in civilian clothes took a stick from behind the stove like the kind in the walls of our tents, that long and thick, and suddenly they threw me on the floor and stuffed my cap in my mouth and started to beat me, I couldn't cry out because the judge sat on my legs and the second one held me by the head and held the cap in my mouth, and I fought back until I tore the cap to bits, and the third torturer beat me the whole time, I got that stick more or less 30 times, and they stopped beating me and sat me on the stool by the wall. I had long hair, and the senior lieutenant grabbed me by the hair and started to beat my head against the wall, I thought that nothing would

be left of my head, he tore the whole clump of hair from my head... they threw me on the ground and started to beat me with a hazel stick, they turned me from side to side and beat me, and in addition two of them were still sitting on me and suffocating me and said that they would finish me off. They kept beating me until they probably knew that I couldn't take anymore, so at last they let me go. They beat me like a cat in a sack, and at the end they sat me on the stool and beat me with the stick on the arms...." (from *W czterdziestym nas matko na Sybir zesłali* [In 1940, Mother, They Sent Us to Siberia], published by the Solidarity Interfactory Structure, p. 82).

I took this text from a collection of accounts prepared years ago for print by Professor Jan T. Gross. When writing his book about Jedwabne, Gross skips over the description of Antoni B.'s arrest and torture, although he quotes other fragments of this account. Why?

The facts leave no room for doubt: the Jedwabne Jews, as in the entire territory occupied by the Soviets, constituted the nuts and bolts of the machinery of repression. Up to the last moment, they were delivering Polish patriots into the hands of the NKVD* and preparing the next deportation transports to Siberia.

The responsibility of historians

Does this mean that Poles burned 1,500 Jedwabne Jews in the barn as revenge? Certain accounts by surviving Jews indicate precisely this. At the same time, however, we know that the German *Einsatzgruppe* *B* was active in this area, carrying out murderous raids on Jews in the surrounding towns. We also know that some sort of formation, called "the Gestapo" by Wasersztajn, was in Jedwabne that fateful day, that the Germans had at their disposal the kerosene used to set the barn ablaze, that German sentries were on duty around the town the whole time, and, to top it off, that a German newsreel team was brought in to document the crime and that the German *gendarmerie* supervised the burial of the corpses. There even exists a description of the course of events, which Gross arbitrarily deems it false: "on the critical day the German *gendarmerie* went with the Mayor and Secretary Wasilewski at their head around the houses, driving the men out to guard the Jews, who had already been herded onto the town square. They also came into my house and found my husband and, with strict orders and threats, gun in hand, they drove my husband out onto the square."

The estimates of the numbers of Germans vary. Gross speaks of a dozen or so *gendarmes* and a few dozen members of the Gestapo. The cook from a *gendarmerie* post, Ms. Sokołowska, testifying at the trial recalled "On the critical day there were sixty gestapo men, because I cooked dinner for them, and there were a lot of *gendarmes* because they came from other outposts." It was probably on the basis of this account that Prosecutor Monkiewicz ascertained that the slaughter was supervised by 232 German *gendarmes* who came to Jedwabne in a column of trucks.

Nevertheless, there has never been a serious inquiry to identify the Germans who planned the atrocity, gave the orders, supervised their execution, and filmed it. The involvement of Poles, although shocking, is definitely not equivalent to the involvement of Jewish police who murdered their fellow Jews in the ghettos, delivered them into the hands of their executioners, and drove them onto the *Umschlagplatz*.* Those who, instead of establishing facts, join in the campaign against the Polish nation by trying to shoulder Poles with blame for the Holocaust under German occupation while "forgetting" that the real perpetrators were the Germans, bring shame upon the profession of historian. Prof. Strzembosz's article restores honor to Polish historians, who previously maintained a cowardly silence in the face of the campaign against Poland and the Poles. I would like to believe that there are also Righteous Ones among the Jews, who have not succumbed to the pressure of the pervasive hatred toward Poland.

Antoni Macierewicz

Zdzisław Krasnodębski

In Darkest Jedwabne

"Znak" February 2001

Jan Tomasz Gross describes the crime that was committed against 1,640 Jewish inhabitants during the war by the Poles of the small town of Jedwabne. Some Jews were beaten or knifed to death; the majority were herded into a barn and burnt alive. The author, relying on documents and accounts of witnesses, carries out a detailed reconstruction of the bloody events. Gross himself captures perfectly the feelings that come from reading this book: "*The murder carried out against the Jews in Jedwabne invokes feelings of helplessness and stupefaction.*" These sentiments result in the fact that even the desire for revenge becomes understandable, which Rabbi Julius L. Baker expresses in the *Jedwabne Yitzkor Book* [Town Memory Book]: "May God revenge their blood"—understandable even when you yourself believe in a God of forgiveness and love.

At the same time, Gross reveals the postwar history of deception about this crime—officially ascribed to the Germans, as it is to this very day in the official inscription on the local monument. In the *Nowa Encyklopedia Powszechna* [New Universal Encyclopedia; 1996], it is possible to read that: "during the Second World War the Germans murdered over 1,600 people in Jedwabne, including around 900 Jews burnt alive."

This is a significant book, one that is painful for the Polish reader despite the fact that, as Professor Tomasz Szarota shows, it leaves open certain questions relating to the details of the massacre. It refutes definitively the comfortable and calming conviction that Poles were only witnesses, that they were never responsible for the crime committed against Jews during the Second World War. This book also invokes more general reflections, and not by accident, as in Gross's previous book *Upiorna dekada* [The Ghastly Decade*]. *Neighbors* is not only the work of a historian, but also a morality play calling for reflection and a coming to terms with our consciences.

It is impossible to avoid asking why this book affects the Polish reader to the core when, for example, Christopher Browning's *Ordinary Men. Reserve Police Battalion 101 and the Final Solution in Poland*, which reveals equally appalling facts, can be read with much more distance. The answer is simple. *Neighbors* invokes the national identity of the reader.

Of course, I can always ask: What has that got to do with me? What do I have in common with Jerzy Laudański, one of the murderers from Jedwabne? The fact that I was born in the same country, use the same language, and grew up in a culture that was to some extent the same—but which I did not choose? If the radical liberals are right in saying that everything is subject to free choice and that it is possible to distance oneself as much as one wants from the national community and the national culture, then I should haven't any problem with this. In this regard, taking the blame, wrongdoing, and obligations are only individual.

In the case of the Jedwabne crime, it is apparent that this is not so. Without the existence of national ties that defy rational analysis, it would be impossible to explain why my attitude to such an incident is different from when I read about crimes committed by, let us say, Lithuanians, Latvians, Ukrainians, or the Germans amongst whom I have lived for ten years and whose culture I have been dealing with for much longer. Nor is it of any help knowing the theory that the nation is only a construct of intellectuals. Even if I were to repudiate such ties, those who belong to other national communities would not believe me. The more I try to deny this, the more I confirm it, as well as my own co-responsibility. When it is said that Poles have done something, this carries over onto me, identified as a Pole, even if an exception were to be made for me.

In contrast to many contemporary Polish writers, Gross refers to the category of collective responsibility and the individual as a collective subject. He writes, among other things: "*When reflecting about this epoch, we must remember that there is no such thing as collective responsibility and that only the murderer is responsible for murder. But there is an insistent need for reflection on what it is that makes us—us as members of a collective that has a separate subjectivity and to which we belong because we feel ourselves to be part of this community—capable of such deeds. As a collective unified by an authentically experienced spiritual bond, which entitles us to a sense of a community of fates—I have in mind national pride and a sense of identity rooted in the historical experience of many generations—are we not likewise responsible for the shameful deeds of our forebears and countrymen?*" [so runs the Polish edition; the corresponding passage of the American edition is provided in a note, since some subtle differences in Gross's formulation of the issues at hand may be found—trans.][1]

It is certainly possible to seek other ways of dealing with this problem. It is possible to negate the facts or lessen them. It is possible symbolically to exclude those responsible from one's group. After all, there are criminals and thugs amongst Poles but their behavior does not testify to the entire national collective. (In this case, however, exclusion is unusually difficult. The genocide in Jedwabne was a collective crime in which all of the small town as it were took part or were at least in passive attendance). In the end, it is not possible to avoid confrontation with this issue. Gross stresses that a painful period of settling accounts is starting in Poland. He writes of the

---

[1] "*When reflecting about this epoch, we must not assign collective responsibility. We must be clearheaded enough to remember that for each killing only a specific murderer or group of murderers is responsible. But we nevertheless might be compelled to investigate what makes a nation (as in "the Germans") capable of carrying out such deeds... if people are indeed boded together by authentic spiritual affinity— I have in mind a kind of national pride rooted in common historical experiences of many generations—are they not somehow responsible also for horrible deeds perpetrated by members of such an 'imagined community'?*" (*Neighbors*, pp. 134–135).

young people in Jedwabne who made a step towards truth by placing information about this crime on the school Internet site, though without naming the perpetrators: "*You have to take your hat off to the young, for a very difficult task waits for them in coming face to face with the crime of their own grandparents' generation*" [the American edition omits any reference to this initiative, which Gross describes as "a step in the direction of truth" in the Polish edition, p. 115—trans.]. In fact, the hope remains that these young people won't say to themselves: Let's choose the future,* let's not worry about secondary matters since we face such important tasks as the economic development of the region, our career, or the integration of Europe.

Relatives wait for the memory of the victims to be restored. In the introduction to the *Jedwabne Yitzkor Book*, Rabbi Jacob Eliezer Baker writes: "Indeed, the murderers did not only humiliate and butcher their victims; they wanted also to blot out their memory. They slaughtered them twice, reducing them in Yedwabne literally into ashes, and then trying to deny their deed. Not to remember our martyrs would mean to become accomplices to the design of their murderers." From the victims' point of view, the denial of memory is to conspire in lies and even to take a symbolic part in the crime itself. He who does not wish to be among the perpetrators should demand the truth.

The matter of the atrocity in Jedwabne calls, however, for a certain wider reflection. I think that one of the principal problems in restoring memory and a sense of responsibility in Poland stems from the fact that the average citizen received and continues to receive conflicting signals from the political and intellectual elites. On the one hand, they say: let's remember what happened during the war; let's remember the dark sides of our national fate and deeds. On the other hand, in the meantime, they announce that democracy involves forgetting, and that in the case of the communist past we shouldn't be too inquisitive or too moralistic.

So I must on the one hand accept partial responsibility as a Pole for nationalist and chauvinist excesses, law-breaking, and crimes—while on the other hand I am told that no one, none of the political parties, no group, and no individual will be responsible for the communist system and for particular deeds committed under it. On the one hand, I am told that I must look the uncomfortable, painful truth in the eye, and on the other that I must accept that everything is an interpretation, that there are various truths.

One of the most brilliant Polish intellectuals, Marcin Król, wrote in his book, *Liberalizm strachu czy liberalizm odwagi* [The Liberalism of Fear or the Liberalism of Courage]: "The controversy about these issues [the memory of the former communist system and the eventual consequences that should ensue from the crimes and injustices remembered] is a controversy that, regardless of its meaning, has an undemocratic nature because memory cannot be fully democratic and there is no question of justice or of equal treatment of all those who deserve to be remembered. Therefore in fact, and not for moral reasons, moderate forgetting is highly conducive to the building of a liberal-democratic society." What sort of forgetting is moderate? Can it relate to crimes such as those in Jedwabne? Is that memory "fully democratic"? Should the act of forgetting only entail crimes and lawlessness committed in the name of reason, progress, emancipation, the workers' movement, and social justice?

In fact, such wrongs become more anonymous with the passage of time, since there is no well-defined collective entity to which to ascribe their legacy. The easiest thing would be to say that the victims of communism were simply victims of history. Not only are the victims anonymous, but it also transpires that no one is responsible. Poles did not become post-Poles, but communists became post-communists, and the past can be treated as a closed book. The post-communists do not inherit any blame or responsibility in a cultural or moral sense, and do not have anything on their conscience. It thus turns out, paradoxically, that voluntary participation in a totalitarian movement is not associated today with any moral or political consequences or responsibilities, while belonging to a national community by reason of birth is all the more so associated with such consequences. The Polish President, Aleksander Kwaśniewski, encapsulated this splendidly when, in a speech marking the thirtieth anniversary of the March 1968 events,* he spoke of the responsibility of the Poles for expelling Jews from the country, but not about the responsibility of the PZPR* and its members.

At times, it appears that the memory of the nation's wrongdoing has not only serve in the fight against nationalism, but also serve in the dismantling of thinking in the categories of the nation [nation meaning "people," in the sense of "the Polish nation"—ed.] itself, and the dissolution of national ties. It appears that only when we dispense with these categories will we be inoculated forever—that we will have a guarantee that ethnic cleansing and genocide will not be repeated. The German Left once reasoned this way. The Germans had to remember about national-socialist crimes in order to stop being Germans. This was not only an ambiguous stance in moral terms, but also a contradictory one. It turned out that the nation was absolutely essential for expiation. It needed to be retained at least as a *Schamgemeinschaft*, a community of disgrace. Nor was this a realistic position, for, as we know, the Germans, too, failed to become post-Germans. Today it is said officially that in Germany the crimes of National Socialism were committed "in the name of Germany" (*"im deutschen Namen"*), rather than simply coming out and saying that Germans perpetrated these crimes. The genocide in Jedwabne was perpetrated by the Polish inhabitants of this small town. In whose name?

This question appears to me to be rather important in deliberations on the theme of responsibility. Jan T. Gross notes that the Jews have even greater resentment towards Poles than towards Germans—because the former murdered not in uniform, not as agents of the state, but of their own free will, out of their own private initiative: *"And if in collective Jewish memory this phenomenon is ingrained—that local Polish people killed the Jews because they wanted to, not because they had to—then Jews will hold them particularly responsible for what they have done. A murderer in uniform remains a state functionary acting under orders, and he might even be presumed to have mental reservations about what he has been ordered to do. Not so a civilian, killing another human being of his own free will—such an evildoer is unequivocally but a murderer."* This is true. On the other hand, however, this civilian to a greater extent represents only

221

himself, and not the collective to which he belongs, the nation or state.

It would be difficult, therefore, to argue that the crime in Jedwabne was committed in the name of Poland or that it was an expression of the political will of the Poles. In principle, its motives were, as Gross stresses, pre-political and pre-ideological. The Germans in uniform represented the German state which was governed by the National Socialists, who were elected and supported by the majority of the German nation. The German nation accepted and carried out Hitler's policies, knew its criminal intentions, and was in a position at least to suspect that they were being consistently carried out. From this point of view, their responsibility as a collective—it was the Germans who planned and carried out the Holocaust—has a completely different quality and dimension, notwithstanding the number of helpers they may have had from among other nationalities. It appears that the descendants of the victims should also understand this fundamental difference.

This does not mean that we should be able to forget about our responsibility stemming from facts such as those of the crime in Jedwabne. Gross's book reminds us of the need to redress this responsibility, and of the obligations that flow from the deeds of our fathers and grandfathers. After the things that happened, we have a particular moral and political responsibility to our compatriots of Jewish origin, to Polish Jews and Jews in general. It is not only the Poles from Kazakhstan* to whom we owe a debt, but all those Polish Jews for whom Poland once failed to become a homeland. This book also reminds us of the need for truth in community life. Gross is right to say: "*And if at some point in this collective biography lies are situated* [in the American edition: "a big lie is situated"—trans.], *then everything that comes afterward will be devoid of authenticity, underlain with anxiety and a lack of self-confidence* [in the American edition: "...authenticity and laced with fear of discovery"—trans.]. That is also why the search for truth about that period, as well as determining and condemning the guilty, lies in our own interests. I am convinced in any case that if Poland had become democratic after 1945, all the perpetrators of this and other similar crimes would have met with the appropriate punishment.

In evaluating the importance of Gross's book, I cannot fail to mention certain doubts which its explicatory layer raises. This is because, aside from the narration of events, the author has yet another aim in mind, which to my mind is completely unnecessary. Namely, just as in his book *The Ghastly Decade*,* he seeks to dismiss the widespread conviction that among the circumstances that may have contributed to exacerbated ethnic hatred and, indirectly, to the massacre, were events from the period of Soviet occupation. The crime in Jedwabne is presented as an inexplicable explosion of dark forces, as a mystery play, as an epiphany of evil. The perpetrators were a dark and benighted force that was unleashed. The pogrom was an incident that seemed to emerge from the shadows of ancient annals. As Gross writes, "*the murder of Jedwabne Jews reveals yet another, deeper, more archaic layer of this enterprise* [the Shoah]." It could be said that this is an incident beyond history, having nothing in common with that which occurred before or after. In principle, it could have occurred at any time. This is how Rabbi Jacob L. Baker presents it. According to him, the crime represented only the surfacing of permanent attitudes: "We are convinced that during the centuries of its existence, Jewish Yedwabne had to face the same kind of rough, inhuman neighbors." The life of the Jewish community in Jedwabne, therefore, was the life of a small group of honorable people among wolves, in constant danger of death.

So as to refute the assumption that it was the Soviet occupation that dug the abyss between the Poles and Jews, Gross points out that in Jedwabne there was no over-representation of Jews in the organs of authority at that time. On the basis of this, he draws the following conclusion: "*[T]here is no reason to single out Jedwabne as a place where relationships between Jews and the rest of the population during those twenty months of Soviet rule were more antagonistic than anywhere else.*" But could they perhaps have been equally bad everywhere? Could the years 1939–1941 have caused such an escalation of enmity and hatred that German consent sufficed for it to end up in a bloody settlement of accounts? No doubt the religious and ethnic enmity at that time played a huge role. One of the Jewish inhabitants of Jedwabne recalls, for example, that only the intervention of the Łomża archbishop saved the Jedwabne Jews from a pogrom at the hands of Haller's army.* It is also characteristic that one of the Jedwabne Jews who converted to Christianity survived, and still lived peacefully in Jedwabne long after the war. It is impossible to fail to notice that the Jedwabne crime fits in with other, similar events that were acts of revenge for Soviet policy. After the invasion by the *Wehrmacht* of territory seized by the Soviet Union in 1939 and the discovery of the NKVD* crimes, anti-Jewish excesses and pogroms occurred in many places. Bogdan Musiał describes them in a book, published this year, about the situation in the eastern lands before the German-Russian war and after it broke out.[2]

Is it therefore really possible to understand those incidents while passing over the years 1939–1941? It is, at any rate, a fact that the motive of settling accounts with the communists was always present in the Jedwabne horror. After all, it is hardly a matter of chance that the Jews were ordered to dismantle and carry a monument to Lenin. Those who survived the pogrom also recall these motives. One remembers: "When Poles saw the oncoming German army they came to the Germans with flowers and shouted 'Heil Hitler, our savior. Down with communism!' They destroyed an enormous stand built by the Russians at the town square. The Poles began forming their government, elected a mayor, town clerk and police. They immediately arranged for all Jews who had collaborated with the Russians to be taken to the town office where they were severely beaten, then let go." As is known, the *Wehrmacht* entered Jedwabne the first time in 1939. Did the Polish people already then greet them with joy? It is certain that only the experience of the Soviet occupation gave them the illusion that the *Wehrmacht* brings liberation.

[2] Bogdan Musiał, *"Kontrrevolutionäre Elemente sind zu erschießen." Die Brutalisierung des deutsch-sowjetischen Krieges im Sommer 1941* ["Counterrevolutionary Elements Must Be Shot." The Brutalization of the German-Soviet War in Summer 1941], Berlin–Munich, 2000.

Rywka Fogel recalls that in the case of Karolak, the Mayor of Jedwabne and a known anti-Semite: "The Germans allowed him to murder only communists. At this time all Jews were considered communists, with the exception of the tradesmen who the Germans needed in their workshops." The Polish population was certainly influenced by German propaganda which ascribed Soviet crimes to "Jewish communism."* Perhaps the ringleaders were only looking for a scapegoat and exploited this pretext in order to settle accounts. But it is highly probable that in the years 1939–1941, not without any real reasons, they aggravated or deepened the abyss between the Polish and Jewish population. This division could probably only have occurred because the Jews, weakly integrated with the Poles, reacted in a different way to the Soviet occupation, treating it simply as still another change of state allegiance, and rather quickly adapted to the situation. This, however, could have been interpreted by Poles as a lack of loyalty or as outright treason. A fact testifying to the role played by the issue of loyalty in Jedwabne was that, despite the complete breakdown of the moral order, Poles wanted to spare the life of a Jedwabne Jew who had saved the life of a Polish officer.

The Jewish population was treated differently by the Soviets than the Poles, though, as we know, the Jews also fell victim to deportation and other repressive measures. Herschel Piekarz Baker, describing the years 1939–1941, maintains that the Jedwabne Jewish population quickly adapted to the new conditions: "It was difficult to comply with the regulations of the communist government. In a short period of time, however, the Jewish community organized itself so as to supply everyday articles that were needed. They baked bread and opened cooperatives, run mainly by Jews. Jews were hired in various positions and institutions. Jewish tradesmen continued their work in shops whose owner was the state, not as before, in their own shops. Earnings were low but the situation was calm. Men who were stronger physically, aged 20–38, were taken into the Russian army."

The Germans, not the Soviets, were a mortal danger to the Jews. The Soviets were the opposite, a guarantee of safety. The author quoted above remembers the following incident: "When the Russians were retreating, Poles plundered the clothing, footwear and food cooperatives as well as robbing Jewish homes. A Russian patrol walked the streets and shot at the looters. Several were killed but the majority ran off with the plundered goods." This incident characterizes the mood of the people and was certainly widely known, also to those responsible for the Jedwabne crime. I must admit that I don't understand why Gross does not refer to these accounts. In a footnote he marks, however, a remark by another Jedwabne resident, Janek Neumark, to the effect that the Soviets confiscated private property and arrested many Jews. There exist many testimonies as well as historical works confirming that the positive attitude of the Jewish population to the new authorities was no exception.[3]

The fact that Gross formulates conclusions of a most general nature in relation to totalitarian and communist regimes based on his Jedwabne research raises even more doubts. He maintains, for instance, that "*Stalinism or Nazism aimed at winning over and keeping power by playing on low instincts; they depended on... exploiting the evil that lies within man*" [this observation from the Polish edition is missing from the American one—trans.]. This is true—but even worse, they also exploited the good that lies within man. Gross suggests that the anti-Semites are to a large extent responsible for communism: "*anti-Semites rather then Jews were instrumental in establishing the Communist regime in Poland... it was indigenous lumpenproletariat rather than Jews who served as the social backbone of Stalinism in Poland.*" It probably was the *lumpenproletariat* that prevailed numerically among those supporting communism. Yet it was not the *lumpenproletariat* that invented this system, introduced it, legitimized it, and managed it. Communist activists introduced and managed it whilst progressive intellectuals legitimized it. Blaming the anti-Semitic *lumpenproletariat* for communism would simply be a falsification of history.

---

[3] Ben-Cion Pinchuk writes about this in *Shtetl Jews under Soviet Rule. Eastern Poland on the Eve of the Holocaust* (Oxford, 1990). The picture that emerges from his description is different from that which Gross presented in *The Ghastly Decade*. See also, for example, Jeff Schatz, *The Generation. The Rise and Fall of the Jewish Communists of Poland* (Berkeley, 1991), as well as Aleksander Wat, *Mój wiek. Rozmowy z Czesławem Miłoszem* (London, 1981), vol. 2.

Among communists and progressive intellectuals supporting communism there were also Polish Jews and Poles of Jewish origin. The argument that communism was unusually attractive to many people wishing to escape from traditional Jewish culture, from the Shtetl, has nothing to do with anti-Jewish ill will. Intellectuals such as Aleksander Wat or Julian Stryjkowski[4], who themselves succumbed for a time to this illusion, repeatedly wrote about it in Polish literature. After the war, furthermore, many Jews and Poles of Jewish origin became communists because of their experience during the occupation. It is possible to demonstrate this, for example, through hundreds of biographies. It is therefore difficult to maintain that this is only a matter of stereotypes or prejudices. Many of these people were driven, for understandable reasons, by a deep aversion not only to the Germans[5] but also to Poles, and especially Poles with right-wing views.

The view that communism was, by all accounts, mainly the work of Jews is an anti-Semitic stereotype and does not deserve to be considered. Yet is it possible to remain silent about communism and the positive attitude to it that appeared amongst the Jewish population when investigating this period? If we justifiably speak of the false perception among Poles that identifies all Jews as sympathizers with Soviet authority, then can't we at the same time admit that the viewing of the communist authorities in a positive light by a significant section of the Jewish population was a mistake fraught with tragic consequences? Can we not admit that this could also have

---

[4] Stryjkowski characterizes the attitude of the hero of *Wielki strach*: "Artur cannot think in general whether this Lwów will be Polish or not Polish. This doesn't concern him at all, for him the most important thing is whether there will be communism or whether there won't be communism. I continually stress that a Jew who becomes a communist ceases to be a Jew" (in: Jacek Trznadel, *Hańba domowa* [Warsaw, 1996], p. 239). The attractiveness of communism appeared even in America in the 1950s, as noted by Peter Novick in his famous *The Holocaust in American Life* (Boston-New York, 1999), p. 92.

[5] John Sack described certain instances in *An Eye for an Eye* (New York, 1993). This book triggered numerous controversies and the author encountered a great deal of unpleasantness although, as far as I know, no one has denied his facts.

been one of the causes of the dissension and growth of ethnic hatred
—despite the fact that a large section of the Polish population,
including the intelligentsia, also quickly accepted the new regime
and were inclined to collaborate with it?

I am convinced that, when speaking of the Holocaust, true reconciliation and "overcoming the past" will be possible only when, while
demanding commemoration and justice for the victims, we will no
longer be able to remain silent about the complicated motives, about
the various behaviors and attitudes of the Jews in *The Ghastly
Decade*.* Only then will we manage to convince everyone that the
issue is the truth, rather than selective interpretation, manipulation
for short-term political goals, or an appeal to nationalistic arguments. Only then will we truly leave the past behind. Unfortunately,
silence and resentment are still obstacles. There is, however, one
consolation: despite all differences we are in agreement that nothing
can justify crimes like the one perpetrated in Jedwabne, and that the
truth should be revealed and the guilty punished severely. I am
convinced that, if Poland had become a free and democratic country
in 1945, this would already have been done and, today, we would be
able to read Jan T. Gross's book in a different light.

Zdzisław Krasnodębski

STEFAN WILKANOWICZ

A FEW REFLECTIONS ON
RESPONSIBILITY AND PATRIOTISM

"ZNAK" FEBRUARY 2001

It is good that Zdzisław Krasnodębski has clearly posed the issue of grandchildren's responsibility for their grandparents and the responsibility of the nation for smaller or bigger groups belonging to it. Krasnodębski has also made it clear that there are contradictions within this emotionally painful problem.

In discussions about the massacre in Jedwabne (and in other discussions about the Holocaust), a constantly recurring theme is responsibility—not collective responsibility by any means, but nevertheless a responsibility that somehow extends to various communities, be they local or national. We cannot, of course, speak about any legal responsibility for the sins of the forebears (unless we have profited from their sins, at the cost of someone else). Nor do we bear any direct moral responsibility—the fault is not ours.

But we must ask ourselves a question: what sort of links bind us to our ancestors?

For me, it is gratitude and solidarity that are in play here. Gratitude for the valuable things that have been passed on to us, for equipping us with different types of tangible and intangible goods. But there is also the conviction that the evil they have done must be made up for in some way, even if this is to be a symbolic way of naming the tragedy and expressing regret for it. At times, material compensation is also needed. We do not hesitate to demand compensations from contemporary Germans who, after all, are not guilty of Hitler's crimes. And far from making money on those crimes, on the contrary, they suffered enormous losses, and the madman would surely have destroyed them if he could, for they proved to be unworthy of him.

This particular responsibility for our ancestors has yet another dimension, a metaphysical or spiritual one, because the catastrophe of the evil cries out for good, and requires some sort of answer even if it is hard to speak of making up for the evil.

Christianity goes even further. We all are bound by spiritual ties and that is why we pray for each other, why we pray for those who have passed away and for those who are to come. We pray for those who died long ago and for those who are to be born centuries hence. We pray because time does not exist for God, and our deeds and prayers form a spiritual capital that He "distributes" according to His wisdom and love.

We can make up different theories regarding relations between people but we are bound to each other whether we like it or not, and whether we know it or not. We help or harm each other even when we know nothing about each other.

This solidarity with our ancestors is connected with something else—with our solidarity with those who will come after us. We want to pass on to them all the best of what we have, and warn them against the dangers that could threaten them. This is why we must examine the evil that has been done, because they will need knowledge about it in order to be able to avoid it. That is why we voluntarily do penance for the sins of our ancestors, so that we can leave our successors with a sense of responsibility and a response to evil, a response that offers hope.

We love our grandchildren, and that is why we feel responsible for our grandparents.

Pondering over attitudes of those Jews who welcomed the Red Army units with bread and salt we do not forget about those who greeted German units the same way—for they saw them as their salvation from an evil that seemed absolute to them. Metropolitan Bishop Szeptycki* wrote to Pius XII that he could not image a greater evil than the Bolshevism, and that is why he treated the Germans as saviors. It took a few months for him to become convinced that the saviors were even worse.

We understand such an attitude, but we draw from it a somewhat different moral than the usual one. Namely, that we have an obligation to absorb and pass on even the most uncomfortable and challenging information. This is a general obligation that stems not only from our self-interest properly understood, but also from a sense of responsibility and solidarity with others. This applies particularly to teachers and journalists, who cannot confine themselves to simply conveying information but must also, in the old-fashioned way, inculcate wisdom—even if they do not receive the appropriate gratification for doing so.

In our civilization, the degree of ever-widening interdependence is constantly growing, while at the same time it is becoming more fragile and more vulnerable to perturbation. Today, the "man in the street" has far more ways of doing harm to even the whole of humankind than our ancestors had of doing harm to their village. Let me only mention terrorists of various stripes, and even more so the hackers and designers of computer viruses—today we cannot even imagine the future impact of their deliberate acts or spontaneous stunts. This civilization is in an ever-greater need of a sense of responsibility and solidarity, of more and more knowledge, of psychological health and the skills of cooperation. Today's patriotism should be at once local, national, and global.

It looks as if love of one's neighbor—even a very distant neighbor —has become a patriotic obligation. It is also an expression of sensible self-interest.

We will probably never learn the whole truth about what happened in Jedwabne. We will learn about various circumstances that are more or less important, that favor now one view and now the other, that make our judgments now softer and now harsher. But none of this will change my basic opinion that what happened in Jedwabne demands some sort of reply, some manifestation of the good, and that it must be a reply that cries out loud enough to be heard everywhere. I do not know what it should be, but I know that it should be both local and nationwide. Young people in Jedwabne have already made a first step. What will the next steps be?

I am reminded of a young girl of eighteen who came to Auschwitz years ago with the *Aktion Sühnenzeichen** group to work and pray at the site of the concentration camp in order to do penance for the crimes of the Germans. When her father learned about her intentions, he slapped her in the face. Yet she came to Auschwitz in spite of his reaction. Could this have been because she loved her father? Could she have been thinking about her future children?

Stefan Wilkanowicz

JERZY JEDLICKI

HOW TO DEAL WITH THIS

"POLITYKA" FEBRUARY 10, 2001

1. The book *Neighbors* by Jan T. Gross has inspired heated debates and disputes. Its publisher, *Fundacja Pogranicze*, planned its circulation poorly: the book sold out just when sales peaked. No wonder. It speaks of an event that is quite incredible: about how, on one summer day in 1941, supervised by German occupation troops, the Polish residents of a certain little town outside of Łomża murdered over a thousand of their Jewish neighbors, showing unusual cruelty and not sparing a soul. It also speaks of how reports of the event were silenced for over sixty years.

It would be rather strange if the book aroused no emotions. This, however, is not the first time we have seen such excitement. One need only recall the agitation spurred by the publication in *Tygodnik Powszechny* in 1987 of the article "Poor Poles Look at the Ghetto"* by Jan Błoński, the publication in *Gazeta Wyborcza* several years later of an article by Michał Cichy* on the killings of Jews during the Warsaw Uprising, or the film *Shoah* by Claude Lanzmann. Every time someone presents the public with texts or images casting a shadow on the Polish treatment of Jews under the German occupation, a wide range of emotions springs back to life. Some experience pangs of conscience and shame, while others claim fabrication or even libel, and still others cite mitigating circumstances that reduce the guilt or portray the incidents as only marginally significant. Despite the time that has elapsed, there is perhaps no other historical issue in Poland that plays so powerfully on hidden sensitivities and resentments. Magazine editors know what huge volumes of emotionally charged mail they receive after publishing such articles.

Why is this so? The responses certainly go beyond disputes over facts. It is noteworthy that some information, including the history of pogroms in the Łomża Province, has remained hidden in archives for a long time—this in itself is something to think about—yet there is little that can surprise the professional historians of the period. The volume of scholarly writing on the German occupation in Poland has been growing exponentially. The only differences in opinion among historians concern minor details. The real barrier is being erected between the body of well-evidenced historical knowledge and popular beliefs formed by the passing of available information through a thick filter of preconceived notions, prejudices and personal recollections. Some items of information never make it through the filter, while many of those that do are rejected as contradicting generally accepted opinions.

Bookstores have offered many titles that should shatter public opinion or at least inspire serious reflection. The first one of them is *Stosunki polsko-żydowskie w czasie drugiej wojny światowej* [Polish-Jewish Relations During World War II] by Emanuel Ringelblum, a leading Jewish historian and founder of the Warsaw Ghetto Archive, who managed to complete the book in 1944 in a Grójecka Street shelter before he died with all its inhabitants as the result of being informed on. Marked with an admirable care for fairness, the book took many years to pass through the barbed wire entanglements of censorship. Professor Artur Eisenbach finally published it in 1988, but it did not make much of a splash. A 1992 collection of articles by Krystyna Kersten entitled *Polacy — Żydzi — komunizm: anatomia półprawd 1939–68* [The Poles—the Jews—Communism: An Anatomy of Half-Truths. 1939–1968] attracted more attention. The collection did not touch directly on the Holocaust but rather confronted documented knowledge with stereotypes deeply rooted on both sides. Then came a series of publications analyzing images of the Holocaust and accompanying events retained in the memories of survivors and external witnesses, as well as how such memories turned into the collective "recollections" of entire communities, or coagulating into those communities' versions of history. *Zagłada i pamięć* [The Holocaust and Memory] by Barbara Engelking (1994) and *Pamięć żydowska — pamięć polska* [Jewish Memory—Polish Memory] the proceedings of a colloquium, published by the French Institute of Cracow (1996), are two examples of publications that went practically unnoticed by the press and the public.

We are still waiting for the release of the serious and unbiased book *Bondage to the Dead: Poland and the Memory of the Holocaust* by Michael Steinlauf. Meanwhile, the collection of articles by Feliks Tych, *Długi cień Zagłady* [The Long Shadow of the Holocaust] published in 1999 by the Jewish Historical Institute* and exploring the same regions of Polish memory, historical consciousness and educational stereotypes, has also failed to stir interest so far. The thin volume *Upiorna dekada: trzy eseje o stereotypach na temat Żydów, Polaków, Niemców i komunistów 1939–1948* [The Ghastly Decade: Three Essays on Stereotypes Concerning the Jews, the Poles and the Communists. 1939–1948] by Jan Tomasz Gross, which preceded *Neighbors* by two years, fared better. It was noticed by *Gazeta Wyborcza*, while *Więź*, invaluable in its sensitivity to such issues, discussed it at some length. Nevertheless, the reception of this book gave no indication of the way that *Neighbors* would be talked about.

I refer to these books because the portion of source and interpretative materials contained in these and other titles already suffice to make us ask whether the time has come for a reassessment of the received views on the wartime deeds of certain Polish circles. No such reassessment, however, has yet been performed. It took a blow as powerful as the news of what happened in Jedwabne to break through our defensive walls and stir the garrison of the Polish stronghold. It is still too early to predict how successful this breach of the wall will be (for it was not the first such breach to be opened). Not to be ruled out is a scenario in which, after an exchange of arguments, each side sticks to its own version of the truth, the well-entrenched convictions in which it has invested too much faith and emotion to now call them into doubt.

2. As it is, we have several thousand "Righteous among the Nations," and probably several times as many who deserved that tile, if only they had lived long enough or if someone had remembered them. Considering that the punishment for hiding a Jew in Poland was death, the merits of those who took the risk are all the larger and more praiseworthy. It is fortunate that their valor has been commemorated in collections of reports compiled by Władysław Bartoszewski and Zofia Lewinówna (theirs were the first to be published), Szymon Datner, and more recently Elżbieta Isakiewicz in *Ustna harmonijka: relacje Żydów, których uratowali od Zagłady Polacy* [The Harmonica: Reports of Jews Saved from the Holocaust by Poles], not to mention the great many diaries that convey testimony of gratitude.

The question is: Who is entitled to take pride in the rescuers' acts after all these years? After all, diaries and reports show, as is remembered well by those who lived in the General Government,* that it was not only the Jews in hiding but also their benefactors who trembled under the prying eyes of neighbors, the inquisitive gaze of janitors, store-keepers, and passers-by.... If there had only been the Gestapo, how much easier it would have been to survive in hiding and count on a network of human solidarity, how much less need there would have been for the constant changing of hideouts.

What then counts in the general, nationwide balance sheet? Heroism or baseness? Compassion or a lack of mercy? Both count; there is no way one can subtract one from the other or offset one with the other. There will always be two separate ledgers. However, while being happy to preserve the former in our memories, we would rather forget the latter, or consider it marginal in terms of numbers and social significance. But the problem was not marginal and, even if it were, it would still cast a dark shadow over all of Polish life under the occupation. It is also difficult to forget 1968*, when a new generation of *szmalcownicy** and police agents staged a national anti-Semitic campaign that filled us and the rest of the world with the worst associations. They had the nerve to protest against the "anti-Polish" response that they provoked and to appeal to the merits of the Righteous—which also happens today.

Inconveniently for us, the things we would rather ignore or forget are known and remembered by others. We cannot have the one ledger without the other—psychological comfort is no more available to us than it is to other nations that were conquered at the time. If we are the heirs of previous generations, then there is no way around it: upon us fall both their greatness and their baseness, their honor and their disgrace.

Nevertheless, the two ledgers, that of the rescuers and that of the denouncers to the Nazis of hidden Jews, represent two small sections of society: the opposite extremes. Which one you ended up in depended more on your character than your social background. The people who put their lives and their families' on the line to save friends and strangers because they strongly believed that it was the right thing to do came from all walks of life. So did people for whom the Nazi invasion and the sea of human suffering provided an excellent opportunity to do business. Both groups lived in a social environment which, as has been said repeatedly with a mix of sorrow and reproach, was indifferent to the fate of their Jewish neighbors. Yet this is exactly the place where a question mark needs to be placed.

3. Poles were indifferent to the Jews—in a benign way, or with contemptuous indifference—as long as it was clear that the social status of the Jews ranked below that of the gentry, the Christian *bourgeoisie,* and the intelligentsia. The indifference disappeared when the Jews, at different times in the different partitions,* began to claim equal legal, and sometimes civil, rights, and then the equal treatment of their language and culture, as well. The more collective dignity they gained, the more of a nation they became (as opposed to being just followers of the Old Law), and the tenser their relations grew with Polish circles that turned out to be reluctant and, in their view, unable to support such aspirations. Added to these developments was the influence of a wave of racist anti-Semitism from the

West, which sought to block all possibilities of assimilation in the sense of integration with the surrounding people in terms of customs or, in some cases, of consciousness, to the point where any distinguishing features, often including religious denomination, vanished. The zealous champion of anti-Semitism in Poland, as is known, was the National Democracy.* However, yet dislike and even animosity toward the Jews spread to other political groups, except for those on the left, and to the Catholic Church. Shortly before the First World War, the struggle against the Jews became an obsession, garnering more coverage in the Warsaw press and stirring up more emotions than any other issue.

So it has been ever since, with fluctuating pulsations of intensity. This is not the place to describe the history of this frothing torrent or its most dramatic episodes, including the assassination of a president, the exclusion of Jews from Polish professional institutions, "ghetto benches" at the universities, and finally bloody pogroms. Nor is there any reason to idealize the Jews of Poland or anywhere else: they were as diverse as any nation, representing all possible classes and political views, they were deeply religious or completely secularized, nationalistic or totally polonized, immensely wealthy or starving to death, brilliant and primitive, full of virtues and vices. However, regardless of who they were, what they did, or why they deserved credit or condemnation, all were targets of demeaning accusations and insults from all sides, just because they had been born Jewish. The recent book *W jednym stali domu... Koncepcje rozwiązania kwestii żydowskiej w publicystyce polskiej lat 1933–1939* [Of the Same House... Concepts for Solving the Jewish Issue in Polish Publications from 1933 to 1939] by Anna Landau-Czajka provides extensive documentation of a phenomenon that today, in hindsight, seems to have been a madness that spread to a large section of the intelligentsia, the Church and public opinion.

Needless to say, none of the above was unique to Poland. One might say that, to a varying degree, nearly all of Europe fell victim of the psychological and mental pathology that, even before the war, was used in Germany (and in Austria after its annexation) to justify the totalitarian order. This, however, is little consolation. Poland was unquestionably one of the countries most affected by the obsession. Its ideological leaders never ceased developing ideas to deprive millions of Polish citizens of their rights and property and banish them from the country. The only groups to actively oppose such ideas were the socialists and communists and the liberal fraction of the intelligentsia, which explains the inclinations of assimilating Jews to seek refuge and support in these circles that did not treat them with aggression and contempt.

This, in a nutshell, is an overview of Polish-Jewish relations at the time of the Nazi Germany and the Soviet Union invasion. It would be extremely idealistic to imagine that Polish attitudes toward the Jews changed overnight just because both ended up under the oppression of the same invader. In the Soviet zone, some Jews, especially those who had suffered severely and sympathized with the left wing, had their hopes for safety and decent treatment revived. It soon turned out that the expropriations, the shutting down of places of worship, and the deportations to the East proceeded regardless of nationality. Under German rule, no one would feel safe in the face of the terror of the occupation regime from the very beginning, but it soon turned out that there were many circles in this hell, and the denizens of the better circle saw no reason at all to renounce their long-established biases against the even more severely persecuted *Untermenschen*.

In his recently published book *U progu zagłady* [On the Threshold of Destruction] which was recently discussed in *Polityka*, Tomasz Szarota presents a vast and meticulously documented panorama of "anti-Semitic incidents and pogroms in occupied Europe" in the years 1940 and 1941, from Paris to Antwerp, from the Hague and Amsterdam to Warsaw and Kaunas. The book is no less moving than Gross's. It offers copious evidence of the fact that wherever the German occupation forces attempted to instigate unrest against the Jews and demonstrate that the invaded populations were ready to volunteer for a settling of scores, they found people eager, or even overly eager, to comply. Warsaw was no exception. Such attitudes could be found both among proponents of political ideas who (mistakenly) saw their advancement by the Germans as encouragement to collaborate, and among Polish civilian "squads" for whom an opportunity to humiliate, beat and rob Jews with total impunity was a pleasure in itself.

The situation deteriorated drastically from the day when the Germans invaded the Soviet Union. Szarota presents serious evidence for the view that the decision to exterminate the Jews must have been made in Hitler's leadership clique on the eve of the invasion. At any rate, the first act of the "final solution" played itself out in the East. The entire operation was assigned to special task forces named *Einsatzgruppen.** At least in the first days of the invasion, these units were to encourage local volunteers to stage "self-cleansing" operations. Wherever they succeeded (e.g. in Kaunas), the pogroms of the summer of 1941 were extremely bloody and cruel. By all indications, Jedwabne became a part of that plan.

Regardless of how many of them were present at the scene of the crime, there is no doubt that the Germans played the role of instigators of the massacre. Historians are still arguing about how many Germans were there. The occupying forces encouraged such acts, guaranteed impunity and, most likely, provided rewards. Evidently, they found a group of eager accomplices in Łomża district who, having tasted blood once, proved impossible to restrain from an orgy of mass murder. Nor do any known reports speak of anyone in the town endeavoring to stop them.

4. The extermination of the Jews led to a fragmentation of Polish opinion in a way that did not always correspond with previous divisions. For many people, the plan carried out by the Nazi occupation regime was monstrous in its inhumanity. The response of moral protest and compassion for the victims inspired attempts to provide shelter and do all that could be done to help. In addition to thousands of individual acts, such sentiments also took the form of pleas for help voiced by some underground publications, and in particular by *Biuletyn Informacyjny.** They also led to the establishment in 1942 of the Council for Aid to the Jews, known by its code-name *Żegota.** However, a large portion of society did not share such sentiments. While the occupation forces were, of course, held to be the enemies

of Poland, what they did to the Jews did not necessarily meet with objections. If only it had been mere indifference. Unfortunately, when the Warsaw ghetto was burning, sneers at the dying or laughter and relief at the sight of this uncommon spectacle were heard in the streets of Warsaw, on trams, in stores and schools, rather than compassion or horror. I am not talking about solidarity, for solidarity could not be expressed out loud. I am talking about responses expressed among acquaintances and legitimized by a large part of the underground press, in those many clandestine newsletters where the main concern of the editors was how to cleanse Poland of Jewish survivors of the extermination, once the war was over. As we know, such ideas would be realized, some shortly after the war, some not until 1968.

The Holocaust therefore failed to bring about any dramatic transformation of Polish attitudes, although it did exacerbate existing divisions. What for some was the most dreadful event of the twentieth century remained for others an episode devoid of any greater significance. Still, even in the souls of people whose racial and religious biases are so deeply engrafted in their brain tissue that no experience will ever root them out, the Holocaust has left a certain dissonance: namely that admitting to anti-Semitism has become highly indecent anywhere in the world. All the more so, even the slightest suspicion of having supported the Nazi plan for eradicating the European Jews had to be shunned as a calumny. There thus arose a language of camouflage in which feelings and beliefs were no longer communicated directly, but in a roundabout way.

On the other hand, some people began to worry, justifiably, that Poles would be remembered in the world not for the noble courage of the Righteous but rather for the snickers of the on-lookers at Krasińskich Square [near the Warsaw ghetto—ed.] and for the howling of the Kielce* mob on July 4, 1946. It is also thought that it takes time to get over feelings and attitudes, and that such work cannot be completed when society is in the pillory. Furthermore, who has the right to make accusations? And whom can they accuse? In a word, it is better not to stir things up, but rather to wait until a new generation, with no bad memories, takes over.

Such fears are not groundless; they are familiar to any nation bearing the stigma of having participated even in part in acts which, years later, turn out to be shameful—even if they did not look that way to their perpetrators. All those defense mechanisms, those half-conscious concealments and lapses of memory are comprehensible in psychological terms, even if they defer the moment of facing up to the dark episodes in one's history. Such episodes always come to light in the end, and often catch us off guard. Could such things happen? Were Poles really capable of throwing infants into the flames? While others watched? Germans, certainly. Lithuanians, of course. Ukrainians—who would expect anything different from them? But Poles? It is far from easy to find out half a century later that no one earned a certificate of collective innocence. This is precisely the basis of infection with hatred and contempt.

We do not have to do penance for murderers and collaborators who, sixty years ago, incited by invaders, volunteered to perform a task that would horrify any normal human being. What must be noted, however, is that, along with its many noble elements, the baggage of historical tradition handed down to us also includes a moral culture that made such crimes possible and helped justify them or pass them over in silence. We will bear responsibility for what we make of our past, for how we reconcile its glory and its shame, for the way we relate it to ourselves, and for the conclusions we draw.

We are not the first in Europe and certainly not the last to go through a process of reexamining our own legends. The process is difficult for any nation, just as it is difficult and painful to review one's life story when, in the light of new experiences and values, it becomes necessary to change the way one looks at deeds from the past. It is always difficult to admit that we have failed honorably to pass some tests in our lives, and that some of our most cherished convictions have turned out to be illusions or frauds. The same is true for national history. The case of Jedwabne gives us an opportunity to undertake such work in a significant way in at least one aspect. We may, of course, continue to sidestep the issue. We may say it is too early, that reports are unclear, that there is no exact count of the murderers or the victims, that one set of archives or another still needs to be investigated. Investigation is always worthwhile; it should have been done many years ago, but it will not change a thing. The truth will not become any more pleasant than it is now, and sooner or later we are going to have to deal with it.

However, I hear yet other doubts. I hear fears that the whole controversy stirred up by Gross's book will only elicit an anti-Semitic response and that in general dragging such bad memories into the light of day will not do anyone any good, especially if imprudent generalizations are made. I do not wish to underestimate such fears. They were expressed recently by Jacek Żakowski, a journalist who can hardly be accused of bias. As it turns out, however, sleep therapy is also ineffective. The virus of anti-Semitism has crept in to infect the young generation who have no knowledge or experience of the topic but whose members respond to the appropriate signals and slogans. Let them at least know what they are talking about and what they think they believe in. It is time to start calling a spade a spade.

Then there are also, as they say, assaults from abroad meant to defame Poland's good name and its history, and Jews are playing no small role in this. So it is. Statements that do not steer clear of fabrication and slander can be read in American newspapers or heard in the Israeli *Knesset*. We no longer experience any consternation at the lawyerly practices that exploit the Holocaust in the totally worldly interests of heirs. Everyone knows that those who are accused, whether individually or collectively, think first of a defense rather than of their moral responsibility to the past.

It should be noted, however, that it is not without reason that bitter disenchantment has accumulated on the Jewish side over the years. Our own settling of accounts with our history and with our streetcar mentality are not what fuel Jewish complaints and stereotypes. On the contrary, if anything fuels them, it is the obstinate denial of Polish guilt, the refusal to admit the unpleasant parts of the Polish legacy. And finally, this is not about foreign countries, it is about being able at long last to speak openly among ourselves. This is the only way to break free of fears and complexes.

Jerzy Jedlicki

243

JAN TOMASZ GROSS

MRS. MARX'S PILLOW

"TYGODNIK POWSZECHNY" FEBRUARY 11, 2001

S aul Friedlander, an expert on the Holocaust period, ends the first volume of his study *Nazi Germany and the Jews* with a description of what must have been a typical little set piece from those times in Germany. The morning after the November 9, 1938 *Kristallnacht,* when the Nazi authorities instigated anti-Jewish pogroms across the country (it is called *"Kristallnacht"* because the broken glass from thousands of shattered shop windows literally covered the streets of German towns the next day), half a dozen battered men stood on a truck in the square of the little Mosel town of Wittlich. Among them was the butcher, Marx, whose despairing wife stood nearby, wailing hysterically and stretching her hands out towards the faces of the neighbors watching the scene from behind the closed windows of the houses surrounding the square. "Why are you tormenting us?" she cried, "Have we ever wronged you?"

More than half a century later there was an unexpected echo of her cry in Hamburg when, after delivering a lecture, Friedlander was approached by a young man who passed on a greeting from his grandmother, a resident of Wittlich. Seeing the surprised reaction of the lecturer, who had never heard of her, the young man explained that his grandmother had been Mrs. Marx's neighbor before the war. Like many other local people, she had taken over "formerly Jewish property." It so happened that she was still in the possession of a pillow that had belonged to Mrs. Marx. She kept it in the bottom of her wardrobe and, troubled by her conscience, had no idea what to do with it.

Mrs. Marx's pillow came to my mind last spring when I read an article by Jerzy Robert Nowak in the May 14, 2000 issue of *Nasz Dziennik*.* I learned from the article that my description of the homicide in Jedwabne is intended to justify Jewish efforts to obtain compensation for losses suffered during the war. This argument did not come as a surprise to me, since circles ideologically close to the *Nasz Dziennik* commentator generally and spontaneously associate Jews with money. Some time later, mass-circulation Polish newspapers started voicing anxiety over what would happen after *Neighbors* was published in English. After reading Paweł Machcewicz's December 11, 2000 article in *Rzeczpospolita*, I wondered why making a good impression abroad should be the dominant concern of an academic responsible for the education department at the Institute of National Remembrance,* which deals with teaching Polish society about its own history. Then Ryszard Bugaj, the historic leader of the Union of Labor,* reacted to the news of the tragedy of the Jedwabne Jews in a way similar to the *Nasz Dziennik* commentator. When the president of the Administrative Body of the Institute of National Remembrance, Sławomir Radoń, seconded Machcewicz's views in the January 20–21, 2001 issue of *Gazeta Wyborcza*, I realized that we were dealing with a case of basic conceptual confusion. I believe that Jan Nowak-Jeziorański drew similar conclusions from his reading. In his article "The Need for Compensation" in the January 26 *Rzeczpospolita,* he worried that "the debate (on the Jedwabne affair) is beginning to turn in the wrong direction." Therefore, I too will join in trying to untangle a few of the threads are knotted up in the articles by the above-mentioned writers, to clarify what our attitude towards Jedwabne has to do with aspects of the "formerly Jewish property" issue and the image of Poland abroad.

We should begin by stating that it was not *Neighbors*, but rather the commission of genocide in Jedwabne, that created the problems that Bugaj, Jerzy Robert Nowak or Machcewicz write about. Reading their articles, we may have the impression that the problem is not the consequences of acts committed half a century ago, but rather the texts that describe those deeds. Only through profound reflection on our own history will we be able to come to terms with the consequences of those acts. Press comments full of hand-wringing on the topic of "what others will say about us" are rather out of place: at best, they offer further testimony to the alienation of the collective Polish identity caused by the falsification of Polish-Jewish relations during the war.

I have written "further" because this is not the first such reaction of concerned Polish patriots to the persecution of the Jews in Poland. The Zionist *Opinia* wrote on July 25, 1946, that "at protest meetings after the Kielce pogrom,* Polish speakers kept repeating 'What will the foreigners think about us?' How glad we would be to hear a question that is simple but ever so sweet to our ears: 'What will our Jewish compatriots think about us?'" The point is that the foundations of a free and creative common life cannot be shored up by nervously monitoring our own reflection in the eyes of others. At best, this is a way of depriving ourselves of authenticity by somehow handing over to strangers—and why, of all people, to those American Jewish circles that are ill-disposed towards Poland?—the power to determine who we really are. It is, in fact, by our own efforts that we must reconcile our difficult history with our image of ourselves. We must understand the collective biography that bonds us through the generations. The most important thing is whether we are able to confront our own past—not what others may say about us. We will earn the respect of others, in any case, only when we stop being afraid of our own history. This is a long and time-consuming task, but there is no other way.

The question for political commentators alarmed about Jews suing "Poland," as Bugaj put it, is: Why shouldn't people settle contentious issues in court? Isn't that the Poland and the regulated international order that we were fighting for? Weren't we fed up with the lawlessness of despotic party officials and the law of the jungle, which guarantees that might makes right? The alternative is the rule of law and the settling of disputes by independent courts, according to fixed, clear, and generally accepted principles. It is an imperfect solution, but none better has yet been devised.

So let's calm down. There is nothing scandalous about people settling their disputes with the help of lawyers. We dreamed of a world where we would be under the jurisdiction of independent courts, rather than a pliant political police force. And we managed to achieve it by way of the sacrifices made by many courageous people, as well as a chain of miraculous coincidences. The fact that we can claim our rights, and strive for compensation for wrongs that until recently we had to bear in silence, is part of this joyful new reality. And because today's laws apply by their very nature to all people, irrespective of their religious denomination or social background, a Jew has the same right as any other apartment-house owner or dispossessed member of the landed gentry to go to court and try to get his own back.

Besides, it should be pointed out that it is not "the Jews" who are taking "us" to court, but concrete Jews who are suing concrete legal entities—individuals or institutions—over concrete pieces of property. Furthermore, in dealing with claims of a general nature, as for example the ownership rights of Jewish religious communities, we also know perfectly well what the point is. This, too, is a concrete matter and it is analogous to, for example, the claims of the Roman Catholic Church. In both cases, legal questions of a general nature relate to the laws and expropriation practices accepted in communist Poland by the communists—who, as we know, had a special attitude towards private property. Solutions to this aspect of social life, as implemented by the communists, surely cannot be defended to the bitter end either by the nationalist patriots from *Nasz Dziennik,** or even by politicians from the Union of Labor.*

We also remain mindful of the fact there is no analogy between Jewish claims against "Poland"—to use the emotionally loaded formulation that appears in the papers—and claims once made by the State of Israel or Jewish institutions against Germany. The reason is simple: the Polish state never instigated the murder and plunder of the Jews. This point has recently been dealt with by Jacek Kurczewski, who summed it up in a few short sentences in the newsmagazine *Wprost*. The murdering and looting of Jews by their Polish neighbors during the occupation was a spontaneous action carried out on individual initiative and was at the most, as in Jedwabne, coordinated by local authorities established under Nazi auspices.

The problem is that the seizure of Jewish property was so widespread that the scale of claims is potentially huge. ("All the local scum turned out in the streets of town," writes the outstanding diarist, Dr. Zygmunt Klukowski of Szczebrzeszyn. "Many horse-driven carts from the countryside arrived, and they all waited almost the whole day long for the moment when they could start plundering. News about some Poles behaving shamefully and looting abandoned Jewish flats was heard from different sources. Our locality will not lag behind in this respect.") Today we simply face one of the consequences of the general debasement of morality during the occupation, and there is no point in blaming Jews for the fact that the anti-Semites acted in precisely this, and no other, way.

Half a century after the end of the war, the time has come to get rid of various uncomfortable objects that became our property as a result of tragic historical circumstances that often give us no reason to feel proud. This was not property that belonged to no one, and we must be prepared to give it back. We have already made use of a good deal of the property in question, much of it is worn out, and in any case no one will ever turn up to claim a great deal of what remains in our hands. However, without a clear willingness to compensate, we will not be able to bear the burden of the seized property, even if it is no heavier than an eiderdown pillow. Simply put, after all, we are dealing here with a question of ethics, and not of accountancy.

Money cannot replace repentance. Compensation cannot be purchased. However, we should not cherish any illusions—the bill that history has written out and that we will have to pay for the moral debasement of a generation of our ancestors (those involved in homicide in different ways, even if all they did was to mock and rub their hands together while watching a tragedy of human suffering that cried out to the heavens for revenge) will come due, but we will not be able to pay it with money. We are going to have to cover ourselves in mourning and weep over the cruel fate of our Jewish fellow-citizens.

My point is that it will take spiritual evolution, and not new entries in the deed books, to deal with the heritage of the Second World War in the area of Polish-Jewish relations. The multiplication tables will not do us much good, and we are going to have to reach for the Tablets of the Ten Commandments. To cope in dignity with the past, it will be necessary to internalize the enormity of the tragedy that befell our Jewish fellow-citizens back then. It is only the lack of sympathy and mourning for those who were murdered that makes Jewish claims for the return of their plundered property, lodged by the heirs of the victims, so vexing and irritating a problem—"poor Poland," as Bugaj writes, at the mercy of Jewish attorneys from New York. Nor are our parents and grandparents blameless. Please only recall whether what they taught us about the Jews was above all melancholy and sympathetic reflection on their tragic fate, or perhaps rather some other kind of knowledge about the Jews and attitude towards the Jews.

But I am quite sure that those who finally weep over the fate of their Jewish fellow-citizens under the occupation will follow in the footsteps of the resident of Wittlich and will part with "Mrs. Marx's pillow" without a trace of regret. And if the voice of our hearts does not tell us what to do in such a situation, then we should be guided by cold analysis. The choice we face—whether to take the side of the heirs of the Polish citizens who came into possession of property by plundering and, in not a few cases, murdering their fellow citizens, or rather to take the side of the heirs of the people who were robbed and murdered (and who, it should be added, were also Polish citizens)—is not difficult.

Of course, what the world says about "us" has great importance for Poland. And although we can neither turn back the clock nor change the course of events that took place 60 years ago, we do have substantial influence on the image of Poland that people form in the perspective of the Jedwabne crime. Polish society will be judged according to its reaction to the newly acquired information about this act of genocide. And although it may sound paradoxical,

Jedwabne offers us a chance to reestablish credibility in the area of Polish-Jewish relations—provided that we accept the knowledge of this tragedy with humility and a sense of responsibility.

When the American edition of *Neighbors* comes out, almost a year will have passed since its publication in Polish—from May 2000 to April 2001. This is a very important year, as it has offered us the opportunity to consider together the case of Jedwabne, to discuss it publicly and, to some extent, to learn to live with it. We should be aware of the fact that we owe this year of consideration to the descendants and survivors of the Jedwabne Jews, who were guided by the understanding that today this case is, above all, part of Polish history, and who found my idea of publishing the book first in Poland convincing. The pain and despair caused to them by the fact that the case was hushed up for decades is something that ought to be easy for us to imagine, since we ourselves were unable to speak the truth about Katyn* out loud, or to draw the world's attention to it.

We should remember that, for Jews, the anonymity of the death of millions of their brothers and sisters is one of the most painful curses of the Holocaust, and for my interlocutors these were the people they held dearest. Neither the New York lawyer Ty Rogers, who maintains the internet site of the Jedwabne *landsmannschaft*, nor Rabbi Baker (whose real name is Piekarz), the publisher of the memorial book about Jedwabne, ever sent journalists to lie in wait for me or insisted that I publish the English-language edition of the book as quickly as possible, despite the fact that both of them had been engaged for years in the effort to increase awareness of the nightmarish fate of their loved ones.

Whether or not we have made good use of this year is not something for me to judge. The year, indeed, is not yet up, and the discussion continues, and will continue.

The immediate reaction of journalists to the news about the massacre in Jedwabne was very encouraging—I am referring chiefly to excellent reports published in *Rzeczpospolita* and *Gazeta Pomorska*, which were followed by the opening of serious, many-sided debates in *Gazeta Wyborcza, Rzeczpospolita*, and the newsmagazine *Wprost*. When I said during public appearances in the United States and Israel that the issue was not being dodged in Poland, but, quite the opposite, was being written about—with no punches pulled—in the largest-circulation newspapers, what I said was greeted at first with incredulity, and later with great respect and relief.

And that is why I would like to express the hope that we will soon hear the voice of Church authorities in the discussion on Jedwabne. In any case, it is not only words from the Church that matter here, but also actions, no matter how modest, no matter how symbolic. For instance, couldn't a special collection be announced in the churches of the Łomża diocese some Sunday for cleaning up the Jewish cemetery in Jedwabne and erecting a new monument to the victims? The eloquence of the message that such a gesture would send to the world and to Polish society is enormous. Everything else aside, some priests ought to assure today's residents of the little town of Jedwabne, themselves hardly guilty of anything, of pastoral care and support. Unfortunately it does not seem, if the January 23 article in *Wprost* is anything to go by, that the local priest will be of much help in this regard.

Looking back on the past century from the perspective of a new millennium, it should not come as any surprise to us that neighbors murder each other. We know full well that no one has a monopoly on savagery, because the list of societies where the moral brakes have failed in one set of circumstances or another is a very long one. We shall not be judged by the deeds committed by our grandfathers—some of our grandfathers—in moments when they went berserk, but rather by whether or not we have managed to discern and give a name to their bloodthirsty madness, and to make use of it for spiritual transformation. The genocide committed in Jedwabne is a challenge to us for the present day, and not merely an old bill that has suddenly fallen due. There is a great deal that we can accomplish here. It is up to us either to bear this burden and, along the way, to recover faith in ourselves and credibility "under western eyes," or to sink into a defensive gesture of confused embarrassment, deeply convinced that everyone is against us anyway.

Jan Tomasz Gross

ARCHBISHOP JÓZEF ŻYCIŃSKI

THE BANALIZATION OF BARBARITY

"WIĘŹ" MARCH 2001

When I came to Tarnów as bishop in 1990, people still remembered Otto Schimek, a *Wehrmacht* soldier in World War II who was shot for insubordination. According to the romantic version of his death, having perceived the immoral nature of the war started by the Nazis, he refused to shoot Poles and paid for this with his life.

During the martial law* period, the memory of Schimek inspired young people to protest against the violence practiced by the authorities at the time. The supposed site of Schimek's grave was visited by pilgrims from the farthest reaches of Poland who came to pay their respects to a young soldier who had valued the voice of his conscience so highly that, at a time of a total disrespect for moral principles, he was capable of drawing a clear dividing line between honor and barbarity.

At that time, there were ideas of having Schimek canonized as an example of how a strong personality can guide itself by its own conscience, even under the most difficult circumstances when human rights are being trodden underfoot. However, such plans had to be abandoned when I received files on the sentence by the court-martial that had sentenced Schimek to death. According to these files, prepared for internal *Wehrmacht* use, the reason for Schimek's death was rather more mundane than the legend would have us

THE BANALIZATION OF BARBARITY

believe. Apparently, Schimek was a rouge who broke all the rules of military discipline.

This was one of those cases, present in popular tales, of finding one just man in Sodom. Once again, it was a beautiful legend, but far removed from the reality. However, in such tales we find expression of our search for the kind of patterns of human dignity in which not even an aggressive outburst of barbarity is capable of destroying elementary human solidarity.

Godot instead of Schimek

The inhabitants of Jedwabne were unable to emulate the patterns of behavior commonly attributed to Schimek. There are no documents showing that, on that tragic day, the inhabitants tried to express fundamental solidarity with their Jewish fellow men. One can pursue never-ending discussions on the extent to which that barbaric situation was the result of Nazi provocation and to what extent it reflected the individual sentiments of the Polish inhabitants of Jedwabne, but this will not alter the fact that waiting in Jedwabne for the style of behavior attributed to the Schimek of popular legend was just like waiting for Godot.

I am inclined to believe that, on that fateful day in Jedwabne, various feelings permeated the crowd of people watching the anguished figures screaming in pain among the flames. Some of them saw the dying victims as recent supporters of Bolshevik rule, whereas others saw them as local businessmen who had enjoyed economic success until quite recently. There must also have been people whose feeling of shame was combined with a sense of fatalism in the face of relentless events over which the inhabitants of small towns have scant influence. Any attempt to establish the mathematical proportions of these feelings is doomed to failure. In any case, they would not contribute anything to a moral assessment of the situation, since it would be madness to suggest that could have existed any justification for the mass burning to death of human beings inside a barn.

Attempts at reconstructing mechanisms of crowd psychology that might mitigate the dramatic import of that situation change little, because reference to crowd psychology can be used in the attempt to excuse the most shameful behavior. The society or local community of Jedwabne was no anonymous crowd of spectators bearing grievances sparked by prior resentments and prejudices. Its cultural environment should also have been inspired by Christian ethics. Father Maksymilian Kolbe, who lived by these ethics, was able to lay down his life in Auschwitz for a fellow man who had been sentenced to death. It is true that we cannot expect the inhabitants of provincial localities to display on a day-to-day basis the kind of heroism manifested in the lives of the great saints. Yet there were reasons, in that situation, to expect a basic human solidarity that proved lacking.

At a time when many values are becoming blurred, the border between heroism and barbarity often proves difficult to establish immediately. The case of Jedwabne is a warning to all those who, claiming to be masters of relativism, would like to erase these borders. Even if establishing a dividing line between good and evil is sometimes more difficult than we think, Jedwabne is an example of moral evil in which that indifference that is explained by powerlessness leads to embarrassment and a feeling of shame.

Getting used to barbarity?

The helpless acceptance of barbarity as a means of action evokes a feeling of powerless inside us, as well as giving rise to the question: "Why is it so easy to accept and become used to primitive displays of aggression towards our fellow human beings?" This question has been asked by many people who examined the mechanisms behind the trivialization of evil. One of those who asked it, in the pages of *Słonecznik* [The Sunflower], was Simon Wiesenthal. In this book, he describes a community of petty timid conformists in the 1930s, in which the average German stifled his conscience by means of the pragmatic principle: "We have to live with Hitler somehow because millions of others are doing so. The neighbors are watching us." Looking to one's neighbors, who helped make up the mindless crowds, made it easy to silence one's conscience—at least for a while. Only after many years did "good boys" from bourgeois families admit in the hour of their death: "I wasn't born a murderer. They made a murderer out of me...." This anonymous "they" is easily identifiable with the term *man,* as used by Heidegger. It effaces the shape of the individual responsibility of those who succeeded in extolling an ideology of hatred by exploiting the convenient indifference of their immediate environment.

There are situations where psychologically easy indifference turns out to be a crime. In order to learn any lessons from the painful spread of barbarity, one must know how to place one's personal moral responsibility above the anonymous mentality of a crowd, in which moral choice is supplanted by the automatic copying of our neighbors' conformism. Barbarity can be accepted by average people who have no intention of excusing genocide or destroying humanistic culture. Wiesenthal recalls several SS-men who loved the music of Bach, Grieg and Wagner. Even SS-*Untersturmführer* Richard Rokita, well known for his sadism and cruelty, used to wipe the tears from his eyes whenever he listened to the *Funeral Tango.*

The insane plan to exterminate the Jews did not, therefore, appear out of nowhere as the product of someone's sick mind; neither was it fuelled by a disdain for the European cultural heritage. It assumed a much more subtle form, in which the supporters of insane ideas were sometimes able to appear in the role of intellectuals, quoting the words of persons of authority who were regarded as symbols of courage and engaged in a creative search for new directions. They cited not only the racist anthropology of Gobineau, but also the great works of Heidegger or Nietzsche's ideas about the *Übermensch*, whose rhetoric still fascinates many people today. The background to these peoples' ideas was supplied by broad circles of conformists who drew comfort, under the influence of facile optimism, from the fact that Hitler would do all the dirty work and then "shuffle off the stage" because the German nation was too great to entrust its long-term future to psychopaths. This background was also eked out by influential intellectual circles that created a climate in which absurdity, barbarity and sadism lost their previous significance and became capable of providing the foundations for a new world built by *Übermenschen* deprived of elementary logic and traditional morals.

Eventually, the spreading barbarity reached the inhabitants of small towns, who calmly silenced the voices of their conscience by referring to the authority of those who were acting as the ultimate experts on the subject of the Jewish question. Genocide—trivialized at a certain stage of social control—started a chain reaction that spread beyond the confines of political systems and cultural traditions. The *ad hoc* pollution of the intellectual environment by ignoring the truth and shunning moral responsibility permitted the uninhibited growth of all kinds of distortions, including the excusing of barbarity by small-town communities that had previously only read about barbarity in the papers.

Empirical anthropology

The drama of Jedwabne bears a bitter lesson of truth about mankind. It is particularly bitter for those who consider the barbarity of Nazism as nothing other than a local variety of genocide, horrifyingly alien to the commendable remainder of humanity. It transpires that the truth about human nature is much more complex. The victims of barbarous aggression can easily grow accustomed to it, and end up applying new aggression against the innocent. The spiral of evil knows no ethnic restrictions, and we cannot consider any environment to be immune to the radiation of primitivism. This bitter truth affords protection against ideological delusions whereby some people attempt to extol blood ties or cultural affinities. These values cannot be worshipped as contemporary deities because human susceptibility to evil transcends all the borders of the categories we hold dear.

Does a realization of this bitter truth have to lead to pessimism or even to relativism, in which our faith in man disintegrates? I think not. We can learn the painful truth of the entire complexity of human nature from the biblical story of King David. David, the author of the consummately poetical Psalms, was unable to follow the voice of his conscience when Bathsheba appeared in his life (2 Book of

Samuel, chapter 11). His world went haywire; in the face of a cataclysmic situation, the entire system of previously recognized values lay in ruins. The radiation of evil, assuming the form of a chain reaction, induced him to intrigues that cost Uriah, Bathsheba's husband, his life (2 Samuel 11,15–17). How many Uriahs does David have to destroy before we view David's tragedy the same way we view the tragedy of Jedwabne?

An important quality of David is that he was capable of admitting his own fault. "And David said unto Nathan, I have sinned against the Lord. And Nathan said unto David, the Lord also hath put away thy sin" (2 Samuel 12,13 ff.). What is significant is that David does not attempt to seek excuses for his deed. He does not argue that he found himself in a qualitatively new situation in which he lost his wits and his elementary sense of moral responsibility. His remark "I have sinned against the Lord" remains a clear, manly sign of moral responsibility. It liberates us from delusions according to which there are people, and perhaps entire nations, that are a pure embodiment of moral good.

In our world, good is mixed with evil—just as it was in the life of King David. However, this does not excuse us from moral responsibility, nor does it make a virtue of indifference to evil. Therefore let us not search for some imaginary historical documents that could turn the tragedy of Jedwabne into a commonplace event. Such documents cannot exist, because the death of innocent beings can never be reduced to the status of an incident.

Today, we need to pray for the victims of that massacre, displaying the spiritual solidarity that was missing at the hour when they left the land of their fathers. In the name of those who looked upon their death with indifference, we need to repeat David's words: "I have sinned against the Lord," regardless of whether any protest from the onlookers might have been efficacious in that situation.

Archbishop Józef Życiński

A ROUND-TABLE DISCUSSION

JEDWABNE—CRIME AND MEMORY

"RZECZPOSPOLITA" MARCH 3, 2001

Rzeczpospolita: The subject of our discussion is the events in Jedwabne in 1941, with all the surrounding circumstances and consequences. As a newspaper, we consider this matter very important, and we have been taking part in the public debate in Poland on this subject ever since the first publications by Professor Gross appeared. We would like to start with a straightforward question that has probably still not received a definitive answer. What really happened in Jedwabne on July 10, 1941?

Jan Tomasz Gross: I have described this matter and I think most of the historians who have spoken out on this topic do not question my basic findings. What happened in Jedwabne was genocide. It cannot be called a pogrom because it involved more than just a small group of riffraff. In fact, an enormous part of the local population took part. All day long, the Jewish population was cruelly murdered and tormented in the most refined ways, and at the end of the day all those who had not been murdered were burned alive. We cannot say exactly how many people died. The number given on the monument and in many reports is 1,600, but that is just an approximate number of victims of this terrible killing. This crime was the work of the local Polish population.

Tomasz Strzembosz: I am in a weaker position than Professor Gross because my only sources are his article, his information on the reports on which he based his book, and a group of reports I gathered from people who were in Jedwabne at the time. I am not acquainted with the records of the 1949 and 1953 court cases, and I am not acquainted with the materials of Prosecutor Monkiewicz.

As we know, eyewitness accounts are often varied and may be questioned. I do not have many of them—five—but as someone who has been collecting them for forty odd years, they seem genuine to me. Each of those people saw Germans in Jedwabne. One German took a young girl of 12, living near the town square, for a Jew and dragged her to the square. She was saved by her mother and an acquaintance. Germans were also seen on other streets. People say that they surrounded the Jews who were working on the square. They were seen clearing out Śleszyński's barn of its contents. They were also seen later, during the burning. One account even says that they acted as the perpetrators.

An atrocity by Poles or Germans?

Rzeczpospolita: Let us therefore ask: Was the massacre of the Jewish population an independent action by Poles in which the Germans only played a passive role, or was it stage-managed by the Germans themselves, who used the Poles for the actual dirty work?

Andrzej Żbikowski: Professor Strzembosz is dealing with reports obtained today, 50 years after the event. I am using mostly Jewish reports that were submitted immediately after the war in 1945 and 1946. It is worth giving some thought to their reliability. This is fundamental because, for instance, if Wasersztajn had not submitted his report, the Jedwabne atrocity might never have come to light. I took the trouble to count the number of Jewish accounts we have. The archives of the Jewish Historical Institute* have 36 reports from the area of Radziłów, Jedwabne and Łomża, concerning 19 places and written during the first two years after the war. Mass murders and the burning of Jews in barns occurred in only two places— Radziłów and Jedwabne. True, we do not know much about the authors of these accounts, but there is no evidence that these people were dishonest or politically involved in any way. They were ordinary, average people. All the reports were collected and written down in Yiddish. As far as Radziłów and Jedwabne are concerned, neither of the two main witnesses—neither Wasersztajn nor Finkelsztajn—was in the barn itself or anywhere near it, and could not have been there. The person nearest the barn in Radziłów was Finkelsztajn's wife, Chana, some 100 meters away. From that distance, she saw exactly what was happening. A dozen or so Jews survived the pogroms of Jedwabne and Radziłów. They lived together for two years afterwards. The reports of Wasersztajn and Finkelsztajn are a generalized record of these peoples' recollections, the result of their collective memory. This is, in any case, shown by the language of these accounts. Wherever they recall individual murders that they witnessed, the style of writing is sharper and more detailed. In those parts where they describe what happened in the barn, they present more generalized views. One can see that this is no eyewitness account. The same applies to the reports by Hersz Piekarz and Rywka Fogel in the *Yedwabne: History and Memorial Book.* These are important accounts, despite the fact that neither of the authors were eyewitnesses and did not see the burning barn.

Rzeczpospolita: Do the Germans appear in these reports?

Andrzej Żbikowski: No, these accounts mention no Germans. As for Radziłów, Finkelsztajn implies that the Germans herded the Jews onto the town square and then left. It seems to me that the situation was as follows: In the Białystok area, in Tykocin, Wizna and other places, the Jews were murdered mainly by Germans. There is a lot of evidence for this. Only in Jedwabne and Radziłów was the situation different. There is no doubt that the Germans were there earlier, but they left before the massacre itself.

Paweł Machcewicz: I would like to return to the general question of what we know about the events in Jedwabne and what facts we can all agree on. I also want to stress, like Prof. Strzembosz, that I, too, have never done any research on the matter. Such an investigation has now been taken up by the Institute of National Remembrance.* Perhaps they will confirm Prof. Gross's claims and permit a few corrections to be made, perhaps they will reveal new facts. In my analysis, I can base what I say on Prof. Gross's book and on articles about this book by historians.

It seems obvious that a massacre was carried out on the Jewish population in Jedwabne and that Jews died at the hands of Poles. However, what needs to be clarified is the role of the Germans. Did the Germans merely approve the deed, did they inspire it, or did they indeed participate? We know that these were not spontaneous events because there was a film crew in Jedwabne, or perhaps just a few Germans with cameras. There are a lot of different currents to which it is worth paying attention, even in the materials cited by Prof. Gross. Wasersztajn himself says at one point that the things that happened were on orders from the Germans.

Various reports contain conflicting information about the presence of Germans in Jedwabne. One of those interrogated says that there were 60 Germans there. Others also mention that the Germans helped or even drove the Poles onto the town square to make them carry out the atrocity. I think this issue must be clarified—a search of German archives should be made. And that is what the Institute of National Remembrance plans to do. It has submitted queries to these archives, asking if there is any material on the Jedwabne atrocity. We have also commenced talks with German historians, who have provided us with valuable advice, so that we might be able to say more about this topic in a few months' time.

Another issue not fully clarified is who actually did the murdering. Even if we agree that it was the Poles, the question remains: Was it a group of ruffians, social outcasts consisting of, perhaps, several dozen murderers, or was it the entire Polish community, or society, as Prof. Gross claims? The 1949 trial raises a lot of doubts. We know that evidence in that trial was forced out of the witnesses, which Gross admits. My question is: To what extent can we rely on these materials and believe that the trial singled out the people who were actually responsible and that these people actually carried out the murders? Prof. Gross writes that the municipal authorities planned and coordinated the murder with the Germans. I think the terms "municipal authorities" and "town councilors" are misleading to an extent. The truth is that when the Soviets pulled out, a certain group of people came together on their own and took over authority in Jedwabne, but I do not think they had any right to act as municipal authorities.

And one more thing. There are accusations that delving into details is an attempt to conceal the truth and shift the blame from the Poles. I disagree with this most strongly. As a historian, it is my duty to investigate the truth, and the truth consists of a lot of details that are essential in order to present a full picture of events. Such details do not relativize Polish responsibility at all. As researchers, it is our duty to discover what part the Germans played in these events. But our delving into details is not intended in any way to diminish the responsibility of the Poles for this massacre.

Radosław Ignatiew: I have been listening carefully to what you are saying. Without wishing to infringe upon the confidentiality of the investigation, I only wish to say this: I realize what a painful issue this is for Polish-Jewish relations. However, I view the matter solely as an investigator, and as an investigator I remove the matter from its historical context because for me this is a question of victims and criminals. The nationality of the victims or the perpetrators is not the most important thing in my work. I question everything. So if there are reports by victims, I doubt their credibility because victims were naturally shaken up by what happened. If I listen to the testimony of witnesses, I doubt the authenticity of what they are saying because witnesses reconstruct observations after a period of time has passed. So it is possible that some details are made up while others are forgotten. The witnesses may also be telling lies. Everything has to be checked.

I interviewed one eyewitness three times. His final account diverged from his first. I think I discovered why he changed his testimony. As for the report of Jan Neumark, I came across a witness who says that Neumark was not in Jedwabne at the time. In June 1941, a German tried to shoot him, so he fled and hid with his sister. All these accounts have to be checked.

As for the 1949 trial, I would say this: I do not have enough data to prove conclusively that the law was broken and that unacceptable methods of obtaining testimony were applied. What I can say is that the trial was conducted in a slipshod manner. My task is to establish what material from the trial can be used to arrive at the truth. I have already contacted people who took part in the trial, both as defendants and as witnesses.

I interview witnesses very carefully, asking them about all sorts of details, and I do not limit myself to July 1941 because there is a hypothesis that the outburst might have been the result of collaboration between one of the injured parties and the Soviet authorities. I also ask about the entire period of Soviet occupation. I also try to get hold of documents from that period, in order to verify this issue. And I can tell you this: the work is such that, having clarified one matter, I immediately come across two or three others that also need clarification.

Rzeczpospolita: Does your work so far make any essential changes to the way events are portrayed in Prof. Gross's book and in Rzeczpospolita *articles?*

Radosław Ignatiew: Of course I can present some thesis, but as a prosecutor I will not defend such a thesis. I can formulate a thesis and defend it against all attacks if beforehand I establish the evidence precisely, backed up by more evidence, and state why that evidence is credible and cannot be refuted. For example, there is an account that someone saw a column of German vehicles in Jedwabne. That is a piece of information which must be verified because I cannot immediately tell if the witness who saw the German vehicles is telling the truth, is not mistaken, or whether he is in a position that forces him to defend the Poles. In any case, here too I am following in your footsteps, gentlemen. I have made a very careful analysis of Prof. Gross's book, and it will be helpful in the investigation, together with all other publications, including those that the gentlemen present here have written.

Rzeczpospolita: Prof. Gross, what kind of role do you assume the Germans played in the Jedwabne massacre? Do you think the reports mentioned by Prof. Strzembosz alter the picture?

Jan Tomasz Gross: To be honest, I am surprised that Prof. Strzembosz considers modern reports as a serious counterweight to the evidence gathered in 1945, 1949 and 1953. Accounts provided 50 years after the event are not worth much. You come from a family of lawyers, Tomasz, so ask your brother [former president of the Supreme Court—ed.] if this sort of formulation after 50 years has any weight, and whether it can stand up to 50 accounts. My book was not based on the reports of victims and would-be victims. It was based on the reports of those who committed the atrocity and of witnesses, Poles, who gave evidence in 1949. Of course I realize that that was the Stalinist period, so since we are dealing with a trial that took place then, we have to look at these materials with a critical eye. And my book says a lot on this subject.

The first thing I considered was whether this was a political trial. As the Prosecutor said a minute ago, the trial was held in a hopelessly shoddy manner. But there is no doubt that it was not a political trial. Back then, no one cared about whether the Jews were murdered by the Poles or by anyone else. That was 1949, when Stalin was already fiercely anti-Semitic. What did the Auschwitz museum look like in those days? Anyone who did not know what happened in Auschwitz would never have guessed during a visit that Jews had died there. That is how the Stalinists portrayed the history of the German occupation. So this was not a political trial.

Rzeczpospolita: I repeat my question to Mr. Gross. What role do you ascribe to the Germans?

Jan Tomasz Gross: The role of the Germans has been described by several dozen witnesses. Apart from a *gendarmerie* outpost where ten or twelve men were stationed, there were no Germans in Jedwabne that day. We know this from Poles who worked at the *gendarmerie* post. Witnesses say the Poles did it and that there were no Germans around, apart from a dozen or so *gendarmes*. What is more, if we examine the manner in which the Germans murdered Jews during that period, Jedwabne is qualitatively different. Up to the middle of August 1941, the Germans did not kill women, children and old people *en masse*, they only killed men. That is what happened in Wizna, among other places, where they shot several dozen men. The victims there were also rounded up by the local Poles because Jews in that area were physically indistinguishable and could not be identified because they were not a Hasidic community.

If the murder in Jedwabne had really been carried out by the Germans, we would have had evidence of this in the reports on the operations of the *Einsatzkommandos.** These reports are very detailed. No German *Einsatzkommando* commander would have missed the opportunity to boast that he had murdered 1,600 Jews in a single day.

Andrzej Żbikowski: I agree with Prof. Gross. In my work as a historian, I try not to use modern accounts. If one does, one is dealing not with history, but sociology, a completely different subject. The 1945 instructions of the Jewish Historical Committee on the method of gathering memoirs contain the following point: "All phenomena in this sphere must be noted; both positive ones, for example about help given to Jews, and negative ones, for example about the participation of certain sectors of society in anti-Jewish actions." In 1945, the Commission was led by people who left Poland soon afterwards, except for Szymon Datner. These were not anonymous figures. They are well known, with great moral stature.

As far as the Germans are concerned, I am not saying that they played no part in this all. The following record of events in Radziłów exists: After some sort of meeting between the Poles and Germans, numerous groups moved off to the town, each consisting of one German and one member of the town council or some other trusted person. The Germans were present in both places for a while, but certainly not during the actual murder. Finkelsztajn clearly writes that in Radziłów, the Gestapo handed out weapons to their supporters among the local population, left a man in Polish uniform, got into their cars and said, and I quote: "You have three days to take care of the Jews." Afterwards, there were only Poles present. The Jews were lined up and driven into the barn, and murdered. That is the story, which no one has refuted yet because there is no evidence against it. Of course the Germans murdered Jews, but not in that way. They tried to do everything in an organized manner—just as in subsequent years—in other words, round up the people, preferably on the town square, and then transport them outside town, shoot them and bury them. That is how they did it in Tykocin, for example. From the middle of August, the Germans also started to murder women and children. They gathered all Jews, took them away and murdered them.

Historians have written a lot about two orders issued by Heydrich to the *Einsatzgruppen** on June 29 and July 1, 1941, in which he said that if a pogrom can be arranged, so much the better. I found no confirmation in Jewish reports from that time that the Germans managed to arrange such pogroms frequently. Of course they did, but rarely.

The credibility of the sources

Andrzej Kaczyński: I am rather surprised by the dispute about which accounts are more important, the older or the more recent ones. Every source deserves criticism. Of course, reports gathered recently have to be subjected to particularly severe criticism. During the months when I visited Jedwabne, Radziłów and Łomża and gathered various accounts, I noticed that later ones already bore the hallmark of newspaper articles.

Accounts from 1945 should also be corroborated. For instance, Finkelsztajn talks about a delegation of Jews from Radziłów who went to the bishop of Łomża to ask him for protection, taking valuables and silver with them. Well, they couldn't have reached the bishop because he wasn't in Łomża at the time, he was in hiding. In any case, it is unlikely that the bishop would have been able in that situation to accept the proposition that he ensure the security of the Jews.

Paweł Machcewicz: I would like to return to the question of the credibility of the accounts and investigative materials from the trial of 1949. Prof. Gross writes in his book that, during the trial, each defendant claimed he had been beaten during interrogation and, in this way, forced to give evidence. A few pages further on, the author nevertheless concludes that the investigative materials can be used to reconstruct the truth. This surprises me. The materials on which Prof. Gross bases his findings contain various threads, and some reports contradict each other. This is not unequivocal material. There are many threads that require investigation, for example the statement that the Germans—the Gestapo or *gendarmerie* took part in driving the Jews onto the town square.

One more remark. Of course, Prof. Gross is the only historian to have used this material, and that is your advantage, Professor, but I wish to remind everyone that for the past few years, historians have not been able to use these materials because first of all, the Main Commission for Investigating Crimes against the Polish Nation* being liquidated following the passage of the law to set up the Institute of National Remembrance,* and you were the only one who had access to them. Later, the materials were also used by Prosecutor Ignatiew. I have only now received permission to release the materials to historians. Our task at the Institute of National Remembrance is to publish these materials. Then we will hold a debate about the material stemming from these investigations.

As far as the presence of Germans is concerned, I think that for the time being we are simply not fully acquainted with the documentation, and the statements of Prof. Gross seem too categorical.

Why was there silence?

Jan Tomasz Gross: I have one question, which can serve as a reply to Mr. Machcewicz's remarks. How is it that for 50 years, not a single historian dealing with the German occupation and Polish-Jewish relations has uttered so much as one word on the dramatic fate of the Jews in Jedwabne? This is question is addressed to you in particular, Tomasz, because as a historian you cover not just that period, but that very region. Why have you never written about it? Didn't you know anything about it? In 1966, Mr. Datner published a long article on the murder of Jews in the Białystok area in the *Bulletin of the Jewish Historical Institute*.* That article says in no uncertain terms that in Wąsosz, Radziłów and Jedwabne, the murders were carried out by Poles. Mr. Machcewicz says that no one has had access to records for the past 18 months because everything is under wraps. Fine, but for 50 years everything was accessible, yet no one tackled the subject. That is a great question which Polish historiography will have to struggle with.

Tomasz Strzembosz: There are two things I would like to discuss. A report from 1945 need not necessarily be accurate, and a report from 50 years later need not necessarily be inaccurate. I am capable of describing my wedding day 44 years ago in perfect detail, because that was an important day for me. And for many people, the murder in Jedwabne was also a very important event. The fact that today, after 60 years, the prosecutor is investigating these matters and talking to people confirms the view that later reports possess importance. I am not saying they are of decisive importance; merely that they possess some importance. It is not true that the Germans did not burn Jews. If one reads Jewish reports contained in the Eastern Archive, describing the situation of Jews in the Lublin region and in eastern parts of Warsaw province, one comes across descriptions of the mass burnings of synagogues, and on many occasions of people dying in these synagogues. There is also the case of the burning of 50 Jews beneath the bridge at Pułtusk, repeated in many reports. And that was in 1939. Not only men were murdered. Jewish accounts speak of children being shot, mass murders, people being shot with machine guns while trying to cross the San River, though the Soviet Union did not want to admit them on the other side. The same thing happened in the Augustów area. So it is not true that up to a certain point, the Germans only killed adults, and children later.

Jan Tomasz Gross: Why didn't you write anything about this for 50 years?

Tomasz Strzembosz: Because I was out on a limb. Between 1982 and 1990, I wrote no letters and made no phone calls. I was engaged in matters which the [Communist—ed.] system considered to be treason against the Polish state. In other words, I was examining the Polish resistance to and armed struggle against the Soviet occupation regime between 1939 and 1941, before the Jedwabne massacre. If I had gone any further, I might have been found dead in the mud. That was made clear to me. And aside from that, I am not a historian of Polish-Jewish relations.

Rzeczpospolita: The question about the silence of Polish historical writing does not concern only, or even chiefly, Prof. Strzembosz. It is more appropriate to Dr. Żbikowski.

Andrzej Żbikowski: In 1990 I got to know Prof. Gross and he talked me into specializing in the eastern marches* and in Polish-Jewish relations during the Soviet occupation. In 1990 and 1991, I wrote my first and, for a long time my only, sentence in which I said that apart from the pogroms in the Ukraine, in June and July 1941, pogroms also occurred in Podlasie, Wizna, Wąsosz and Jedwabne. I provided references to the reports at the Jewish Historical Institute,* but to be honest, I did not really believe that such things could have happened on such a scale. I was completely unprepared for it.

I think we will be discussing for a long time yet whether Jedwabne is the most important episode in Polish-Jewish relations during the occupation. I do not think it is, though of course the case has to be examined very closely. The wave of murders in June and July 1941 occurred during a transitional period, when the Russians had left and the Germans were only just arriving. And that is when the murders occurred, along the entire belt of land previously held by the Soviets.

These crimes have a certain context. On the one hand there were, let us say, economic reasons, envy of possessions and a desire to get hold of them. I think that was the strongest motive. But on the other hand, there was an ideological motive, a tendency to blame the Jewish people for the Soviet occupation. The Jews became a scapegoat.

Paweł Machcewicz: Up to 1989, there was no freedom to engage in research, and the communist authorities wanted to hush up sensitive issues. But I agree with Prof. Gross that, first, historians committed gross negligence by failing to write about this topic after 1989 and, second, that even if they did write about it, like Andrzej Żbikowski, they were unable to get through to public opinion. The Jedwabne memorial book was published in the United States in 1980. Before that, there was a memorial book for Grajewo, published in the early 1950s. But knowledge of the murders did not penetrate to Jewish historians, either.

In an interview for *Gazeta Wyborcza,* Prof. Gutman said that when he learned about Jedwabne, he felt as if he had been hit over the head with a hammer. It seems that none of us were prepared for such facts, which have altered our picture of Polish-Jewish relations during the occupation. If society is incapable of accepting certain controversial ideas, there will be no discussion about them. To come to a reckoning with one's own past, and not just in Poland, one has to follow a very tortuous route. In Germany, the great debate on the subject of Nazi atrocities did not start until the 1960s, and in France the debate on the Vichy regime started even later—in the 1980s. Therefore, in their attitudes towards their own past, the Poles are no exception.

Radosław Ignatiew: I would like to refer to two matters—the accounts from 1945, and those gathered sixty years later. I treat both with the same degree of seriousness, regardless of how sensational they sound, because, as Prof. Strzembosz has said, one can remember certain traumatic events 60 years later even if they did not affect one directly. However, after a short time one also remembers such events.

Szmul Wasersztajn's report is a typical example of how collective memory works. This man and six others were themselves saved by hiding beneath a barn for 26 months. Janek Neumark writes that the Poles drowned two unfortunate women with their children. But Rywka Fogel claims that the women had attempted to commit suicide, and that the Poles dragged them out. This shows how a view of events can be distorted by the subjective point of view of the observer.

As for traces of Germans, which I am also investigating, we can forget about *Einsatzkommandos** from Group B. At that time, they were already in the east, somewhere near Mińsk. In Białystok, there were only rearguard units. In his 1966 article, Szymon Datner also suggests that Wolfgang Birkner and his *Kommando Białystok* was engaged in the extermination of Jews between June and August 10, 1941. Datner even says that that Kommando was responsible for the Jedwabne massacre. All this has to be checked.

One cannot say that July 1941 was a period of anarchy. I have materials which show that there was a German *gendarmerie* post in Jedwabne even before July 10. They arrested someone there and killed someone. There were already some Germans in Jedwabne during that period. The question is, just how many Germans were there and what was their role? Were they passive observers of the crime, or active co-perpetrators?

Let me get back to the 1949 trial. I have reliable knowledge on this because I have read the court materials many times. None of the 22 perpetrators was charged with the murder of Jews. They were merely charged with broadly-understood aiding and abetting. Aiding and abetting whom? The Germans, by escorting the Jews onto the square and guarding them there, and leading them to the barn. One cannot ignore the fact that the same court materials contained the names of persons who had committed acts of violence or homicide on persons of Jewish nationality. But the trial did not deal with this fact at all.

Andrzej Kaczyński: Let me tell you how I learned about Jedwabne. I first read about it in Prof. Gross's article contained in a book dedicated to Prof. Strzembosz to mark the forty-fifth anniversary of his scholarly debut. The article cited Wasersztajn's entire, shocking report, which Gross furnished with a rather general commentary and reflections. The things I expected from a historian and sociologist, i.e. criticism and a verification of sources, were absent. I was disturbed by the fact that he had not compared this account with others. I thought to myself, well, if Gross has not done so, then I will. So I went to Jedwabne. In the space of several hours I succeeded in obtaining quite convincing accounts which confirm a major part of Wasersztajn's facts. In the end, people said, with pain: It was not the Germans who did this, it was our people....

The Germans were already in Jedwabne before the massacre. There was a police outpost there. Some uniformed Germans arrived from outside. That happened over two weeks after the front line had passed through. But the residents said that the murder was perpetrated by Poles. Some people remembered individual uniformed and armed people, but rather as spectators, onlookers rather than perpetrators and leaders. This information usually came from the lips of people who were too young to have taken part in the atrocity or even to have been present on the square. No, they witnessed some fragments, for instance they watched from behind the curtains, or from behind the fence, as the Jews were herded to the site of the massacre near the Jewish cemetery, for as soon as the parents had learned what was going on that day, they shooed their children into their houses and locked the doors. Later I met people who had seen more. Besides direct testimony like this, the truth of the crime has been passed down in oral tradition. It is a paradox that, as long as the circumstances of the massacre of the Jews in Jedwabne were not generally known, it was a public secret, the townspeople kept the truth to themselves and repeated it among themselves, but as soon as the truth came out into the open, many people became determined to deny it.

As for the negligence of historians, the *Bulletin of the Jewish Historical Institute* * containing Szymon Datner's essay on the massacre of Jews in the Białystok area is dated 1966, but that particular volume was not published until 1969. That may explain why the fragments that concern Jedwabne and Radziłów are ambiguous. He wrote that in both those places, and in several others, the Germans managed to induce a certain number of local Polish hooligans, riff-raff and criminals into carrying out the crimes. This is formulated in such a way that a reader not prepared to take in such information may understand that here, like everywhere else, the perpetrators were mostly armed Germans, assisted by a small number of Poles.

Andrzej Żbikowski: The situation with the Datner report is complicated. Most of the books were published in order to rescue the Jewish Historical Institute and the entire community in 1968.* That was a difficult situation, and the point was to rescue Jewish institutions. It wasn't so much a matter of committing falsification, as of reaching certain compromises.

Jan Tomasz Gross: There is one thing I cannot understand. In our assessment of the Jedwabne events, what difference does it make if the Germans were, let's say, twenty kilometers from Jedwabne, or had only just arrived, or had only just left? We know they were there. We know they wanted to terrorize the population and perhaps involve it in the massacre, and we also know that they themselves murdered the Jews *en masse*. That is a fact. But at the crucial moment, they were absent from Jedwabne. They never issued any order which, if disobeyed, might have put anyone in danger. It's not true, there is no evidence of such an order.

Paweł Machcewicz: We are not discussing a moral assessment of the atrocity, we are wondering whether it was perpetrated by the Poles independently, or under German influence. If we want to investigate everything, it is important to know whether the Germans were thirty kilometers or five hundred meters from the events. I think we have to pay attention to details.

Collaboration with the Soviets: perpetrators and victims

Rzeczpospolita: Let us consider the origins of this crime. Mr. Żbik-owski said that the chief motive of the perpetrators was greed. Professor Strzembosz said that one of the motives could have been revenge for the fact that some Jews had collaborated with the Soviet authorities.

Tomasz Strzembosz: I never said that. I do not link the burning of the Jews in Jedwabne to what happened there before June 22, 1941. The killings that occurred earlier might have been acts of vengeance, but the burning of everyone in the barn exceeds any measure of revenge for the actions of the militias, etc.

Rzeczpospolita: The dispute is that Mr. Strzembosz claims that during the Soviet occupation, many Jews in this area, in cooperation with the Soviet authorities, took an active part in persecuting the Poles. However, Mr. Gross basically denies this.

Paweł Machcewicz: Even accounts now to be found in the Eastern Archives of the Karta Center contain opinions that in various places, including Jedwabne, the Jews were the most visible group collaborating with the Soviets and the NKVD.* An examination of the very events of July 10 shows that elements of vengeance existed there. The Jews were forced to dismantle Lenin's statue, carry the red flag, sing "This war was through us," etc. So the problem seems to exist.

Jan Tomasz Gross: You are absolutely right. This problem exists in many different guises. It was revealed recently in an interview with Maria Janion in *Gazeta Wyborcza*. She cites Konstanty Jeleński from 1956: "A favorite argument of Polish anti-Semites is that the Jews joyfully welcomed the Red Army entering eastern Poland in 1939.

In any case, it seems absurd to level accusations against those citizens whose collaboration can be explained by self-preservation. Jews would have been less attracted to communism if Poland had not shunned them for so many years."

So the population generally believed that the Jews had collaborated with the Soviets. That is the same thing as saying that the Polish population was anti-Semitic. For this is an anti-Semitic stereotype that is firmly rooted, and of course one has to pay attention to it. One cannot talk about the events in Jedwabne and gloss over the fact that there was anti-Semitism and that the National Democracy* was the leading ideological force which penetrated the minds and moods of the local population. It is not without reason that they murdered Jews rather than, say, old people.

In your article, Tomasz, published in *Rzeczpospolita* under the title "Covered-Up Collaboration," you say a lot of things that are obviously untrue. First of all, from beginning to end you use large-scale quantifiers such as: The Jews persecuted the Poles, the Jews sent Poles into banishment, the Jews shot at the Polish Army. This is the mirror image of Shamir's famous remark about the Poles drinking in anti-Semitism with their mothers' milk. Your image of Jews is that they are Pole-haters. I wonder what kind of sensitivity enables us to reverse stereotypes in that way.

Secondly, when you say the Jews sent the Poles to Siberia, you are uttering downright lies. There were proportionately more Jewish victims of these deportations than Polish victims. Between one-fourth and one-third of the deported civilians were Jews. Your article says: The Poles are persecuted by the Jews, the Jews send them to God knows where. Well, it was not like that. The Jews suffered just as much as everyone else under the Soviet occupation, if not more. The whole stereotype of Jews supporting the Bolsheviks and communists is nonsense. They supported them to such an extent that they demonstrated their antipathy toward the Soviets *en masse*, for which they were punished terribly.

Tomasz Strzembosz: These are two completely different issues—someone's attitude towards the USSR and the communist system on the one hand, and the attitudes of the Soviets to that person on the other. This problem arises when the Jews flee from the Lublin region across the San River but are greeted with machine gun fire. They choose the Soviet Union, but the Soviet Union does not want them. These are two totally different matters. If the Jews collaborate with the Soviets, and I know of several such cases, and are subsequently deported into the depths of the USSR, it does not mean that they are merely victims and never perpetrators. Besides, Yezhov, the head of the NKVD,* was also shot. What does that make him, a perpetrator or a victim? He was both. Polish Gulag inmates met NKVD there, and these were sometimes murdered later by their fellow prisoners. Many Jewish communists also abandoned their communist ideology once they were in prison or banishment. But that does not mean that all Polish Jews were communists. It is like saying that no Poles were communists.

However, it is a fact that a lot of Jews worked in the militia, both uniformed and plainclothes, and not just in Podlasie. In accounts gathered in Palestine in 1944, in other words at a very early stage, Jews who had survived the USSR themselves say how many of them had joined the militia in the Lublin area which was taken over by the Red Army in late September and October 1939, even though the Red Army ruled over them only for a few weeks. This confirms Polish reports, by the way. But what troubles me is not triumphal arches, but the fact that in 16 places in so-called Western Belorussia, the Jews opened fire on the Poles.

That is why information about 30, 40 or 5 percent of the Jewish being deported is no answer to the question about the extent of their collaboration with the occupation regime. Why? Because that was a system that devoured its own children.

Jan Tomasz Gross: Do you think Wanda Wasilewska, one of the main collaborators, attended synagogue? And what about Felix Edmundovich Dzherzhinsky, who founded the KGB?

Tomasz Strzembosz: One can cite other cases, this time Jewish ones. There was a something which, in my opinion, equaled the phenomenon of *szmalcownicy:** representatives of Jewish communities collaborated with the Soviet authorities and handed Poles over to them.

275

Jan Tomasz Gross: In Jedwabne, the Poles delivered fellow Poles into the hands of the Soviets. Mr. Laudański was an NKVD agent. He said so himself.

Tomasz Strzembosz: You are mistaken. The case of Laudański and others is linked to Kobielno. The Jedwabne Jews are not guilty of betraying the partisan base in Kobielno. But they blamed for the arrests that occurred in Jedwabne from 1939 onwards, including the great arrest on the night of June 16–17 preceding the Kobielno operation, and for involvement in the deportation on 13 April 1940 and 20 June 1941. In any case, vengeance for collaborating with the NKVD did not apply only to the Jews of Podlasie. It also applied to Polish peasants throughout the Jedwabne area. We know of many cases.

Andrzej Żbikowski: As far as the Soviet occupation and the collaboration of Jews is concerned, it is necessary to clarify a few matters. What is collaboration? It is cooperation. So if it is cooperation, it has many shades, and various groups of people cooperate in various forms. If we are talking about cooperation with the apparatus of repression, then of course a group of Jews collaborated, but a group of Poles, Belarussians and Ukrainians collaborated as well. I think one can talk about overrepresentation of Jews in the sense that in Jedwabne there were more or less as many Jewish agents as Polish ones. The Soviets only needed a dozen or so agents. I know a lot of reports, submitted during the war by Jewish *bezhentsy* w*ho escaped from German occupation, and these reports mention groups consisting of one NKVD agent, one Jew and one Pole. Such groups went around together arresting people. But in small towns, groups of several or a dozen or so Jewish agents, and similar ones consisting of Poles and other nationalities residing in the area were organized.

As to the number of Jews deported, the Soviets deported Jewish *bezhentsy* not because they were Jews, but because they were *bezhentsy*. And they wanted to solve the problem of these *bezhentsy* in their own way. First, they wanted to send them for "voluntary labor" in Belorussia and the Ukraine. Several thousand Jews went there. Some of them returned, so that did not work. Then they were given a choice: either return to the General Government* or take Soviet citizenship. Most of them, some 80%, refused Soviet citizenship. Why? Because they were scared that if they did, they would never leave Russia again. So they were punished by being deported under the same terms as the Poles, Ukrainians or Belarussians before them.

Jan Tomasz Gross: What I meant was that the Jews under Soviet occupation were treated the same way as others. Yet before that they were discriminated against, like all other minorities in these areas, because the Polish Government between the wars practiced discrimination. But communism discriminated against people on a class basis, not on a religious or ethnic basis. The Jews under Soviet occupation were attacked in various ways for being Jews. Zionists were persecuted and members of the *Bund** were locked up. Religious life, so important to the Jews, was completely destroyed, etc.

Andrzej Żbikowski: Concerning Polish-Jewish relationships under Soviet occupation, the welcoming of the Red Army is not the most important matter. The Red Army was welcomed by a handful of people, mainly Jews, but not many. The problem was a shift in the situation of people during the occupation. Poles suffered the most persecution because they were citizens of a defeated country. They were removed from positions of authority. The Jews reaped certain benefits from the situation. Social space does not tolerate a vacuum. If experts are required, and no Poles are employed and there are no Belarussians or Ukrainians with the right qualifications, then the jobs go to, for instance, Jewish doctors. From the sources, one can also discern a rather visible *schadenfreude* on the part of the Jewish population.

Paweł Machcewicz: The question of Jewish relations *vis-à-vis* the Soviets is more than just the number of NKVD* agents of Jewish origin on the one hand, and the number of Jewish deportees on the other. But it is true that numerous accounts, e.g. many reports by the Polish Underground State* or Karski's* report, keep repeating that the Jews built triumphal arches welcoming the Soviets. We also know that in September 1939, in eastern Poland, the Jewish population took part in many acts against the Polish authorities. We know of

277

various kinds of militias that collaborated with the Soviets, and in which the Jews took active part. I wish to ask Prof. Gross, are all these the accounts of anti-Semites?

Jan Tomasz Gross: I have read practically every single report at the Hoover Institution on this subject. I have been dealing with this subject for 20 years. When did the collection of these accounts begin? Very early. The head of the Institution has written the following memorandum: The anti-Semitism of the remarks we have gathered is so all-embracing that before the texts are published, we should seriously consider editing them. As far as the anti-Semitism of the people in General Anders's army* is concerned, we do not have to reach for the archives. You can read about it in plenty of works on the subject of Anders's army. Anders even issued a special order on this matter—anti-Semitism was that widespread.

The exception or the rule?

Rzeczpospolita: To what extent does the history of the atrocities in Jedwabne and Radziłów compel us to take a completely different look at the history of the occupation in Poland, especially the history of Polish-Jewish relations? To what extent were the things that happened in Jedwabne and Radziłów an exception?

Andrzej Żbikowski: I have read many thousands of Jewish accounts in various languages, and in none them did I find a single mention of burning people alive in barns. This must be the tip of some pyramid. At the bottom of the pyramid, Polish-Jewish relations spread out on other levels. Usually, these relations are vexed. I do not think the episode of one single month in 1941 is the biggest problem. The problem is the attitudes connected with the conceal-ment of the Jewish population, with the lack of help, and with widespread indifference. This indifference forms the base of the pyramid whose apex is Jedwabne. Very few organizations or political forces were involved in helping the Jews. The heroism of the *Żegota** activists and of all those righteous people who already have or should have a tree planted in their honor is, of course, commendable, but these were just a drop in the ocean. Most of the population was indifferent. Acts of hostility, envy, blackmail and betrayal were much more numerous than we had previously thought.

Paweł Machcewicz: For me, the most controversial part of Prof. Gross's book were his remarks towards the end. I felt he was metaphorically extrapolating his specific analysis of the events in the two towns to the whole of Polish-Jewish relations and to the general attitudes of Poles toward the Holocaust. He said the following, and I quote: *"In collective Jewish memory this phenomenon is ingrained —that local Polish people killed the Jews because they wanted to, not because they had to.... After all, Jedwabne—though perhaps one of the most excessive (the most excessive, it must be hoped) of all murderous assaults by Poles against the Jews—was not an isolated episode."* In the light of what Andrzej Żbikowski said just now, I think this is wrong. Jedwabne and Radziłów were exceptions. The opinions of Prof. Gross are expressed in a way I find unacceptable.

Andrzej Kaczyński: It seems to me that the question of whether we should adopt a new approach towards history, different from what has previously been regarded as canonical, because of Jedwabne and Radziłów, is badly posed. History never ends. It is always being written anew. Numerous new facts and phenomena, not just on Polish-Jewish relations, are now coming to light which no one has ever investigated before. I consider this a challenge. They must be described and explained. It is necessary to continue to investigate the events in Jedwabne and Radziłów—not just with the help of the prosecutor and Institute of National Remembrance,* but also with the help of journalists. Many of the assessments that have been plentiful in the media on the present debate are, in my opinion, premature.

Tomasz Strzembosz: After this discussion, I still do not know what happened in Jedwabne. I have encountered reports which seemed to me much more credible than Wasersztajn's. And these reports all told me something different. I cannot ignore them completely. Also, just like other Warsaw historians, I do not have the UB* documentation.

Jan Tomasz Gross: Jedwabne and Radziłów are a phenomenon that goes far beyond anything else that happened in this area. This is because of the pure tragedy of a situation in which the Jewish population of those towns was murdered by their Polish neighbors in such a cruel and final way. This is an event that, to my mind, creates a completely new way of recording the history of the occupation.

As far as Polish-Jewish relations are concerned, we have a great deal to do. The Poles, themselves the victims of the German occupation, behaved with indifference toward the Jews, and displayed no sympathy for their suffering. The Jews were in a lower circle of hell, and this fact was exploited. I am very pleased that Mr. Machcewicz, who will be engaged in education and is responsible for this at the Institute of National Remembrance, promises that these matters will be investigated and that we will learn everything. I hope he is right. Because we have never properly mourned over the fate of our Jewish fellow citizens. We have not suffered through and lamented the Jewish disaster during the war. I would like to believe that the Jedwabne affair will represent an opening in that direction, because it is so exceedingly dramatic.

The discussion was chaired by Jan Skórzyński and Paweł Lisicki

TOMASZ SZAROTA

THE NATIONAL DEBATE
ON JEDWABNE

REFLECTIONS OF A HISTORIAN AND SPECIALIST
ON NATIONAL STEREOTYPES

"WIĘŹ" APRIL 2001

S ince May of last year I have been following with great attention
the discussion on the "Jedwabne issue." I have voiced my
opinion on it a few times myself. The issue is being discussed
not only in the Polish media. Articles on the events at Jedwabne
started appearing in foreign newspapers before foreign editions of
Jan T. Gross's book called *Neighbors* have been published.

The historians' input to this discussion is visible, but it is not
dominant. A certain Polish German-studies specialist is misleading
the German public, informing the readers of the *Frankfurter Allge-
meine Zeitung* that we are dealing here with *einem polnischen Histo-
rikerstreit* [a Polish historians' controversy]. In reality, a public debate
is being held in Poland—stirred up by Gross's text and successive
opinions expressed by partakers in the discussion—and who knows,
perhaps it even deserves to be labeled as national debate. Scientists,
journalists, publicists, writers, politicians, and clergymen are participating in this discussion, as well as ordinary people who send letters
to editors with their own comments and thoughts. When I speak of
a national debate, I also mean that the events at Jedwabne have

become the subject of heated debates among members of Polish families, among friends, colleagues, and acquaintances.

Why are historians needed?

When reading some newspaper articles written by some participants in the discussion on Jedwabne, I feel sometimes not only that we—the historians—are redundant, but also that our work, the objective of which is to determine all the circumstances and events preceding the extermination of Jedwabne Jews on 10th July 1941, is starting to be treated as an embarrassing attempt to lessen the crime committed by the Polish inhabitants of this town against their Jewish neighbors.

One of my polemicists implies that in my discussion on Gross's book I point at "missing details which... should be taken into account." The following assertion follows: "It seems that all these details are part of the sphere of 'wishful thinking.'" Another partaker in the discussion expresses a similar opinion: "We may, of course, continue to sidestep the issue. We may say it is too early, that reports are unclear, that there is no exact count of the murderers or the victims, that one set of archives or another still needs to be investigated. Investigation is always worthwhile; it should have been done many years ago, but they will not change a thing. The truth will not become any more pleasant than it is now, and sooner or later we are going to have to deal with it."

Here is my answer: many, a great many details which Gross did not include or which it was possible to ascertain after his book was published, are historical facts and not part of any "wishful thinking" mandated by any "obsession of innocence" among Polish researchers. Criticizing source materials or querying archives, placing events at Jedwabne in the broader context of the extermination of the Jewish population in territories occupied by Germans after June 22, 1941, as well as taking antecedents into account, i.e. the thirties and the period of Soviet occupation—this is not evasion!

When I read that "they will not change a thing," I wonder if there is any sense at all in my continuing to work as a historian. On that same principle, one can also question the justification of the all-new investigation of the subject being carried out by the Institute of National Remembrance.*

What role did the Germans play?

Jan Tomasz Gross writes in his book that: *"At the time the overall undisputed bosses over life and death in Jedwabne were the Germans,"* and elsewhere he adds: *"What we would like to know, however, with as much precision as possible, is this: What specific role did the Germans play in the implementation of the massacre?"* Unfortunately, despite these declarations, we learn little from this book about the Germans who were present in Jedwabne.

As I write this text, I still have no access to full documentation concerning the realization of the first stage of *Endlösung** in the Province of Białystok in the summer of 1941. We know that police battalions No. 309, 316, 322, special operational groups of the Sipo* and SD,* and probably some *Wehrmacht* squads participated in these criminal acts, along with, unfortunately, local civilians. I suppose, although I am not able to verify it yet, that the events which took place in Wąsosz (July 5), Radziłów (July 7), and Jedwabne (July 10) are connected to the activities of *Einsatzkommando** 8 (*EK8*), commanded by SS-*Sturmbannführer* Bradfisch, which was a part of *Einsatzgruppe** B, commanded by SS-*Gruppenführer* Arthur Nebe, and which arrived in Białystok on July 1, or with the special *Kommando Białystok*, of which we still know very little, which was commanded by SS-*Hauptsturmführer* Wolfgang Birkner from the Warsaw Gestapo. This latter formation was established as a result of an agreement between the Sipo and SD chief Reinhard Heydrich and his representative in the General Government,* SS-*Brigadeführer* Eberhard Schöngarth. Birkner's squad left Warsaw on July 3, 1941.

One of the tasks of *Einsatzgruppen* was to organize the so-called *Selbstreinigungsaktionen* [self-cleansing actions], after June 22. This mainly involved "initiating" pogroms against the Jewish population, which were supposed to create an impression "that it was the local population which out of its own initiative took the first steps as a natural reaction to decades of Jewish oppression and to the communist terror." In a report dated October 15, 1941 by the commander of *Einsatzgruppe A,* stationed in Lithuania, we read: "It was quite significant to create certain facts that would be possible to be proved in *the future* which would demonstrate that the liberated populace resorted to the most abrupt measures against Bolshevik and Jewish opponents, whereas *orders* given by the Germans *would not be identifiable"* [emphasis added—T.S.].

With regards to using Poles in these "self-cleansing" operations, the idea came from the commander of the 17th German Army operating in the vicinity of Lwów at the end of June 1941 (his name was General Karl-Heinrich von Stülpnagel, from February 1942 *Militärbefehlshaber* in France, then member of the anti-Hitler conspiracy, hanged in Plötzensee prison on August 30, 1944). The proposal reached Reinhard Heydrich, who, on July 1, 1941 ordered commanders of four *Einsatzgruppen* to do the following:

"Poles residing in the newly-occupied Polish territories may be expected, on the basis of their experiences, to be anti-communist and also anti-Jewish. It is obvious that the cleansing activities have to extend first of all to the Bolsheviks and the Jews. As for the Polish intelligentsia and others, decisions can be taken later, unless there is a special reason for taking action in individual cases considered to be dangerous. It is therefore obvious that such Poles need not be included in the cleansing action, especially as they are of great importance as elements to initiate pogroms and for obtaining information. (This depends, of course, on local conditions)."

We may also assume that this order, through official channels, reached the above-mentioned commanders of *EK8* and *Sonderkommando Bialystok,* whose names are not mentioned in Gross's book. If Wolfgang Birkner, like the commander of *EK3* operating in Lithuania, Karl Jäger, had survived the war and were able to be interrogated, then we would know a lot more about the events of the first ten days of July 1941 in the Province of Białystok. Birkner was killed in the Pomorze Province on March 24, 1945 and—if I am not mistaken—it has not been possible to obtain statements from any of his subordinates. I know, however, that Bradfisch was tried before a court in the Federal Republic of Germany.

In the weekly magazine *Kontakty* of Łomża, in 1988—twelve years before Gross's book appeared—a report on Jedwabne, written by Danuta and Aleksander Wroniszewski, was published. It describes the crime committed there by the Poles. Here, for the first time, voluminous fragments of Szmul Wasersztajn's 1945 testimonies were published. It is surprising that this report did not reverberate throughout the nation, and that Jan Tomasz Gross did not get hold of it (in the USA, almost no one took notice of the 1980 publication of *Yedwabne: History and Memorial Book*). One of the interlocutors of the Wroniszewskis, a witness to the events, Jan S., quotes the words said to him on the morning of July 10, 1941 by mayor Marian Karolak, the central figure in the pogrom soon to be commenced: "You know, today they are going to either burn them or shoot them." There is not a shadow of a doubt that he was referring to the Germans and their Jewish victims.

Unfortunately, it turned out that the Poles did the "dirty work" for the Germans. Their participation in the extermination of the Jews was condemned by the clandestine press—one of the fundamental media channels at the disposal of the Polish Underground State.* In the publication *Prawda* [The Truth], an organ of the secret Catholic organization called the Front for the Rebirth of Poland (the current Polish Minister of Foreign Affairs, Władysław Bartoszewski, was one of those involved), in the May 1942 issue, (the second issue), we read: "*We must take all possible steps to prevent a similar disgrace recurring. We must make people aware that they are becoming Herod's myrmidons, we must condemn it in the secret press, we must appeal to the people to boycott the butchers, we must threaten and foresee severe legal actions against the murderers by the courts of the free Republic of Poland. So far no one is taking up this issue; the press is timorously stifled, and the evil is spreading like an epidemic, crime is turning into a habit. Under no circumstances can we allow for the plague of sadism, which turns people into animals, to spread to us.*" Unfortunately this could not be prevented.

TOMASZ SZAROTA

What happened earlier?

As a historian, I express the view that, in order to explain certain events, it is always good to say what happened before. Of course, one may ask how far back it is necessary to go. I found out recently that many "stiletto wielders" were recruited in Jedwabne for the [Polish—ed.] national organization in the January Uprising of 1863, and their names later appeared on lists of Siberian exiles. In the period between the First and Second World Wars, the marshes of the Biebrza—where it was possible to hide out of the reach of the police—favored the proliferation of crime in the area. At the same time, the Province of Łomża was an area of significant influence of the National Democracy* movement and the very radical youth wings allied with it.

When we think about the late thirties in Poland, there are associations with the increasing wave of anti-Semitism, "ghetto benches" at educational institutions, and anti-Jewish excesses. Reflections that the Second Polish Republic* was a nation of laws, actively opposed to the activities of the extreme right wing, are much less prominent. In the effort to ensure order, there was an effort to suppress anti-Jewish incidents, and to bring agitators who exacerbated nationalistic tensions, including Catholic priests, to justice. In the Bereza Kartuska camp, members of the far-right opposition were imprisoned alongside those from the left.

We surely forget too often that the *Sanacja** governments in Poland were considered by nationalist groups to be centers of Jewish and Masonic influence and obstacles to the process of creating a Catholic Polish "national state." In the view of the nationalists, these were not governments capable of carrying out the slogan "Jews to Madagascar." It was the German occupation regime that suddenly created an opportunity to eliminate the "foreign element."

In areas that were under Soviet control from 1939 to 1941, Polish--Jewish conflicts intensified greatly. In *Neighbors,* Gross cites the following message sent from Lwów to London on December 8, 1939: *"Jews are so horribly persecuting the Poles and everything that is connected to Poland under the Soviet occupation... that at the first op-*

*portunity all the Poles, from old men to women and children, will take
such a horrible revenge on them as no anti-Semite has ever imagined
possible"* [printed in a footnote in the American edition of *Neighbors*—trans.]. Jan T. Gross comments on this passage: *"As a description of reality this text was wrong, but as a forecast of things to come it
was prescient."*

In my opinion, unfortunately, the "description of reality" truly
reflected the prevailing atmosphere. The same atmosphere in the
territory occupied by the Soviets was documented by Jan Karski,*
who wrote in his January 1940 report that "In principle all Poles are
embittered and disappointed with the Jews—the majority (mostly
young people of course) is literally waiting for an opportunity to
wreak 'bloody vengeance.'"

Poles about themselves

From the point of view of a researcher of national stereotypes,
one can wonder how the "issue of Jedwabne" will influence the
historical consciousness of the Polish populace and the Poles' own
image of themselves, as well as how information about a crime
committed 60 years ago will influence today's image of Poland and
Poles as seen from abroad.

It is indisputable that, between 1945 and the time when Poland
regained full sovereignty in 1989, the portrait of our times, and
particularly the most tragic period, World War II as an age of heroes
and martyrs served—as the tales of Sienkiewicz once did—"to
strengthen hearts." Everything that called to mind our sins, shameful
or disgraceful deeds, clashed with that idealized picture of the past.
The censorship in effect in Poland at that time did not allow, indeed,
for the "blank spaces" to be filled in. That is, it did not permit writing
about injustice done to us by our neighbors from the East (I also
would like to point out that, after the [communist—ed.] German
Democratic Republic was formed, it was forbidden to write or speak
of the German occupation and German crimes, but only to use the
corresponding terms "Nazi occupation" and "Nazi crimes"), but the
same censorship did not allow Poles to "foul their own nest."

In 1990, censorship disappeared and the Poles have slowly been getting rid of their complexes and are becoming a normal nation, in the history of which, as in the history of any nation, there are events to be proud of and events to be ashamed of. Signs of the courage to talk about the evil and painful pages in our history and of a willingness to discover the truth about it now are books that are appearing in Poland, such as a two-volume (so far) edition of sources *Niemcy w Polsce 1945–1950* [Germans in Poland 1945–1950], *Zemsta ofiar* [Revenge of the Victims] by Helga Hirsch, or *Neighbors* by Jan T. Gross.

Confessing to the sins that were committed, and even the crimes committed by Polish hands, modern Poles have a right to be proud of having been the first ones to say no to Hitler in 1939, of phenomena such as the Polish Underground State* and its armed forces—the Home Army,* as well as two uprisings (since the uprising in the Warsaw Ghetto was the work of Polish Jews), are something to be proud of, along with the fact that, of the approximately 16,600 people awarded the Righteous among the Nations of the World medal, almost one in three is a compatriot of ours.

At the same time, the world should remember that, although without a doubt the Jews suffered the most, the Poles also suffered. Almost every Polish family lost someone close in World War Two as a victim of one of the two totalitarian systems. Poland emerged from the wartime conflagration as a country of ruins and devastation, a country betrayed by its Western Allies and given over to foreign rule.

Poles in the eyes of others

Just recently, I had the opportunity to take a look at results of opinion polls carried out in the last two years in a few European countries, commissioned by the Polish Institute for Public Affairs. In connection with our efforts to become a member of the European Union, the polls were supposed to show how Poles and Poland are perceived in Austria, Spain, Sweden, France, and Germany. The results are not promising.

It turns out that the world not only does not remember our heroism and martyrdom during World War Two, but has also forgotten—so quickly—the contribution of Poland's *Solidarność* movement to overthrowing the communist regimes not just in Poland but in the entire Soviet bloc. Instead of obvious Polish successes in the field of political and economic transformation, our country and our people are associated with backwardness and anti-Semitism. Let's not have any illusions: information about crimes committed by Poles 60 years ago will only strengthen long-established stereotypes, and will worsen our not-very-positive image in the world.

I am not saying that this was the intention of the author of *Neighbors*. However, I am convinced that such intentions are fodder for foreign journalists and publicists, for whom the "Jedwabne affair" provides an opportunity to show Poland and Poles in the worst possible light. How else can you explain the behavior of the Frenchwoman who put the following title on an article published on December 1, 2000 in the *Libération*: "*55 ans après, et toujours le refus d'affronter son passé. Jedwabno* (sic!), *le trou de mémoire polonais*" [55 Years Later and Still Refusing to Confront the Past: Jedwabno, a Gap in Poland's Memory].

Neither the title nor the content of the article, which takes up two columns, upsets me much. The thing that I consider most perfidious is the placing in the text a map of our country sent by an *envoyée spéciale* from Warsaw, showing the outline of our country with only three cities on it: the capital, Jedwabne and Kielce.* And consider that, in the most recent public opinion poll, dated October 2000, the French placed second when Poles were asked which nations they had the warmest feelings towards.

How to eliminate anti-Semitism?

Yet what is to be done about our poor anti-Semitism, which still exists and still makes itself felt? What to do with a phenomenon that feeds on human stupidity, but is also nourished by those who use it to attain their political goals? What to do so that those distasteful and disgraceful slogans and graffiti disappear from our streets? How to achieve a state in which each anti-Semitic statement made in Poland is immediately condemned by listeners and readers? How to achieve a state in which each Polish anti-Semite finally understands that he is committing a sin by violating the moral norms that apply to a member of a Catholic community? If *Neighbors* leads to a spiritual shock in Poland, then it will do us a great favor.

I remember that many years ago, during a televised discussion, my Ph.D. adviser, the late Prof. Franciszek Ryszka, was asked how to eliminate anti-Semitism in Poland. He answered succinctly: "Stop being an anti-Semite!"

Tomasz Szarota

A DISCUSSION ABOUT JEDWABNE IN JEDWABNE

WE ARE DIFFERENT PEOPLE

"WIĘŹ" APRIL 2001

Participants in the discussion held at the Municipal Offices in Jedwabne on February 22, 2001:
* Krzysztof Godlewski, mayor,
* Stanisław Michałowski, chairman of the town council,
* Father Edward Orłowski, parish priest,
* Stanisław Przechodzki, director of the Łomża branch of the Podlasie Public Health Center,
* Senator Stanisław Marczuk, chairman of the Białystok chapter of *Solidarność* from 1981 to 1991,
* *Więź* editors—Jacek Borkowicz, Father Michał Czajkowski (cochairman of the Polish Council of Christians and Jews) and Zbigniew Nosowski.

Zbigniew Nosowski: *We have come together to talk about how to deal with memories of the tragic events that took place here 60 years ago.*

Krzysztof Godlewski: In broad terms, the entire "Jedwabne case" has two aspects, a moral one and a political one. Both of these aspects constantly permeate each other and mingle in discussions on this subject. For several months, we have been playing host to a series of journalists. Some of them have come to us in order to learn the truth, whilst others have come in order to write a sensationalist article. Articles like that cast a very unfavorable light on the entire debate surrounding Jedwabne. The first question on the list is: How many people died and where did they die, and was this possible? Only at the end of the list do the murdered people themselves appear. A game of numbers begins: Did 500 people die, or 1,600? The tragedy is becoming a game in the hands of the media and politicians.

Stanisław Przechodzki: Some people are trying to profit from this tragedy. The tragedy of people—the tragedy of those who died then, the tragedy of those who were guilty, and the tragedy of those who are still alive today—somehow gets lost in the rush of words. Jedwabne is a small place, everyone here knows everyone else, and the tragedy concerns everyone. Arguments are revived, and both anti-Semitic voices and voices accusing the Poles are being heard again. No one should be written off. Those who might think in an untruthful way today, but who follow their own consciences and believe what they are saying, might change someday.

There is no anti-Semitism in Jedwabne. I say so with full deliberation. I have encountered symptoms of anti-Semitism in larger towns. But simple people live here. Nevertheless, certain anti-Jewish elements remain inside them, shaped by the history of the inter-war period or the war itself. But this is not the aggressive anti-Semitism that can be found among certain political groups or in some newspapers.

Jacek Borkowicz: *How did the people here remember the events of July 1941 before May last year, in other words before the appearance of Andrzej Kaczyński's article "Burning Alive," which sparked off a series of publications about the massacre?*

Stanisław Przechodzki: I am, and I feel myself to be a Jedwabne man, though I have been living in Łomża for a dozen years or so. My forebears settled here. My family lived right on the town square. My parents told me about the events when I was still a boy. I did not find them all that interesting. For most young people here, they were so remote that they seemed to have occurred hundreds of years ago. They were in the past, and that was that. In any case, our parents did not want to tell us everything; they did not want to damage us emotionally. We used to go to the so-called "tombs," that is, the Jewish cemetery, and our parents shouted at us whenever we gathered nuts there. We did not realize what we were doing, though we knew that beside the cemetery there was a barn in which the Jews were burned.

Only later, when I visited Jedwabne as a student, did the time come to read up on the subject and reflect upon it. That was when I discovered a few more details. Towards the end of my mother's life I knew much more, but I still did not know all the details which I read about in Gross's book. However, I know a lot of details which do not appear there. But they make no difference to the letter and spirit of that book.

Stanisław Michałowski: I, too, was born here. My family has lived in Jedwabne for three generations. When I was eight, I witnessed a conversation between people who had taken direct part in the massacre. Names were mentioned, details given…. I did not identify myself with the events. I did not comprehend them. Years later, a very clear memory of what I once heard came back to me. The words I heard have a completely different dimension today.

Stanisław Przechodzki: Those who live here and come from here will never be the same people that they were a year ago. Even at home, among my family, I feel different than the way I felt last year, even though I am not to blame for what happened 60 years ago. The Jedwabne that existed before May 2000 is gone.

The people of Jedwabne are in for a difficult task. They will have to accept the truth of the events which, though they happened in the distant past, are nevertheless a tragedy that is very close to them today. But before that, they will have to prepare themselves by undergoing an internal mental change.

One must remember that the overwhelming majority of the population here consists of ordinary people. They are no better and no worse than the inhabitants of many Polish towns. It is a downright lie to portray them in some publications as simple peasant folk who do not read and who live in a village dominated by the all-encompassing weight of the church.

Zbigniew Nosowski: *When you said, "We will never be the same again," everyone nodded in agreement. What has changed?*

Stanisław Przechodzki: Most of all, Jedwabne is no longer just another Polish town, one of thousands. One can say without exaggeration that we are now on the lips of the world. That creates a very onerous psychological burden. The people of Jedwabne now have to consider how much they are capable of changing and what sort of truth they should accept. Can we stand up to the things that will surely happen over the next few months? In some people, knowledge of the tragedy, even though it happened so long ago, still rouses misgivings. They try to interpret them in their own way—not always in accordance with the truth—with the intention of protecting their families. These people will find it difficult to change and to accept the fact that certain events are irreversible. One always tries to seek an excuse.

But there is no excuse for what happened on July 10, 1941, never mind how difficult the period of Soviet occupation was. My parents and sister were on the deportation list, but at the very last moment, on June 20, 1941, they were warned about this and hid in the forest. Specific individuals and the entire Soviet system are responsible for the tragedy of the people who were deported from this area and mistreated. We know that in those areas where Russians were not the dominant ethnic group, the Bolsheviks systematically recruited, first of all, members of ethnic minorities for the NKVD.* The reason was clear. Should it be necessary to disclose the crime, the minority could always be blamed. For instance, in the days of Dzerzhinsky, the second largest ethnic group among the *Chekhists*—after the Russians—was the Poles. A similar mechanism was applied to the Jews. I do not know how many Jewish Soviet militiamen there were in Jedwabne, and how many Jewish informers. Perhaps a few, perhaps over a dozen. But all the rest of the Jews were poor, simple people. We do not suspect that a list of Poles to be deported was prepared in every Jewish household, just as we do not suspect that every Polish household thought about how liquidate the Jews.

After reading some articles, one might get the impression that eastern Poland in the period 1939–1941 was under Jewish occupation, and not Soviet occupation. I did not think it possible to alter history so much in the space of a few months.

Stanisław Michałowski: My parents were deported. These days, people say that the Jews handed Poles over to the NKVD, but my family, unfortunately, was handed over by a neighbor, a Pole. What's more, after my father had been deported (he was taken at night, one of the first to go), the Russians came the next morning, threw everything out, drove us out of the house, and ordered us not to enter the property. They were accompanied by another neighbor, also a Pole.

Stanisław Przechodzki: One cannot blame the entire Jewish community of Jedwabne for the deeds of a few Jews during the Soviet terror. Yet the same applies to those who took part in the crime of July 10. This was a not an entire "society," as Jan T. Gross says in *Neighbors* [in the Polish edition, Gross writes that the crime was committed by "society," and in the American edition by the "neighbors" of the Jedwabne Jews—trans.]. They were just individuals, perhaps several dozen of them, perhaps more, perhaps fewer. Of course, in a certain sense, the remainder are also responsible. They may not quite have been capable of preventing it, may not have done all they could have done, or did not offer shelter.

But generally, after 60 years, it is difficult to judge the acts of our parents and grandparents. The situation was different then. One occupation had passed, and another was beginning. No one knew what Nazism would bring, so the German forces received a warm welcome in many places. They were treated as liberators from Soviet occupation.

Stanisław Michałowski: What happened in July 1941 is regrettable, but undeniable. In a certain sense, it also concerns me, and I too bear moral responsibility, even though I am in a "comfortable" situation arising from the fact that my family was neither directly nor indirectly involved in those events.

I feel very sorry to say this, but I think the Poles played a certain part in the atrocity. But on the other hand, I do not agree that the involvement of the Germans was marginal, or even non-existent. Even Professor Gross has written in his book that were it not for Hitler and the war, the atrocity would never have happened. The Germans organized everything. There was a group of people, 92 of them, whose names and addresses are known, who came out onto the square to guard the Jews who were under escort. Most of these people were acting under pressure, they were in the pillory [the speaker may mean "in the yoke"—ed.]. One wonders what would have happened to them if they had refused to come. Could they have helped? I suspect not. The element of fear which paralyzed the Jews also affected the Poles in a certain sense. There was a group of some thirty persons whose participation in the crime is irrefutable and—to be honest—was ruthless. They included people known for an inclination to hooliganism and banditry before the war.

I grieve over what happened—and in our own town at that. But I have never agreed, and still do not agree, with attempts to implicate the whole town in this business. One should not apply collective responsibility. Over 95 percent of Jedwabne's present population came here after the war. These people have no connection with the events of summer 1941.

Father Edward Orłowski: At this point I would like to correct a certain distortion in Gross's book. He writes that, when they sensed danger, the Jews of Jedwabne asked the bishop in Łomża to shelter them. They were supposed to have offered him silver candlesticks in return for this help. The bishop supposedly kept his word, but only "for a while." His appeal to the Germans proved to be of no avail and he did not prevent the massacre.

Well, nothing of the sort happened. When the occupation came [in 1939—ed.] and Poland was divided up, the bishops went their separate ways. The auxiliary bishop went to live in Ostrów Mazowiecka, under German occupation, while Bishop Stanisław Łukomski hid from the Soviets in Kulesze Kościelne. He returned to Łomża on July 8 or 9, just before the Jedwabne murders, but he did not actually take up office until August, because the vicarage and bishop's palace had been commandeered by German troops. It would have been practically impossible for Jedwabne Jews, under conditions of wartime isolation, to have contacted the bishop before July 10.

Father Michał Czajkowski: *Mr. Przechodzki said: "Accept the truth." Jesus said that the truth shall make us free. The quicker we accept* *the truth, the sooner we will be liberated from this nightmare. You will be different, but the important thing is, how? Does change mean an apologetic attitude, a closing of your eyes to the truth—or does it mean liberation, which brings with it the courage of acceptance? The good must be given a chance, so that the world does not associate Jedwabne solely with the evil that happened here.*

Krzysztof Godlewski: One could accept the truth if only we knew it in full. For instance, if the exact number of Jews were established. But that unfortunate number of 1,600 Jews has been pulled out of a hat!

We want to bring this issue to a close, although it has gotten too big for me, as it has for some others among us. Whatever I say anything on this subject, I offend someone's sense of what is sacred. Are we still the "royal Piast tribe"* that we are proud of being? I was brought up on Mickiewicz,* on the song of the *Pierwsza Brygada* [First Brigade*]. My father was in the Home Army,* and did time in Wronki* prison. When I ask such questions, I enter unwillingly into a conflict with my own father.

Zbigniew Nosowski: *The Pope talks of an examination of conscience by the Church, for in the Church there is a link between present and past generations. We bear all the good, and also all the evil previously done in the name of the Church. I think one can view the nation in a similar way—after all, this concept also possesses a spiritual dimension.*

Father Edward Orłowski: Let us tell the whole truth—change must occur on both sides, and not just one. For dialogue applies to both sides. By blaming only one side, we will always be biased.

When the two totalitarian states divided Poland between themselves, they took advantage of ethnic minorities in order to set them at odds with each other. Here, the Jews and the Poles co-existed well. Things began to deteriorate only after the outbreak of the war, and the conflict reached its peak when the Germans attacked the Soviet Union. We must admit the whole truth—young Jews supported communism, and the Soviets used the Jews against Poland. Later, when the Germans came, they tried to use the Poles against the Jewish community. One cannot say that the crime was committed by the Poles. What happened in Jedwabne also happened all over Europe. However, it cannot be excluded that some Poles were compelled to take part in this crime, others felt like exacting vengeance on the Jews, and some may have been downright criminals. It is also difficult to accept that Polish society as a whole treated the Jews so cruelly. If it is only individuals who did so, then they did it as part of German operations.

I worked with Father Józef Kembliński, who was the priest here throughout the occupation, when I was vicar in Lipsk on the Biebrza River. We went to Jedwabne then, looked at the monument at the site of the burned barn, and talked. He always said that the murder was carried out by the Germans. I know from his account that the Jews asked him for protection from destruction. They were prepared to give him gold and other valuables. Father Kembliński talked to the *gendarmes* because he spoke German well, and asked if anything could be done. They replied that it was impossible. They had been given orders—the Jews must die! Father Kembliński did not accept the gold.

Father Michał Czajkowski: *And what did he say about the murder itself? Where was he at the time?*

Father Edward Orłowski: For three days, the Jews were rounded up to weed the grass and clean the park. No one in town knew how it would end because on the critical day they, too, were herded onto the square. On the day when that unfortunate barn burned, the parish priest stood at the gateway leading to the church and watched. The town square was almost empty. People were only peeking out the windows or around corners. The fear was pervasive.

Father Michał Czajkowski: *Couldn't he have intervened?*

Father Edward Orłowski: I know that, before the burning of the barn, he went up to an officer who had arrived in Jedwabne that day and said: "What harm have the women and children done to you? Spare them at least!" to which the officer replied: "Maybe you don't know who's in charge here. Clear off, if you want to keep your head on your shoulders!"

Zbigniew Nosowski: *The factual plane and the moral plane keep getting entangled here. What exactly happened and what can be done* *now? Father, you are speaking about motives that can explain the events. But can they justify them?*

Father Edward Orłowski: Nothing can justify murder, absolutely nothing.

Zbigniew Nosowski: *Apparently, Rabbi Baker, who was born in Jedwabne under the name Piekarz and is today an old man living in New York, has indicated that he could come here and talk to people, young people, but that he would like to be accompanied by the local priest.*

Father Edward Orłowski: The Rabbi has never asked me, but if he wants, then I am ready to meet him. Human fellowship is built not only on the basis of religion, but also on the basis of culture and a general sense of humanity. He is invited to the rectory!

Jacek Borkowicz: *The afterword of Gross's book* [reference is made to the Polish edition; the American edition of *Neighbors* does not contain the words of Rabbi Baker—trans.] *contains a message from Rabbi Baker in which he asks the people of Jedwabne to tend the Jewish graves and commemorate the site of the synagogue. Would this be possible—not so much in the financial as in the psychological dimension?*

Father Edward Orłowski: I realize that, as parish priest, I am responsible not just for the Roman Catholic cemetery here, but also for the cemeteries of other communities within the parish. We have a German cemetery here, and I never permit the old graves to be destroyed by burying people there. When, in 1991, there were plans to set up a market square close to the Jewish cemetery, I protested from the pulpit and said that it would be a sacrilege. I suggested that the marketplace be moved elsewhere, and I offered 1.1 hectares of parish land in exchange. Thanks to the exchange, neither the Catholic nor the Jewish cemeteries have been trampled. True, the Jewish cemetery is overgrown, but we have so many unemployed people here. If the Jewish community provides the money and employs them, they will tidy up the cemetery.

Father Michał Czajkowski: *But here we are talking about a community gesture.*

Father Edward Orłowski: At this moment, that is perhaps impossible.

Krzysztof Godlewski: As for looking after the Jewish graves, there might still be some psychological barriers in the minds of the people of Jedwabne, but I see no such danger in the minds of young people. They already think in different terms, for them there are neither Jews, nor Romans or Greeks.* That initiative could launch the building of not just one, but several small memorials in the hearts of these young people, much more durable than stone.

However, there is a polarization of views. On the one hand, we are defending ourselves against historical accusations, and on the other hand the government is preparing major ceremonies on July 10. What would happen if it turned out that we here are in opposition to all this? Something important is due to happen on July 10, so let world opinion see us as open-minded and responsible Catholics. But there is no sense in our doing anything that runs contrary to our convictions.

Jacek Borkowicz: *The people of Jedwabne should be aware that a gesture on their part does not mean they are confessing to the crime, but is merely an expression of responsibility for the place where they live.*

Krzysztof Godlewski: I remember how the government's proposed version of the inscription on the monument ended: "Forgive us, as we have forgiven others!" But if we do not think we share any guilt, then what is the sense of that sort of "forgiveness"? If the July 10 ceremonies are meant to be simply a general reminder of the death of Jews, after which we all go home, then it would be better not to have any ceremonies at all.

On the basis of what Father Orłowski says, we bear practically no guilt at all. Father Orłowski has his information, and we have ours. How are we to tell who is right? I am convinced that the Poles played a considerable part in this crime. But if this participation was only sporadic, then it would be a grave mistake to say that the whole town was involved. We would only be wronging the residents.

No one is criticizing the people of Jedwabne for being forced to leave their homes and guard the Jews. The complaints are about the ones who were over-zealous. They should be named, and they alone should be tried. Except that no one is able to do this.

Father Edward Orłowski: They are either dead, or old.

Krzysztof Godlewski: The question remains: Do we, the Jedwabne community, accept the legacy of those 30 people? Do we distance ourselves from it? Do we apologize for those 30 people?

Stanisław Marczuk: I agree with the mayor. There are no good or bad nations, only good and bad people.

Jacek Borkowicz: *In the same way that there are no good or bad towns.*

Stanisław Marczuk: The Pope stresses that one cannot blame the entire Jewish people for the death of Christ. I think the same principle ought to be applied to Jedwabne—individual Poles were guilty, yet there were people with various mentalities among the general Polish population of the town. Their attitudes to the murder of the Jews could not have been identical.

Zbigniew Nosowski: *How do children and young people ask their parents today about what happened in 1941?*

Stanisław Michałowski: I witnessed a five-year-old child listening to a conversation among adults, and then asking: "Listen, grandfather, was it you who murdered those Jews, or your dad, or my dad?" When you hear such questions, you cannot brush them aside, unless you are totally thick-skinned. Most of us are experiencing this matter profoundly, each in his own way.

Krzysztof Godlewski: Before today's talk, I didn't sleep all night. Whenever I think seriously about this crime, I lose my equilibrium, and emotions get the upper hand. This is not something about which one can talk coolly, calculating and jotting down figures. On July 10 last year, as we were laying a wreath at the memorial, two elderly ladies were talking about what happened 60 years ago. At one point, both of them burst into tears. No one who has the tiniest bit of sensitivity can talk about this normally. We cannot lose sight of this in our talk.

We in Jedwabne don't need either psychologists or sociologists. Anyone who is incapable of reacting to these horrors on their own is beyond integration with society. For others, it is enough if, when they walk past the monument, they think about things—and then go back, in their thoughts and more than once, to the entire episode and digest it. Their consciences will be enough to remind them to do so.

Zbigniew Nosowski: *Mr. Mayor, I understand you wanted to name the local school after Antonina Wyrzykowska, who rescued seven Jews during the German occupation. Has this proposal been considered in the school?*

Krzysztof Godlewski: To my surprise, I found that the children knew nothing at all about this subject. Should we therefore "make them happy" by digging up old matters?

Father Michał Czajkowski: *The children will find out anyhow. I do not think this can be kept hidden from them. Besides, they probably know a lot already. They must, or else a five-year-old would not have asked who carried out the murder. One should not hide the dark side of local history from children, but one should also show them the beautiful parts of that history.*

Krzysztof Godlewski: The suggestion of naming the school after Mrs. Wyrzykowska was just an idea I tossed off the top of my head. The school is not yet ready for it. Remember that the school is an organism consisting of the Teachers' Council, the Parents' Committee, and the pupils. The new name cannot be imposed by an administrative decision. Internal changes have to occur first. And that is a long educational process in which the family and the home must also play their part.

Jacek Borkowicz: *Gross writes about the Wyrzykowski family in a footnote to* Neighbors, *describing them as wonderful people, and I hope a book will also be written about them one day. But at the same time I do not think anyone will ever write such a book. That is how the logic of the media works, unfortunately. Evil is more attractive than good. That is why commemorating Mrs. Wyrzykowska by naming the school after her would somehow fill this gap.*

Krzysztof Godlewski: Let me tell you one thing: I consider it my duty to mediate. Wherever I encounter racial or religious hatred, or other kinds of hatred, I will try to overcome it within the limits of my modest abilities. In this way I want to repay the debt that is owed to those who were murdered. This shall be my absolution and …how shall I put it? ...my penance for the death of those people. What I mean to say is that the death of those people should somehow pay off. If we all make sure that such events as in 1941 never happen again, those deaths will have not been in vain.

Zbigniew Nosowski: *Do you pray for the murdered Jews, Father?*

Father Edward Orłowski: I feel responsible for the entire history of my parish. Ever since I became parish priest, I have been praying for all its residents living and dead, regardless of their creed. Yes, I do pray for the Jews, but I also pray for the Germans, for the Russians, for all those whose bodies lie in our parish soil. That is my duty. War set these people against each other, and they resorted to atrocities, to death. But that death has reconciled them. They have stood, deeply shamed, before the same God.

Father Michał Czajkowski: *It's a shame that they were only reconciled after their deaths.*

Father Edward Orłowski: If necessary, I will take up a collection in my parish for a monument to the murdered Jews, then I will take part in a procession with my parishioners and sing the *Angelus*, and then we will pray at the stone where those who were burned in the barn are buried.

Krzysztof Godlewski: The Church is imbued with the wisdom of two thousand years, but today's times are a time of change. I have three children, whose religious attitudes are different than mine, and completely different from my father's. Certain steps and gestures can only do us good. You, father, are the highest authority in Jedwabne, and have the greatest opportunity to work a gradual change in people's hearts.

Father Michał Czajkowski: *The acts of contrition proclaimed by the Pope do the Church good, because they make it credible in the eyes of others. Perhaps there is no such thing as collective guilt, but every community needs a kind of collective responsibility, felt by everyone who considers himself a part of this community. Can anyone say that the Pope does not love the Church because he discusses its sins? He discusses the inquisition, the pogroms, and the expulsion of the Jews from Spain precisely because he feels such a strong attachment to this Church. It is the same when we talk about own sins. We do not do so* *because we are bad Poles, but because we love Poland so much. Gentlemen, you feel so closely linked to this place and experience its history so deeply because it is your town, your life.*

Krzysztof Godlewski: Resolving this issue and explaining it in full, even if it is painful to do so, will give us more benefits than keeping it a secret.

Stanisław Przechodzki: Of course. There can be only one truth in a fundamental issue. The murder was carried out by some neighbors. That was the main murder—the burning in the barn—but there were also many, very many individual murders. There is no doubt that they were committed with the approval of the Germans. But to talk of dozens or hundreds of armed *gendarmes* in Jedwabne is a mockery of the victims. There was no cordon of Germans around Jedwabne. Just before the barn was burnt, my mother, with a baby in her arms, walked through the entire town and left it unhindered. Nowhere did she see any Germans. One kilometer away from Jedwabne, she heard the screams of the burning victims. It was so piercing that she remembers it to this day.

Stanisław Marczuk: 35 year ago, Polish bishops addressed the following famous words to the Germans: "We forgive and we ask for forgiveness." There was a heated reaction to these words at the time. People said, why should we apologize to the Germans? And yet as a result of this message, the attitudes of Germans towards the Poles changed, and this was confirmed by surveys. Sometimes we apologize not because we owe someone a debt of guilt, but because we require purification. He who utters these words first is the wiser. We apologize not because we are guilty. We apologize simply in the name of love.

Father Michał Czajkowski: *No one expects the parishioners here to go to the confessionals and confess to the evil of 1941 as their own personal sin. There is a kind of solidarity; not just a surface layer, but one that reaches deep down. In the name of this solidarity we ourselves should commemorate the victims, and not just follow instructions from foreign journalists tell us to do.*

Stanisław Michałowski: But these instructions sometimcs smack of blackmail. Being continually lectured to arouses a feeling of being under threat in the local community. And a person who is being attacked naturally begins to defend himself.

Jacek Borkowicz: *Jedwabne is becoming a symbol, whether we like it or not. An important part of this symbol is the things which we Poles find the most difficult to enunciate. Irrespective of the number of perpetrators, irrespective of the amount of German inspiration, and irrespective of whether there was any coercion and how strong it was, we cannot deny that the murder was perpetrated by Polish hands. The murderers were Poles. I do not agree with the reverend Father that the same thing happened all over Europe. Jedwabne is not typical—if it were, it would never have become the symbol it now is. Of course, Jedwabne is no exception either—similar events occurred along the entire front, in Lithuania, the Ukraine and Moldavia, not to mention in the neighboring towns of Wąsosz and Radziłów. But a characteristic feature of a symbol is that it "falls" on one place, in this case Jedwabne, and we have to come to terms with that, because what is done will not be undone. But now we can exercise some influence, albeit restricted, on the form of this symbol. Soon it will be too late to do so.*

Stanisław Michałowski: But such reflection cannot be introduced by external laws and decisions, even if they are wise. It must start inside people.

Stanisław Przechodzki: The atrocity occurred 60 years ago, but a rejection of the truth of it, and even more an acceptance of this truth, will change the people here. It will also determine the way in which the outside world looks at Jedwabne. Let us leave it to historians to discover the causes of those conflicts. They had but one outcome—a tragic one. If the people of Jedwabne do nothing but entrench themselves and defend themselves against attacks, if they shut themselves up in their own hell, their defense of the good name of their town will be nothing but a mockery of a defense. On the part of the people of Jedwabne themselves, there should be more sensible, premeditated actions. We should show that we have already understood something and that we have changed.

At the same time, we should be bold. A single bold thought, a single bold deed causes the wave of criticism to disintegrate. And very often a small gesture suffices, one which does not cost much, but is a Christian gesture and very needed. Finally, we should bear in mind that we have children and grandchildren. Our parents did not deal with this issue. True, the conditions for doing so did not exist, but these conditions have existed now for eleven years. If we do not deal with this issue, it will pass to the next generation. And why should our descendants have to be tormented? It is enough that we ourselves are tormented....

Edited by Jacek Borkowicz

AGNIESZKA MAGDZIAK-MISZEWSKA

THE MOST SERIOUS TEST

"WIĘŹ" APRIL 2001

For the majority of people born and raised in communist Poland, it was always obvious that one of the characteristic features constituting the reality of this state was the falsification of history. This applied in particular to the most recent history and, above all, to Polish history. With the knowledge we brought with us from our family homes, we distrustfully approached the interpretations of the history of the prewar Second Polish Republic,* the years of war and occupation and, of course, the "liberation" by the Red Army, that were imposed upon us.

For my generation, the true heroes were those who were relegated to the fringes of our school history lessons: the soldiers of the Home Army,* those of General Anders's army,* the combatants of the Warsaw Uprising, and the Polish officers murdered by the NKVD*, about whom nothing could be said. All of these great people were raised in the Second Republic—which was forcibly presented to us as incompetently governed, weak, poor, a persecutor of its national minorities, and hostile to the Soviet Union for no good reason.

While challenging what they taught us in school about twentieth-century Polish history, we simultaneously accepted, without any particular resistance, the history of Polish splendor and Polish heroism as taught in the same school. This latter history included the tradition of "noble democracy" and toleration on the one hand, and on the other the enormity of the undeserved misfortune that befell us down the ages. In brief, our relationship to our own history—both that learned at school and that learned at home—was above all affirmative and often, in view of our personal relationship to the regime of the day, deeply emotional. The apogee of this affirmation came in the 1980s with the emergence of *Solidarność*, and then resistance toward martial law.* These experiences confirmed the view of Poland and the Poles that we had formed earlier, as freedom-loving patriots who were capable of great acts and great sacri-fices—always, of course "for your freedom and ours."

Overturning memory

The recovery of our independence unexpectedly disturbed our own good feelings about ourselves. Firstly, conflicts that emerged and the divisions that erupted within *Solidarność* itself were increas-ingly personal in character and fueled by ambition, and had less and less to do with substance and ideals. Secondly, national minorities that had been consigned to the margins of folklore in communist Poland now returned to the public scene.

The appearance in Poland of Belorussians, Lithuanians, Ger-mans, Roma, Ukrainians and Jews, differentiating themselves through their language, culture or religion, came as a huge shock to many Poles, who only shortly before had been professing their allegiance to the Jagellonian traditions of a multicultural Republic. Conflicts and resentments that had been frozen by decades of com-munism suddenly saw the light of day. The appearance of minorities evoked consternation in places where these minorities were absent, and caused the revivification of old conflicts in places where the minorities were present. These old conflicts were most glaring in the east, where there was the greatest number of minorities. All of a sudden, it seemed that the rejected communist version of history had taken root in our consciousness in at least one sense: the acceptance of the dogma that Poland is a state belonging to ethnic Poles. There was no reason for anyone else to see that state in a way differently from the way we ourselves saw it. Yet history as told by the minorities often differed from what we considered to be our own history—and therefore the only true one.

The collapse of the Soviet Union brought freedom to our eastern neighbors, but only deepened this historical asymmetry. The confrontation with Lithuanian, Belorussian, or Ukrainian history caused anxiety. It led on the one hand to the reevaluation of our own stereotypes (something we did in *Więź* by introducing the series "Poles in the eyes of their neighbors"), or on the other to defending "our truth" from "others' truth." Both of these stances frequently went to extremes. Sometimes, all virtues and accomplishments were cast in to doubt. Alternatively, anyone who dared question even the most preposterous convictions about the exceptional nature of the Poles might be vilified.

Aside from controversy surrounding the recent history of Polish-Ukrainian relations, the greatest emotions were evoked when discussing the Germans—because of the conviction that we had always been their victims—and the Jews, for whom, we thought, Poland had always been a tolerant homeland, and towards whom the Poles had always been sympathetic neighbors ready to render aid. The discussion that has gone on for several years now on the expulsion of the Germans after the Second World War required us to accept the fact that those who had once been the Germans' victims could also be cruel oppressors. It had taken decades for most Poles to recognize the sense of the Polish bishops' 1965 letter to the German bishops: "We forgive and ask for forgiveness."

We also slowly began to accept the fact that anti-Semitic propaganda did exist in the 1930s, as well as the phenomenon of the *szmalcownicy** and the indifference among a section of Polish society toward the tragedy of the Jews during the Holocaust. Today, these phenomena are taught in many Polish schools. We know, after so many years of silence and lies, that 90 percent of the victims of Auschwitz-Birkenau were Jews. Interest in the history and culture of the Polish Jews is today sufficiently widespread for it to be seen as fashionable (which is not to say that anti-Semitism has disappeared from Poland).

AGNIESZKA MAGDZIAK-MISZEWSKA

Pride and shame

Jan T. Gross's *Neighbors*, a small book published in mid–2000 by *Pogranicze* caused a real shock within Poland. Even among those who had never questioned the painful judgments on the stance of the Poles toward Jews during the occupation and immediately afterward, and who knew full well that Poles sometimes willingly assisted the Germans in plundering and even murdering individual Jews—the truth about Jedwabne was hard to accept.

I do not agree with Jan T. Gross on many specific points, particularly his use of the word "society"[1] at the end of this terrifying book, but I am convinced that *Neighbors* is a book which had to be written and that is needed. Facing up to the painful truth of Jedwabne is, in my conviction, the most serious test that we Poles have had to confront in the last decade. How well we do on this test, will shape—and I do not hesitate in using these big words—our place in the family of free, democratic nations. Each of these nations has in its history dark or, at times, even black stains, but each of them, sooner or later, has been able to come to terms with these.

This test is so difficult because its standard has already been set. In acknowledging the guilt of the Catholic Church toward the Jews, Pope John Paul II has reminded us of the only possible canon for a truthful examination of our conscience: to ask for forgiveness without any conditions or justification. "Forgive, as we too forgive." The real sense of this plea requires an unparalleled double effort—asking for forgiveness and forgiving others at the same time.

Such a task, therefore, faces before us all, irrespective of whether any of us carries any individual responsibility for what happened 60 years ago in a handful of small Polish towns. It is all too human to seek justification and symmetry for our own guilt. The most difficult thing is to admit guilt, to say, simply: so it was. Especially when the admission is accompanied by a justified fear that it will be manipu-

---

[1] In literal translation, the last sentence of the Polish edition says that the Jedwabne Jews were "murdered... by society." The American edition concludes: "...it was their neighbors who killed them." (translator's note)

lated and exploited in order to confirm the already accepted thesis of the collective responsibility of the Poles for the Holocaust.

I shall never be able to come to terms with this thesis, which has been widely disseminated, unfortunately, especially amongst Jews in the United States, nor with the notion of "Polish concentration camps" or "Polish anti-Semitism." Yes, certain Poles murdered Jews. So it was. Many Poles helped Jews, and among them there were those who lost their own lives doing so. If I want to have a moral right to justified pride in the rescuers, then I must admit, to a sense of shame over the killers.

Great nations have a right to be proud of the great episodes in their history, and at the same time they are able to admit to the dark episodes. The test that faces us today will determine whether we are, in fact, a great nation.

Agnieszka Magdziak-Miszewska

February 2001

EXPLANATORY NOTES

1920—in August 1920, the Polish Army, under the leadership of Józef Piłsudski, halted the Soviet offensive outside Warsaw.

1968—see: *March 1968.

1981—in December of that year, General Jaruzelski's regime introduced martial law in Poland and made *Solidarność* illegal.

***Aktion Sühnenzeichen**—Signs of Repentance Action*, a civil movement that arose in East Germany in the 1960s. Its members initiated a movement serving reconciliation with Poles (for example, trips by German youth groups to tidy up the terrain of former concentration camps).

Anders's army—as a result of the *Sikorski–Maisky agreement, some Soviet citizens who had been deported to the eastern Soviet Union during the period 1939–1941 were freed and allowed to join armed forces under the command of the government-in-exile in London. The commander of these forces was General Władysław Anders. The army left Russia and traveled by way of Iran and Palestine to Italy, where it took part in battles such as the capture of Monte Cassino (1944).

Armed Combat Union—a nationwide anti-Nazi underground organization in occupied Poland, under the command of the Polish government-in-exile in London; later transformed into the *Home Army.

"a balance-sheet of wrongs"—an allusion to the poem by the Polish communist poet Władysław Broniewski who wrote, in the face of the German threat to Poland in 1939:

> *"A balance-sheet of wrongs*
> *No foreign hand will right,*
> *But no one will shirk bloodshed"*

"Barbarossa"—code-name for the 1941 German offensive against the Soviet Union.

BCP(b)—Belorussian Communist Party, the name of the Belorussian branch of All-Union Communist Party (Bolshevik), the official name of the Soviet communist party during the Stalinist period.

Berman, Jakub—communist strongman in Poland during the Stalinist period, responsible for the introduction of Soviet ideology; of Jewish ethnic background.

bezhentsy—Russian term used after the 1939 campaign for refugees, mostly Jewish, who fled from the German to the Russian portion of occupied Poland.

Biuletyn Informacyjny—*The Information Bulletin*, the main press organ of the *Polish Underground State.

Blue Police—a popular name, taken from the color of their uniforms, for the Polish police in the service of the Germans in the *General Government.

The Boys from Arms Square—novel for teenagers by the Hungarian writer Ferenc Molnár, popular in Poland.

Bund—the Jewish socialist party founded in Vilna in 1897.

Campo di Fiori—1943 poem by Czesław Miłosz; a poetic coming to terms with Polish indifference to the tragedy of the extermination of Jews.

Chekha—*Special Commission Against Counter-revolution and Sabotage*, the political police in the first years of existence of the Soviet state (predecessor to the *NKVD and KGB).

Cichy, Michał—journalist from *Gazeta Wyborcza* newspaper who wrote a controversial article about incidents of Jews being murdered by the soldiers of the *Home Army during the 1944 Warsaw Uprising.

Citizen's Militia—the police in communist Poland.

eastern marches—the eastern part of the *Second Polish Republic, inhabited by Ukrainians, Belorussians, Lithuanians and Jews, along with Poles.

Edelman, Marek—one of the leaders of ŻOB, the Jewish Fighting Organization, during the Warsaw Ghetto Uprising in 1943; a member of the democratic opposition during the 1970s and 1980s.

Einsatzgruppe, Einsatzkommando, Sonderkommando—special Nazi police units charged with the extermination of Jews in newly occupied territories beginning in 1941.

Endlösung—German for "The Final Solution" ("...of the Jewish Question"), one of the Nazi code-terms for the Holocaust.

"First Brigade"—the anthem of the First Legion Brigade, a military formation led by Józef Piłsudski during the First World War; one of the best known Polish patriotic songs.

first Soviet occupation—1939–41, in contrast to the second, which occurred after 1944.

General Government—the part of Nazi-occupied Poland that was not directly annexed to the German Reich or to the so-called Eastern Lands (*Ostland*); governed by Hans Frank from Wawel Castle in Cracow. All authority was in German hands, exercised by thousands of German bureaucrats who arrived from the Reich, and Poles were subject to terror and extermination.

The Ghastly Decade 1939–1948—title of a book by Jan Tomasz Gross, published in Poland in 1998 and describing—according to its subtitle—"stereotyopes about Jews, Poles, Germans and Communists" during the 1940's.

Haller's army—a Polish military formation during the First World War, popularly named for its leader, General Józef Haller; incorporated into the Polish Army after the recovery of independence (see: *Second Polish Republic).

Home Army—1942–45, the underground nationwide Polish anti-Nazi organization under the command of the government-in-exile in London. It carried out numerous acts of sabotage and armed offensives (Warsaw Uprising, 1944). In communist Poland, Home Army soldiers were persecuted, and some joined the secret organization WiN (Freedom and Independence).

Ingarden Roman—Polish philosopher, a phenomenologist and student of Husserl.

Institute of National Remembrance—the official organ that took over the archives of the communist secret police. Its task is to make these files available to victims of persecution as well as to journalists and researchers investigating crimes committed by the totalitarian Nazi and Communist states against Polish citizens and others of Polish nationality; also charged with conducting research and educational programs on the subject.

Jagielski, Wojciech—journalist for the newspaper *Gazeta Wyborcza,* known for reportage on contemporary armed conflicts.

"Jewish communism"—a long-standing anti-Semitic stereotype blaming the Jews for advocating, introducing, and running the communist system.

Jewish Historical Institute—a Warsaw-based organization, successor to a Jewish educational and research organization that held university-level official status before the war, conducting research on the history of the Jews in Poland.

Kapuściński, Ryszard—reporter, writer and commentator specializing in international issues, and in particular those connected with the Third World.

Karski, Jan—Polish political envoy for the underground authorities in Nazi-occupied Poland who brought information about the extermination of the Jews to the West.

Katyn—a town in Russia where, in 1940, the *NKVD murdered several thousand imprisoned Polish reserve officers; a symbol of Soviet crimes against the Poles. The communist authorities banned the truth about this crime, maintaining the Soviet version that blamed the mass murder on the Germans.

Kielce pogrom—In July 1946, the inhabitants of Kielce murdered 42 local Jews. As a result of the pogrom, a majority of Polish Jews who had survived the Shoah left Poland. There is still controversy over the role of the Stalinist secret police in this pogrom.

Kolyma—a river in eastern Siberia near which the harshest penal camps in Stalin's Russia were concentrated.

Kołakowski, Leszek—Polish philosopher and writer who moved permanently to Britain after *March 1968.

Korczak Janusz (pen name of Henryk Goldszmit)—Polish physician, educator, and press and radio commentator of Jewish ethnic origins, a precursor of contemporary educational practices; he voluntarily accompanied "his" children when they were deported during the liquidation of the Warsaw ghetto and died with them in August 1942 in the gas chamber at the Nazi death camp in Treblinka.

Kultura **(Paris)**—the most important postwar Polish emigre monthly, which published texts that could not be printed in communist Poland because of censorship. Published through 2000.

"Let's choose the future"—electoral slogan of Aleksander Kwaśniewski, the leader of Polish post-communists, during his victorious presidential electoral campaign in 1995 (he was re-elected in 2000).

Main Commission for the Investigation of Crimes against the Polish Nation —formed after the fall of communism fall as the official organ dealing with research on and the investigation (including criminal prosecutions) of crimes committed by Germans occupying Poland as well as (in contrast to its predecessor the *Main Commission for the Investigation of Nazi Crimes in Poland) those committed by the communist authorities during the period 1939–1956. At present, its mission is carried out by the *Institute of National Remembrance.

Main Commission for the Investigation of Nazi Crimes in Poland—the official organ in communist Poland dealing with research on and investigation (including criminal prosecutions) of crimes committed by Germans occupying Poland during WWII. After the fall of communism, fall it was transformed into the *Main Commission for the Investigation of Crimes against the Polish Nation.

March 1968—the student protests against limitations of freedom of speech; after its suppression the communist authorities forced a wave of Jewish emigration from Poland.

March events—see: *March 1968.

martial law—see: *1981.

The Medallions—a collection of stories by Zofia Nałkowska, describing the reality of the Nazi state, including the concentration camps (1946).

Michnik Adam—leading opposition figure in communist Poland, a participant in protests including those in *March 1968. After 1989, editor-in-chief of the newspaper *Gazeta Wyborcza*, the daily with the largest circulation in Poland

Mickiewicz, Adam—one of great poets of Polish Romanticism and one of the most important figures of Polish culture.

Miracle on the Vistula—the popular name given to the battle outside Warsaw in *1920.

Moczar, Mieczysław—pseudonym of the leader of the 'nationalist' faction of the Polish Communist Party who was responsible for the anti-Semitic campaign after *March 1968.

Myśl Polska—a low-circulation, extremely nationalistic periodical.

Nasz Dziennik—a nationalistic Catholic daily.

National Democracy—a general term for parties and groupings with a nationalistic tendency in pre-war Poland.

National-Radical Camp—a political formation in the 30s associated with youthful adherents of the *National Democracy movement; responsible for anti-Semitic acts and excesses.

neither Jews, nor Romans or Greeks—an allusion to two fragments from the New Testament: the epistles of St. Paul to the Romans (10,12) and to the Colossians (3,11).

Niedziela—right-wing Catholic weekly.

NKVD—*The Peoples' Bureau for Internal Affairs*, the political police in Stalin's USSR.

partitions of Poland—between 1772 and 1795, Russia, Prussia, and Austria divided among themselves the territory of the Polish State (First Republic); "partitions" also refers to the parts of Poland under the control of each of these "partitioning powers" until the recovery of Polish independence in 1918.

Poles from Kazakhstan—in the 30's several tens of thousands of Poles, as a "national minority," were deported from the Soviet Ukraine to Kazakhstan; an even greater number were deported during 1939–41 from the occupied eastern Polish territories.

Polish Underground State—the common name during the Second World War for the clandestine army and civilian structures in Nazi-occupied

Poland; the Underground State recognized the authority of the London government-in-exile.

"Poor Poles Look at the Ghetto"—an essay by Jan Błoński, published in the weekly *Tygodnik Powszechny* (1987), analyzing of Polish attitudes towards the extermination of the Jews.

A Pretense of Life—a book of essays and recollections of the literary critic Kazimierz Wyka on the moral dilemmas facing Poles under the German occupation.

PZPR—*United Polish Workers Party*, the ruling party (practically the only one) in communist Poland.

Recovered Territories—the official propaganda term for former eastern territories of Germany that were given to Poland in 1945 on the strength of the agreement in Potsdam. The term referred to the fact that these territories belonged to the Polish state in the Middle Ages. The majority German population there was resettled, mainly to West Germany, and its place taken by Polish settlers, many of whom had themselves been expelled from the formerly Polish lands in the east that were awarded to the Soviet Union as part of the same postwar settlement, which was drawn up by the leaders of the USSR, USA, and Great Britain without Polish input.

Reich-Ranicki, Marcel—the best known contemporary German literary critic; from a Jewish family from Poland.

royal Piast tribe—a fragment of the poem *Rota* by Maria Konopnicka; a popular patriotic song.

sanacja—["reformation"], popular term for the political formation that ruled Poland from 1926–1939; the name derives from the slogan "moral reformation"; established by men closely associated with Marshal Józef Piłsudski.

Schulz, Bruno—Polish-Jewish writer who described in lyrical-surrealistic prose the world of the Jewish small towns of eastern Poland; murdered by a German officer in the Drohobycz ghetto.

SD—*Sicherheitsdienst*, "security service" (political intelligence) of the Nazi Party (NSDAP—National Socialist German Workers' Party).

Second Polish Republic—the Polish state from 1918–1939, reborn after the period of *partitions.

selsovet—[Russian: "village council"] the lowest organ of facade local government in the Soviet state.

Sikorski–Maisky Agreement—In September 1939, the Soviet Union, in an understanding with the Germans (the Ribbentrop–Molotov Pact) using the pretext of the disintegration of the Polish state, took over eastern Poland. After Hitler's attack on the USSR in 1941, the Polish supreme commander and Prime Minister in exile, General Władysław Sikorski, signed an agreement renewing diplomatic relations with the Soviet Union (signed by Ivan Maisky, the Soviet ambassador in England). In 1943, Stalin broke off relations with Poland after the *Katyn crime was revealed.

Sipo—*Sicherheitspolizei* ["security police"], one of political police formations of the Third Reich.

sledovatel—[Russian: "investigator"], in the Soviet State, *sledovatele* carried out investigations and interrogations in political cases and regularly subjected the "suspects" to psychological and physical torture.

spetsposolek—Russian term for a settlement of deportees sentenced by the Stalinist system to banishment in desolate places such as Kazakhstan and Siberia.

Szeptycki, Andrzej—Greek Catholic metropolitan (archbishop) of Lwów, spiritual leader of Ukrainians in Galicia during the war.

szmalcownicy—common, contemptuous term for persons who blackmailed Jews in hiding outside the ghetto in German-occupied Poland, using the threat of informing on them to the German authorities.

Tischner, Józef—Catholic priest and philosopher, one of the leading authorities in contemporary Poland.

UB—Security Office, the political police during the Stalinist epoch in Poland.

Umschlagplatz—the place where, in the summer 1942, the Warsaw Jews were assembled before deportation by rail to the Treblinka death camp.

Union of Labor—small contemporary social-democratic Polish political party.

Volksdeutsch—popular term, derived from German, for a Polish inhabitant of the *General Government who declared himself or herself to be ethnically German by signing the so-called German nationality list (*Deutsche Volksliste*).

With Fire and Sword—a novel by Henryk Sienkiewicz (Polish 1905 Nobel Prize winner) depicting the period of the Polish-Cossack wars in the seventeenth century.

Wronki—a town in central Poland. During the Stalinist period, many *Home Army soldiers and freedom fighters found themselves in the local prison there.

ZBoWiD—*Association of Fighters for Freedom and Democracy*, the official and only permitted organization for World War II veterans in communist Poland.

Zomowcy—derived from the acronym ZOMO, "Motorized *Citizen's Militia Reserves," a riot police formation used to suppress popular demonstrations, especially during the martial law period; see *1981.

Żegota—Council for Aid to the Jews, a voluntary community organization in existence from 1942–1945 as part of the structure of the *Polish Underground State, concerned mainly with the material support and protection of Jews in hiding outside the ghettos.

NOTES ON THE CONTRIBUTORS

Jacek Borkowicz—born 1957. A member since 1995 of the editorial staff of *Więź*, where he is responsible for the *Polacy i ich sąsiedzi* [Poles and Their Neighbors] desk. Author of numerous publications on coexistence between the nations and cultures of Central and Eastern Europe and of the book *Powrót do Sowirogu* [Return to Sowiróg]. Member of the Polish Council of Christians and Jews. He lives in Józefów near Warsaw.

Halina Bortnowska—born 1931. Catholic activist and commentator. From 1960 to 1983, a member of the editorial staff of *Znak*. From 1967 to 1982, she participated actively in the work of the World Council of Churches. From 1991 to 1997, member of the International Council of *Pax Christi*. Co-founder of *Otwarta Rzeczpospolita* [Open Republic] Association Against Anti-Semitism and Xenophobia. She lives in Warsaw.

Father Michał Czajkowski—born 1934. Roman Catholic priest, professor of Biblical studies. He holds the Chair of Ecumenical Theology at the Cardinal Stefan Wyszyński University in Warsaw. Co-chairman of the Polish Council of Christians and Jews, member of the Polish Episcopate's Committee for Dialogue with Judaism, member of the International Auschwitz Council. Church consultant to *Więź*. Author of numerous books, including *Słowo blisko ciebie. Wędrówki po Biblii i biblistyce* [The Word Close to You: Journeys Through the Bible and Biblical Studies], *Lud Przymierza* [The People of the Covenant], *W drodze do Jerozolimy* [On the Way to Jerusalem]. A prolific writer and commentator. He lives in Warsaw.

Adam Dobroński—born 1943. Historian, professor at the University of Białystok. Director of the Institute of Regional History. Author of several scholarly studies and books for a general readership, including *Losy Sybiraków* [The Fate of Those Banished to Siberia], *Łomża w latach 1866–1918* [Łomża between 1866 and 1918]. Editor of the series *Białostoccy Żydzi* [The Jews of Białystok]. He lives in Białystok.

Konstanty Gebert—born 1953. Journalist and writer. Co-founder of the (unofficial) Jewish Flying University (1979) and the Polish Council of Christian and Jews (1980). After avoiding internment in the 1981 coup,

Gebert became—under the pen-name of Dawid Warszawski, which he still uses—well-known as the editor and columnist of *KOS* fortnightly and of other underground publications. In 1989, he joined *Gazeta Wyborcza*, the new independent daily for which he continues to write. He is a frequent contributor to other Polish and international media. In 1997, he founded, and until 2000 was the editor-in-chief of *Midrasz*, the Jewish intellectual monthly of which he is now the publisher. Author of four books, including one on the 1989 Polish round table negotiations and another on the wars in the former Yugoslavia. He lives in Warsaw.

Michał Głowiński—born 1934. Literary historian, professor at the Literary Research Institute of the Polish Academy of Sciences in Warsaw. Author of a number of books on the theory of literature and the history of the Polish literature, as well as one devoted to the language of communist propaganda. In 1998, he published his memoirs of the war-time period under the title *Czarne sezony* [Black Seasons; an English translation is forthcoming]. He lives in Warsaw.

Krzysztof Godlewski—born 1955. Educated in computer science, mayor of Jedwabne since 1992.

Jan Tomasz Gross—born 1947. Sociologist, political scientist, historian. Professor of Political Science at New York University. He left Poland in 1969, after the March 1968 events in which he took an active part. Author of books on recent Polish history including *Polish Society Under German Occupation—Generalgowernement. 1939–1944*; *Revolution from Abroad: The Soviet Conquest of Poland's Western Ukraine and Western Belorussia*; W *czterdziestym nas matko na Sybir zesłali* [In 1940, Mother, They Sent Us to Siberia]; *Upiorna dekada 1939–1948. Trzy eseje o stereotypach na temat Żydów, Polaków, Niemców i komunistów* [The Ghastly Decade 1939–1948: Three Essays on Stereotypes About Jews, Poles, Germans and Communists]. In May 2000, he published the original Polish edition of his book on the murder in Jedwabne: *Sąsiedzi. Historia zagłady żydowskiego miasteczka* [Neighbors: The Story of the Destruction of a Little Jewish Town].

Israel Gutman—born 1933 in Warsaw, he fought in the Warsaw Ghetto Uprising and was later imprisoned in Majdanek, Auschwitz and Mauthausen. After the war, he emigrated to Israel. Professor of History at the Hebrew University in Jerusalem, chairman of the Scientific Council of the Yad Vashem Holocaust Memorial Institute in Jerusalem. Deputy chairman of the International Auschwitz Council. He lives in Jerusalem.

Radosław Ignatiew—Prosecutor at the Institute of National Remembrance Departmental Commission for the Prosecution of Crimes Against the Polish

Nation in Białystok, responsible for the investigation of the Jedwabne murder.

Krzysztof Jasiewicz—born 1952. Historian, political scientist, faculty member at the Institute of Political Studies at the Polish Academy of Sciences. From 1991 to 2000, he carried out research in 26 archives in the territory of the former Soviet Union, and through 1992 was secretary of the Eastern Archive. Author of a number of books including *Lista strat ziemiaństwa polskiego w latach 1939–1956* [Lists of Losses among the Polish Landed Gentry 1939–1956], *Zagłada polskich kresów* [The Destruction of the Polish Eastern Marches], and *Elity sowieckie w okupowanej Polsce 1939–1941* [Soviet Elites in Occupied Poland 1939–1941] (forthcoming). He lives in Warsaw.

Jerzy Jedlicki—born 1930. Historian of ideas. Professor. Director of the History of the Intelligentsia Department at the Historical Institute of the Polish Academy of Sciences. Chairman of the Program Council of the *Otwarta Rzeczpospolita* [Open Republic] Association Against Anti-Semitism and Xenophobia. Author of many books including *Jakiej cywilizacji Polacy potrzebują* (English edition: *A Suburb of Europe*), *Źle urodzeni, czyli o doświadczeniu historycznym* [Born Lost, or About Historical Experience], *Świat zwyrodniały. Lęki i wyroki krytyków nowoczesności* [A Depraved World: Fears and Judgments of Critics of Modernity]. He lives in Warsaw.

Maria Kaczyńska—*Gazeta Współczesna* journalist specializing in regional problems. She lives in Łomża.

Andrzej Kaczyński—born 1948. *Rzeczpospolita* journalist. Editor in 1981 of *Tygodnik Solidarność*, and, after the proclamation of martial law, editor of several underground periodicals. He specializes in reportage describing the relations between different denominational and ethnic communities living in Poland. He lives in Warsaw.

Stanisław Krajewski—born 1950. Logician and commentator. Member of the faculty of the Philosophy Institute at the University of Warsaw. Co-chairman of the Polish Council of Christians and Jews, member of the board of the Union of Jewish Communities in Poland, member of the International Auschwitz Council, co-founder of the Polish-Jewish Friendship Association. Author of the book *Żydzi, judaizm, Polska* [Jews, Judaism, and Poland]. Member of the Warsaw Jewish Community. He lives in Warsaw.

Zdzisław Krasnodębski—born 1953. Sociologist and philosopher; he teaches sociology and the history of culture of Central and Eastern Europe at the University of Bremen (Germany). Author of a number of books including *Rozumienie ludzkiego zachowania* [Ways of Understanding Human Behavior], *Upadek idei postępu* [The Fall of the Idea of Progress],

Postmodernistyczne rozterki kultury [Post-Modernistic Dilemmas of Culture], and *Max Weber*. Author of essays, published mainly in *Znak*. He lives in Bremen.

Jacek Kurczewski—born 1943. Sociologist, professor at the University of Warsaw, he holds the Chair of Sociology of Customs and Law at the Institute of Applied Social Sciences. From 1991 to 1993, he was the deputy speaker of the Polish *Sejm* [parliament]. Member of the Polish Television Program Council, and of the Mass Media Ethics Council. Author or co-author of a number of books on sociology and the sociology of law, including (in English): *The Resurrection of Rights in Poland* and, jointly with M. Maclean: *Family Law and Family Policy in the New Europe*. He lives in Warsaw.

Paweł Lisicki—born 1966. *Rzeczpospolita* journalist, responsible at present for the *Opinie* [Opinions] section. He has written numerous essays and the books *Nie-ludzki Bóg* [An Un-human God] and *Doskonałość i nędza* [Perfection and the Miserable]. Commentator for *Fronda* quarterly. He lives in Warsaw.

Paweł Machcewicz—born 1966. Historian, senior lecturer at the Institute of Political Studies at the Polish Academy of Sciences, director of the Public Education Office at the Institute of National Remembrance. Author of books devoted to recent Polish history including *Polski rok 1956* [The Polish Year 1956], and *Władysław Gomułka*, co-author of the books *Historia Hiszpanii* [A History of Spain], and *Druga Wielka Emigracja (1945–1990)*, [The Second Grand Emigration 1945—1990]. He lives in Warsaw.

Antoni Macierewicz—born 1948. Historian, politician. Activist in the democratic opposition movement under the communist regime, co-founder of the Committee for the Defence of Workers (KOR) in 1976 and later a *Solidarność* trade union activist. From 1991 to 1993, *Sejm* [parliament] deputy for the *Zjednoczenie Chrześcijańsko-Narodowe* [Christian-National Union]. From 1995 to 1997, deputy leader of the *Ruch Odbudowy Polski* [Movement for the Reconstruction of Poland]. At present independent *Sejm* deputy, publisher of *Głos* weekly, and since 1998 chairman of the *Ruch Katolicko-Narodowy* [Catholic-National Movement]. He lives in Warsaw.

Agnieszka Magdziak-Miszewska—born 1957. She has worked for *Więź* since 1984, from 1995–2001 as its deputy editor-in-chief. From 1991–1995, counselor-minister at the Polish embassy in Moscow. From 1997 to 1995, adviser to Prime Minister Jerzy Buzek on Polish-Jewish affairs. From 2000–2001, director of the independent Center for International Relations. Since April 2001, Polish consul general in New York.

Stanisław Marczuk—born 1935. Senator, chairman of the board of the Białystok Region of *Solidarność* from 1981–1991. He lives in Białystok.

Stanisław Michałowski—born 1952. Mechanic. Chairman since 1998 of the Town Council in Jedwabne.

Bogdan Musiał—born 1960. Historian, academician of the of the German Historic Institute in Warsaw. The scientific article in which he proved that the exhibition "Wehrmaht Crimes" comprises materials illustrating NKVD crimes brought him international fame. Author of *Deutsche Zivilverwaltung und Judenverfolgung in Generalgouvernement. Eine Fallstudie zum Distrikt Lublin* [German Civil Authorities and Persecution of the Jews: The Case of the Lublin District]; *"Konterrevolutionäre Elemente sind zu erschiessen." Die Brutalisierung des deutsch-sowjetischen Krieges in Sommer 1941* ["Counter-revolutionary Elements Are to Be Shot." The Brutalization of the German-Soviet War in Summer 1941]; and *Stosunki polsko-żydowskie na Kresach Wschodnich RP pod okupacją sowiecką 1939–1941* [Polish-Jewish Relations in the Polish Eastern Marches Under Soviet Occupation 1939–1941]. He lives in Warsaw.

Zbigniew Nosowski—born 1961. Journalist and commentator. Member since 1988 of the *Więź* editorial board, since 1993 its deputy editor-in-chief. Member of the National Council of Lay Catholics, member of the Board of the Club of Catholic Intellectuals in Warsaw, member of the Polish Episcopate's Committee for Dialogue with Non-Believers. Editor and co-author of the book *Dzieci Soboru zadają pytania* [The Children of Vatican II Pose Questions]. Author and co-author of more than 300 television programs including the series *Boskie i cesarskie* [God's and Caesar's; with Tomasz Wiścicki] and *Rozmowa dnia* [Conversation of the Day]. He lives in Otwock near Warsaw.

Jan Nowak-Jeziorański—born 1913. Courier for the Polish resistance movement during World War II. After the war, he was an editor of the European service of BBC Radio in London and, later, Director of the Radio Free Europe Polish Service. From 1979 to 1992, consultant to the U.S. National Security Council and the National Director of the Polish-American Congress. He has written a number of books and articles for magazines, periodicals and newspapers including *Kurier z Warszawy* [A Courier from Warsaw], *Wojna w eterze* [War on the Airways], and *Polska z oddali* [Poland from Afar].

Father Edward Orłowski—born 1931. Jedwabne parish priest, dean and prelate.

Paweł Paliwoda—born 1963. Historian of philosophy, doctoral candidate at the Institute of Philosophy and Sociology of the Polish Academy of Sciences. Regular contributor to *Życie*, member of the Warsaw Club for Political Criticism. He lives in Warsaw.

Stanisław Przechodzki—born 1955 in Jedwabne. Economist and lawyer. From 1991 to 1997, director of the Provincial Office in Łomża. Chairman of the Organizational Committees that prepared the visits to Łomża by Pope John Paul II (1991) and Israeli President Chaim Herzog (1992). At present, director of the Łomża branch of the Podlasie Public Health Center. He lives in Łomża.

Bohdan Skaradziński—born 1931. Economist and urban planner, commentator, writer, author of historical books. Member of the Editorial Council of *Więź*, regular contributor to *Tygodnik Solidarność* [Solidarność Weekly]. In 1952, while he was a student, he was sentenced to 10 years in prison by the communist military court for "attempts to overthrow the political system," freed in 1956, and later declared not guilty. In the 1960s, he worked as an urban planner in Arab countries in the Middle East. Author of a number of books including *Białorusini, Litwini, Polacy* [Belorussians, Lithuanians, and Poles], *Polskie lata 1919 i 1920* [The Polish Years 1919 and 1920]. He lives in Podkowa Leśna near Warsaw.

Jan Skórzyński—born 1955. Historian and journalist. Author and co-author of publications devoted to Poland's post-war history including *Ugoda i rewolucja* [Compromise and Revolution]. Editor-in-chief of the biographical dictionary *Opozycja w PRL 1956–1989* [The Opposition in Communist Poland, 1959–1989]. Since 1994, a member of the editorial staff of *Rzeczpospolita* and, at present, first deputy editor-in-chief. He lives in Warsaw.

Tomasz Strzembosz—born 1930. Historian, professor at the Catholic University of Lublin and the Institute of Political Studies at the Polish Academy of Sciences. Author of *Akcje zbrojne podziemnej Warszawy 1939–1945* [Military Actions of the Underground in Warsaw, 1939–1945], *Odbijanie i uwalnianie więźniów w Warszawie 1939–1944* [The Rescue and Freeing of Prisoners in Warsaw, 1939–1944], and *Rzeczpospolita Podziemna* [The Underground Republic of Poland]. He also deals with the history of the Polish resistance movement in north-eastern Polish territories under the Soviet occupation between 1939 and 1941. He lives in Warsaw.

Tomasz Szarota—born 1940. Historian, professor at the Historical Institute at the Polish Academy of Sciences, a prominent expert on the history of World War II and the Nazi occupation. The author of a number of books including *Okupowanej Warszawy dzień powszedni* [Everyday Life In Warsaw Under the Occupation], also published in German, English translation forthcoming; and *Życie codzienne w stolicach okupowanej Europy* [Ordinary Life In European Capitals Under the Occupation]. In 2000 he published *U progu zagłady. Zajścia antyżydowskie i pogromy w okupowanej Europie* [On The Threshold of Destruction: Anti-Jewish Riots and Pogroms in Occupied

Europe] about anti-Jewish actions in European cities occupied by the Nazis: Warsaw, Paris, the Hague, Amsterdam, Antwerp and Kaunas. He lives in Warsaw.

Gabriela Szczęsna—born 1955. *Kontakty* journalist since 1983. She deals with local, social and historical issues, as well as nature topics. She lives in Łomża.

Dawid Warszawski—see: **Konstanty Gebert**.

Stefan Wilkanowicz—born 1924. Catholic activist and commentator, long-time editor-in-chief of *Znak*. At present deputy chairman of the National Council of Lay Catholics, president of the *Znak* Foundation for Christian Culture, deputy chairman of the International Auschwitz Council, member of the Polish Episcopate's Committee for Dialogue with Judaism. From 1985 to 1996, member of the Pontifical Council for Laity in the Vatican. Author of the book *Dlaczego i jak wierzę* [Why and How I Believe], editor of *Auschwitz. Konflikty i dialog* [Auschwitz: Conflicts and Dialogue]. He lives in Cracow.

Adam Willma—born 1970. *Gazeta Pomorska* journalist. Author of a series of reports on Siberia, Belarus and Kazakhstan, as well as on the Croatian-Serb war. He lives in Białystok.

Danuta Wroniszewska and **Aleksander Wroniszewski**—journalists; husband and wife. Their most important articles have been cooperative efforts. They published in the Łomża *Kontakty* from 1980 to 1990. After 1983, they also worked for the *Prawo i Życie* [Law and Life] weekly. At present, they work as free-lance journalists. They live in Gorzów Wielkopolski.

Alicja Zielińska—*Kurier Poranny* journalist. She lives in Białystok.

Jacek Żakowski—born 1957. Journalist, commentator for *Gazeta Wyborcza*. One of the founders of the newspaper in 1989. From 1989 to 1990, spokesman for *Obywatelski Klub Parlamentarny* [the Citizens' Parliamentary Group, i.e. the parliamentary caucus of *Solidarność* deputies]. Together with Piotr Najsztub, he launched the *Tok-Szok* TV program. Author of numerous books including *Między panem a plebanem* [The Lord of the Manor and the Vicar; with Adam Michnik and Father Józef Tischner], *PRL dla początkujących* [Communist Poland for Beginners; with Jacek Kuroń], and *Mroczne wnętrza—uwięziony Prymas* [Dark Interiors—the Imprisoned Primate]. Winner of the prestigious "Grand Press" award as the Journalist of the Year, 1997. Since January 2001, anchorman of the radio program *Gość Radia Zet* [Radio Zet Guest]. He lives in Warsaw.

Andrzej Żbikowski—born 1953. Historian, academician at the Jewish Historical Institute in Warsaw and the Public Education Office at the Institute of National Remembrance. Author of scholarly studies including *Ideologia* *antysemicka 1848–1918* [Anti-Semitic Ideology, 1848–1918], *Żydzi krakowscy i ich gmina 1869–1919* [The Cracow Jews and their Community, 1869–1919]; and the popular *Żydzi* [The Jews]. He lives in Warsaw.

Archbishop Józef Życiński—born 1948. Philosopher, Roman Catholic priest, Archbishop Metropolitan of Lublin since 1997 after serving as Bishop of Tarnów from 1990. Professor of the Philosophy of Science, holder of the Chair of Relations between Science and Faith at the Catholic University of Lublin. Member of two Vatican congregations: the Pontifical Council for Culture, and the Congregation for Catholic Upbringing. Member of the Joint Working Group of the Roman Catholic Church and the World Council of Churches. Chairman of the Polish Episcopate's Commission for the Lay Apostolate. Author of over 300 books, including (in English): *The Galileo Affair: A Meeting of Faith and Science*; *The Structure of the Metascientific Revolution*; *The Idea of Unification in Galileo's Epistemology*; *Three Cultures: Science, the Humanities and Religious Values*; and of numerous scholarly articles and commentaries. He lives in Lublin.

NOTES ON THE POLISH PRESS

Gazeta Pomorska—regional daily published in Bydgoszcz (Pomorze).

Gazeta Współczesna—regional daily published in Białystok.

Gazeta Wyborcza—the largest-circulation national daily newspaper, "liberal" in the American sense of the word.

Głos—nationalist-Catholic weekly.

Kontakty—regional weekly published in Łomża.

Kurier Poranny—regional daily published in Białystok.

Nowe Książki—monthly devoted to reviews of new book titles.

Polityka—second-largest-circulation newsmagazine, decidedly liberal (in the American sense of the word).

Rzeczpospolita—one of the major Polish dailies, middle-of-the-road.

Tygodnik Powszechny—Catholic intellectual weekly.

Więź—Catholic intellectual monthly review.

Wprost—largest-circulation newsmagazine, "liberal."

Znak—Catholic intellectual monthly review.

Życie—conservative daily newspaper.

EDITORIAL NOTE

Broad circles of people have been involved in the Polish discussion on the crime that was committed in Jedwabne. A number of them have made important statements. This anthology presents texts chosen from among the articles published by the Polish press. Some of them appeared even before the book *Sąsiedzi* [*Neighbors*] by Jan T. Gross was published in Polish in May 2000.

The reader will note that the articles included in the anthology *Thou Shalt Not Kill: Poles on Jedwabne* are printed in chronological order. Although the first of these articles was published in 1988, the discussion on the crime in Jedwabne started in 2000 and has continued since. The anthology shows how the discussion evolved from its start to the beginning of March 2001 (by which time a total of almost 200 articles had been published). The only exceptions are articles forthcoming in the April issue of *Więź*, which has not yet been published but is ready for printing. This anthology has been prepared by the editorial staff of *Więź*.

The articles presented here were selected so as to provide a representative sampling of the arguments that have appeared in the Polish press. The editorial team, listed below, accepts responsibility for any oversights in the selection of the texts.

Terms that might be unfamiliar to the English-speaking reader are briefly glossed in the "Explanatory notes." Where they appear in the texts, the words described in the notes are marked with an asterisk.

Quotations from *Neighbors* in the body of the text reflect the contents of the Polish edition, *Sąsiedzi* (Sejny, 2000). For the convenience of the reader, the wording from the American edition (Princeton and Oxford: Princeton University Press, 2001) has been used when it does not differ substantially from the Polish edition. When there are differences, this has been noted and the quotation from the American edition supplied in a footnote.

The Polish national debate on Jedwabne goes on. Another wave of new and significant publications on the subject is appearing even as this anthology goes to press. Unfortunately, it is already too late for us to include them in this collection.

Jacek Borkowicz
William Brand
Aleksandra Brochocka
Eliza Chodorowska
Piotr M.A. Cywiński
Agnieszka Magdziak-Miszewska
Zbigniew Nosowski
Tomasz Wiścicki

WIĘŻ is a monthly Catholic intellectual review that has been published in Warsaw since 1958. Its founder and, for many years, its editor-in-chief was Tadeusz Mazowiecki, who later—following the victory of *Solidarność* in 1989—became the first non-communist Prime Minister of Poland after World War II.

The monthly review is an important and interesting publication not only for Catholics, but also for many other readers as well. WIĘŻ deals with issues of crucial significance: themes that arise at the crossroads of religion, culture, society and politics. Its main goal is the deepening of Polish Catholicism in the spirit of Vatican II, with the Church understood as a community and open to the contemporary world.

The name of the monthly ("The Bond") is a part of its program. WIĘŻ wants to serve reconciliation and the overcoming of stereotypes: between Poles and Jews, Germans, Russians, and Ukrainians; between Christians of different denominations; between Catholics and Jews, members of non-Christian religions, and non-believers.

The relations between Christianity and Judaism and between Poles and Jews have always been of significant interest for WIĘŻ. In 1998, the monthly review published a special English language issue, *Under One Heaven: Poles and Jews*. It consisted of the most important texts on these matters published in WIĘŻ throughout its history.

In 2000, the same special issue was published also in German as *Polen und Juden: gemeinsam unter einem Himmel*.

Towarzystwo "WIĘŻ"
Kopernika 34, P.O. Box 209, 00-950 Warsaw, Poland
tel. (+48 22) 827 29 17 or 828 19 06 • fax 826 79 83
e-mail: wiez@wiez.com.pl • Website: http://free.ngo.pl/wiez

THE DEBATE CONTINUES

The Polish national debate about Jedwabne goes on. Another wave of new and significant publications on the subject is appearing even as this anthology goes to press.

Important statements on the issue have been made by Polish President Aleksander Kwaśniewski, Prime Minister Jerzy Buzek, and the Primate of Poland, Card. Józef Glemp. Let us also mention such press articles as:

— a *Rzeczpospolita* interview with Rabbi Jacob Baker, who lived in Jedwabne until 1937 (March 10-11):

"All that we would want is for the murderers, if any of them are still alive, to be punished. They are the ones who deserve punishment. But ordinary Poles, the ordinary residents of Jedwabne? They were decent, and we were good neighbors and friends."

— a *KAI* [Catholic News Agency] interview with Michael Schudrich, Rabbi of Warsaw and Łódź (March 13), printed the next day by all the major Polish dailies:

"Accusing the Poles of participation in the Holocaust is a sin. ... The time has come at which we Jews, if we want the Poles to feel and understand our pain, must understand and feel the pain of the Poles."

— an essay by Adam Michnik in *Gazeta Wyborcza* (March 17-18), published simultaneously in *The New York Times*):

"Certainly I cannot be responsible for that crowd of murderers who set the barn in Jedwabne on fire. ... When I hear a call to admit my Polish guilt, I feel hurt the same way the citizens of today's Jedwabne feel when they are interrogated by reporters from around the world. But when I hear that Mr. Gross's book, which revealed the truth about the crime, is a lie that was concocted by the international Jewish conspiracy against Poland, that is when I feel guilty. Because these false excuses are in fact nothing else but a rationalization of that crime."

— a *Tygodnik Powszechny* interview with Archbishop Henryk Muszyński, Metropolitan of Gniezno, former chairman of the Polish Episcopate's Commission for Dialogue with Judaism (dated March 25):

"The first and essential step on the road to reconciliation is the request for forgiveness. We share with the Jews the commandment: 'Thou shalt not kill.' We must admit to having failed to observe that commandment."

Unfortunately, it is already too late for us to include these articles in this collection.

Editors